Barcode in Back

THE IRISHNESS OF IRISH MUSIC

Dedicated to the Memory of my Father

The Irishness of Irish Music

JOHN O'FLYNN
St Patrick's College, Dublin City University, Ireland

ASHGATE

Published by
Ashgate Publishing Limited
Wey Court East
Union Road
Farnham
Surrey, GU9 7PT
England

Ashgate Publishing Company
Suite 420
101 Cherry Street
Burlington
VT 05401-4405
USA

www.ashgate.com

British Library Cataloguing in Publication Data
O'Flynn, John
   The Irishness of Irish music. – (Ashgate popular and folk music series)
   1. Music – Ireland – History and criticism 2. National characteristics, Irish
   I. Title
   780.9'415

Library of Congress Cataloging-in-Publication Data
O'Flynn, John
   The Irishness of Irish music / John O'Flynn.
      p. cm. – (Ashgate popular and folk music series)
   Includes bibliographical references, discography, filmography, and index.
   ISBN 978-0-7546-5714-9 (hardcover: alk. paper) 1. Music–Ireland–History and criticism.
   2. Music–Social aspects–Ireland. I. Title.
   ML3654.O654 2009
   780.9415–dc22

                                                                                    2008037156

ISBN 978-0-7546-5714-9

Reprinted 2011

Printed and bound in Great Britain by the
MPG Books Group, UK

Contents

List of illustrations		*vii*
List of figures and tables		*ix*
General Editor's Preface		*xi*
Acknowledgements		*xiii*
List of abbreviations		*xv*

1	Irishness and music: Towards an interpretive framework	1
2	A brief and recent history of Irish music	25
3	Mapping the field	45
4	Snapshots	65
5	Ireland in music?	91
6	Irishness and music in a changing society	121
7	The music	145
8	Authenticity and Irish music	173
Conclusion: Irishness and music 'inside out'		197

Bibliography	*203*
Select discography	*225*
Filmography	*227*
Index	*229*

List of illustrations

2.1	The Frames © Friction PR	34
2.2	Altan © Plankton	36
2.3	Bill Whelan © BillWhelan.com	38
4.1	The National Concert Hall, Dublin © John O'Flynn	70
4.2	Cover artwork for The Celtic Tenors' *We are not islands* © Dara Records	85
5.1	Gerald Barry © Clive Barda	97
7.1	Sinéad O'Connor on *The Late Late Show*, 1990 © RTÉ	158
7.2	Cover artwork for *No Frontiers: The Jimmy MacCarthy Songbook* © Waltons Publishing	169
8.1	Cover artwork for the compilation album *The Rough Guide to Irish Music* © World Music Network	191
8.2	Cover artwork for traditional group Cran's *Music from the Edge of the World* © Claddagh Records	191

List of figures and tables

Figures

4.1   Style categorizations and production modes of music in Ireland   66

Tables

3.1   Percentage share of record sales by repertoire in Ireland 1997–2006   57
3.2   Comparison of sales by repertoire between Ireland and a selection
       of other countries for the year 2001   58
3.3   Per capita recorded music sales in Ireland 1989–2006   59

4.1   Traditional music events   68
4.2   Popular music events   69
4.3   Classical music events   71
4.4   Reported music preferences among the entire interview group   89

General Editor's Preface

The upheaval that occurred in musicology during the last two decades of the twentieth century has created a new urgency for the study of popular music alongside the development of new critical and theoretical models. A relativistic outlook has replaced the universal perspective of modernism (the international ambitions of the 12-note style); the grand narrative of the evolution and dissolution of tonality has been challenged, and emphasis has shifted to cultural context, reception and subject position. Together, these have conspired to eat away at the status of canonical composers and categories of high and low in music. A need has arisen, also, to recognize and address the emergence of crossovers, mixed and new genres, to engage in debates concerning the vexed problem of what constitutes authenticity in music and to offer a critique of musical practice as the product of free, individual expression.

Popular musicology is now a vital and exciting area of scholarship, and the Ashgate Popular and Folk Music Series presents some of the best research in the field. Authors are concerned with locating musical practices, values and meanings in cultural context, and draw upon methodologies and theories developed in cultural studies, semiotics, poststructuralism, psychology and sociology. The series focuses on popular musics of the twentieth and twenty-first centuries. It is designed to embrace the world's popular musics from Acid Jazz to Zydeco, whether high tech or low tech, commercial or non-commercial, contemporary or traditional.

Professor Derek B. Scott
Professor of Critical Musicology
University of Leeds

Acknowledgements

First, to series editor Derek Scott for his encouragement and patience, and for reminding me to enjoy the creative process of writing; commissioning editor Heidi May for being equally patient and for making many helpful suggestions; Anne Keirby of Ashgate who promptly responded to my many administrative and technical queries; Barbara Pretty, for her expert guidance during the final stages of editing.

Lucy Green, who supervised the study in its original incarnation, for her clarity of dialogue and for encouraging me to pursue my research idea in actual music 'scenes'; Barbara Bradby and Keith Negus for their insightful remarks on the PhD thesis that was to follow; Ian Biddle and the late Vanessa Knights, whose editorial suggestions on an earlier essay proved helpful when embarking on this book project.

Mary Immaculate College, University of Limerick for the granting of research seed funding; Muireann Joy, Gwen Moore, Gareth Cox, Michael Murphy, Karen Power, Paul Collins, Michael Finneran, Máire Ní Neachtain, Niall Quinn and Michael Wall for their collegial support, and/or for providing materials and suggesting ideas; Sinéad Carey, for assisting with the gathering of photographic material and for her involvement in aspects of formatting and proofreading; Matteo Cullen, who helped with the finer details of the discography and filmography; Elizabeth Brosnahan, Phyllis Conran, Áine Finnucane and Maureen McArthur for their support in accessing published and online materials; Mary Meaney for printing an early draft of the work; other colleagues and friends who suggested useful contacts or provided support at various stages during the course of fieldwork, among them, Zoë Dionyssiou, Miriam O'Sullivan, Philip Shields, Leonard Wilson and Nicola Murphy.

Paul Flynn and Kate Jameson of the Arts Council of Ireland; Dermot McLoughlin, Broadcasting Commission of Ireland; Niamh Nolan, Phonographic Performance Ireland; Daniela Bindl, Irish Recorded Music Association; Rosita Whelan, The National Concert Hall, Dublin; Amy Kerr, Pearl Quinn and Michael Talty of RTÉ; the agencies and/or musicians/composers who generously provided photographic images, namely, Tom Sherlock (Altan), Chloë Brookes, Oxford University Press (Gerald Barry), Aislinn Mehan (Bill Whelan), Pat Egan Management (The Celtic Tenors), Dan Oggly, Friction PR (The Frames), Seán Corcoran (Cran), Gerry Scullion, Waltons Music (*The Jimmy MacCarthy Songbook*), Brad Haynes, World Music Network (*The Rough Guide to Irish Music*).

Pradeeban Paskaran, for his constant support and for inspiring me in so many ways; my mother May, for her patience and understanding and for our lengthy discussions as work on the book progressed.

The musicians who performed at the various events I attended during the course of fieldwork, the experience of which heightened my respect for all those involved in live music production. Finally and most importantly, the many people who agreed to be interviewed, for their trust and openness to the project, and for providing many insightful reflections on musical life in Ireland.

List of abbreviations

ACSS	Afro-Celt Sound System
BBC	British Broadcasting Corporation
BCI	Broadcasting Commission of Ireland
CCÉ	*Comhaltas Ceoltóirí Éireann*
CMC	Contemporary Music Centre
DAST	Department of Arts, Sport and Tourism
DES	Department of Education and Science
EU	European Union
FÁS	*Foras Áiseanna Saothair* (Training and Employment Agency)
FMI	The Forum for Music in Ireland
GDP	Gross Domestic Product
IASPM	International Association for the Study of Popular Music
IBEC	Irish Business and Employers Confederation
IBI	Independent Broadcasters in Ireland
ICO	Irish Chamber Orchestra
IFPI	International Federation of the Phonographic Industry
IMRO	Irish Music Rights Organization
IRMA	Irish Recorded Music Association
MBI	Music Board of Ireland
MEND	Music Education National Debate
MIG	Music Industry Group (IBEC)
MOR	Middle-of-the-road
NCH	National Concert Hall
NSO	National Symphony Orchestra
PPI	Phonographic Performance Ireland
RAAP	Recorded Artists and Performers
RDS	Royal Dublin Society
RnaG	*Raidió na Gaeltachta*
RTÉ	*Raidió Teilifís Éireann*
SMI	Society for Musicology in Ireland
TG4	*Teilifís na Gaeilge 4*
UCH	University Concert Hall (Limerick)

Chapter 1
Irishness and music: Towards an interpretive framework

Introduction

This book is concerned with national identity and music in Ireland, as it comes to be experienced and articulated by way of musical events and products, as well as through the varied and interrelated discourses of consumer, governmental, cultural, academic and industrial interests. Its provocative title can be regarded in several ways, from conceptions of Irishness that arise out of culturally defined fields of musical content and practice to more critical perspectives that avoid any fixed or essentialist interpretations of the same musical and cultural phenomena. The idea of Irishness can also be used in ironic readings of what might be perceived as stereotypical sounds and images of Irish musical culture. In a sense, the book's title embraces all of these, for while I generally adopt and sympathize with critical (and sometimes ironic) standpoints, I also engage with received notions of 'Ireland', 'Irishness' and 'Irish music'. Of course, what counts as Irish music, what is included and what is excluded under that term is very often contested. For example, the choice of an archive photograph of The Corrs for the book's cover might appear incongruous to some, posing questions about the cultural authenticity of that group's particular style and output; for others again, it might seem inconceivable not to include The Corrs in any lengthy discussion about contemporary music in Ireland.

In other respects, the theme of Irishness and music might come across as anachronistic, particularly when considered in the light of contemporary, post-nationalist images of a globally oriented Irish economy. Debates concerning national identity and music, it might be argued, belong to a nationalist past, and in late modern contexts these debates are only relevant to residual ideological factions within an otherwise pluralist and forward-looking society. And yet, looking back over the past decade or so, questions about the Irishness of Irish music seem to have intensified rather than abated. One has to look no further than to past issues of *The Journal of Music in Ireland* to get some idea about the scale of the phenomenon at a discursive level.[1] It seems that many who are involved in music on the island must at some stage consider, first, what is meant by the

---

[1] Established in 2001, *The Journal of Music in Ireland* is a bi-monthly magazine comprising 'a mix of traditional, classical and contemporary music, music history, music education and cultural debate' (*The Journal of Music in Ireland*, n.d.).

term 'Irish music' and second, how their musical endeavours and interests relate to broader issues of identity in Ireland. Quite obviously, there is no one conception of Irishness and music. Nor should we consider that theorizations of national identity and music are confined to music producers, journalists, academics and others with a specialized interest in the field; equally important are the everyday views (or 'commonsense theories') of national identity and music that may arise from social experience, whether through attendance at music events, through other habits and technologies of music consumption, or through broader cultural and educational media.

Music in Ireland at the turn of the twenty-first century

The mid-1990s saw an explosion of celebratory discourse surrounding a number of high-profile Irish music acts. Insofar as some types of music by domestic artists enjoyed a disproportionately large share of international music sales, the general category of Irish music was enjoying an unprecedented success (Goodbody Economic Consultants, 2003: 34). Global markets for traditional groups like The Chieftains and Altan had expanded from a folk niche into the more mainstream category of world music (see Taylor, 1997: 209–30). U2 were purported to be the world's 'biggest' rock band, and the international successes of Sinéad O'Connor and The Cranberries suggested to the outside world that the idea of Irish rock was based on more than a one-act wonder.[2] Arguably, *the* phenomenon of this period was the rise and rise of traditional-derived Irish music productions. Here, I not only refer to the meteoric success of Enya's New Age/Celtic sound and, more recently, the sustained Billboard world music rating of the Celtic Woman ensemble, but also to the wholescale showcasing of Irishness and music through a series of musical mega-productions. Nowhere was this more explicit than in the case of *Riverdance*, a music and dance show that would come to be regarded as the largest cultural export ever to emerge from Ireland (see Kuhling et al., 2006).

Yet, even when all of these high-profile acts are considered together, they represent a very small part of the field of music production in contemporary Irish society. In other words, what is celebrated in terms of Irishness and music is based on a very narrow selection of products. Furthermore, many of the cultural mediators who allude to and assume the inherent ethnicity of Irish music, do so by presuming a number of essential qualities for Irish people and Irish music alike.[3] This suggests a general problem with two major aspects. First, what comes to be celebrated as Irish music does not represent the diversity and totality of musical life in Ireland. Second, where national identity is concerned, the perceptions of the

---

[2]   The Cranberries disbanded in 2003.

[3]   For a humorous deconstruction of many of the myths and stereotypes associated with Irish people, see Eagleton (2001).

majority of Irish people are assumed by a relatively small and unrepresentative group of commentators.

The recent celebration of some types of Irish music has been concomitant with a society that has changed in several respects. Notably, the Republic of Ireland had become progressively less isolationist in outlook from the 1960s onwards. Moreover, during the same period the Republic's economy had advanced from a relatively backward position in European terms to becoming a global economic success. So it would appear that the celebration of Irishness in music and in other aspects of culture is as much involved with economic conceptions of nationality as it is with cultural and/or political ideas. Indeed, the assumed links between cultural exposure and national economic success have come to be interpreted by many commentators in celebratory terms of national identity, with musical 'renaissance' regarded as a signifier of 'national confidence' (for example, Ó Cinnéide, 2002: 1–7; Walsh, 1996: 78). If anything, the intervening years between the mid-1990s and the time of writing have witnessed an intensification of the tendencies already outlined. In socio-economic terms, Ireland has experienced an unparalleled period of expansion and development, changes that have come to be mirrored by increased levels of music production and consumption in general. The ubiquity of celebratory discourse about the success and/or Irishness of (some) Irish music has not diminished; at the same time, a certain degree of critical response to this phenomenon has gathered ground in scholarship and in some journalistic views on Irish cultural life.

Part of the problem with the celebratory discourse about Irish music is the way in which such navel-gazing representations of Irishness can serve to exclude many musical genres, traditions and practices. I speak here firstly about Irish classical music[4] which, as White (1998a, 1998b, 2003, 2005) observes, has largely not been included in explorations of national-cultural identity, whether celebratory, critical or otherwise. This can be considered as anomalous insofar as ideas of other 'national' music(s) often include art music from the countries concerned (Grieg as Norwegian, Bernstein as American, Villa-Lobos as Brazilian, and so on). A second area of the national musical field that has received little or no attention has been the entire range of domestic popular music scenes. Related to this, it could be stated that, with the exception of some amateur practices in traditional music, affirmations of an Irish musical identity have in the main excluded non-commodity musical forms. In other words, very little attention has been given to those aspects of musical culture that have not achieved national or transnational 'visibility' (Slobin, 1993: 17).

---

[4] Throughout the book I use the term 'classical music' in the everyday sense, corresponding with what is generally termed in musicological discourse as 'art music'.

Defining Irish music

The term 'Irish music' suggests many possible meanings. The definition used throughout this book, namely, music produced in Ireland, follows the pluralist position argued by composer/performer and academic Mícheál Ó Súilleabháin (1982a: 919). An obvious limitation of this approach is that it effectively excludes music produced by populations of Irish people living in other countries,[5] although this can be to some extent justified by pointing out that all styles and genres of music produced in Ireland will have continuities and connections with music systems beyond its shores (Ó Súilleabháin, 1982a: 915). Not only that, but in increasingly globalized contexts of music production and consumption, it is arguable that particular genres of music hitherto associated with fixed conceptions of Irish ethnicity, be it in Ireland or amongst the worldwide Irish Diaspora, have to some degree become re-contextualized insofar as the same music is practised and enjoyed by non-Irish musicians and audiences in many parts of the world (see, for example, Williams, 2006).

This book then focuses on music in domestic national contexts. While obviously not the only way that the category of Irish music can be conceived, it is a way that Irish people themselves sometimes demarcate the field. For example, Bradby (1994), in a review of the 'Imagining Ireland' conference held in Dublin, 1993, describes how participants at an open forum on Irish popular music delimited the discussion to popular music produced by the 'Irish-living-in-Ireland'. My reason for focusing the discussion on domestic-produced music is because the subject matter is concerned with a particular society as much as it is with a particular nation; furthermore, I do not assume that this society-nation equates to any singular ethnicity. Thus, Irishness can be regarded as a problematic, rather than as a given concept.

I confine the study to the Republic of Ireland (henceforth 'Ireland') for two principal reasons. First, the book considers governmental and other official constructions of national identity and music within the sovereign Irish state, thereby leaving Northern Ireland (part of the United Kingdom) out of the analysis, or at least those parts that deal with infrastructural elements.[6] Second, I wish to focus on how Irishness, as opposed to Irishness in combination with Ulsterness and/or Britishness, is associated with certain types of music. Related to these points, the book does not engage in any substantial way with the complex issues of cultural identity arising from the sectarian and political 'troubles' experienced in Northern Ireland over recent decades. While this is a topic that has already received some attention (Bracefield, 1996; McCann, 1995; McLoone, 2004; Magowan, 2005;

---

[5]   See O'Flynn (2005a).

[6]   Northern Ireland has its own regional legislative assembly, and is serviced by different broadcasting organizations than the Republic. Furthermore, a number of agencies within Northern Ireland demarcate histories and identities of music that are distinct from those operating in the Republic of Ireland or, for that matter, in Great Britain (see for example, The Northern Ireland Music Industry Commission, n.d.).

Rolston, 1999, 2001; Stokes, 1994: 8–10; Vallely, 2004a, 2006) and undoubtedly merits further investigation, I do not pursue this route, largely because it is not an issue that significantly emerges amongst the various voices represented in this book.

Of course, musical activities are never wholly contained by political boundaries, and in relation to this particular study it is worth noting that many Irish musicians born north of the border are likely to have aspects of their education and subsequent production based in the Republic. Some contemporary examples include singer/ songwriters Juliet Turner and Paul Brady, and the composer/performer Phil Coulter (see Swan, 2003: 173–6; 237–40; 241–6). Furthermore, I acknowledge the interrelatedness and latent ambiguities of Irish, British and other national identities, an issue that is touched on immediately below. Overt and covert political ideas do sometimes come to the fore in the book, but only inasmuch as they are raised in the course of people's opinions about music and cultural-national identity in Ireland.

Identifying styles of Irish music

The broad definition of Irish music used throughout this work is premised on two key principles. First, the demarcation of particular styles and related sets of musical practices in Ireland or anywhere else arise with reference to the entire musical field (Green, 1999; Middleton, 1990: 1–12). Second, and at the same time, there are specific socio-historical contexts that give rise to the identification of three major style categories for Irish music, namely, traditional, popular and classical, and of various sub-styles within these.[7] This approach departs from conventional accounts of Irish music that are framed around a dual content of traditional music and classical music (see pp. 14–15 below), or on categorization systems centred on Western conceptions of a popular/classical split. Under this latter view, the folk or traditional label is regarded as primarily ideological insofar as its discursive origins represent a reaction to the rise of popular and mass-mediated cultural production in countries such as Britain during the late nineteenth and early twentieth centuries (Boyes, 1993; Clampin, 1999; Francmanis, 2003; Harker, 1985; Middleton, 1990; Pickering and Green, 1987; Small, 1987). Indeed, some critics of revivalist and other folkloristic perspectives go as far as to suggest that the term folk – and by extension, traditional – is itself a dubious if not redundant musical category (Boyes, 1993; Harker, 1985; Middleton, 1990).[8] Accordingly,

---

[7] In subsequent chapters I use the general category of traditional (or 'trad') in preference to folk, mainly because it is a more widely used term in the discourse of Irish music, as well as being the preferred term of the International Council for Traditional Music since 1981 (Bohlman, 1988: xiii). However, I also retain the idea of 'folk' as a relatively distinct sub-style of both Irish and international music.

[8] One of the many reasons put forward for the erasure of the folk category is that its various movements originated from concerns about social differentiation and control rather than from existing cultural practice. Furthermore, the distinctions that are often made between folk and popular music on the basis of rural/urban, oral/technological are

the category of folk or traditional can be subsumed within a broader conception of popular music that embraces all vernacular musical practices in differentiated modern societies (Middleton, 1990; Pickering and Green, 1987; Small, 1987). This re-alignment of the major categories allows us to interpret the dominant ideological interests of modern musical history through the dichotomous conceptions of high and low culture or, in the specific case of music, through the seemingly antithetical categories of classical and popular. However, this is a position that can be challenged, particularly with reference to music in Ireland over a similar historical period.

Certainly, it is possible to find parallels between historical accounts of antiquarian, revivalist and folkloristic movements in England and those that obtained in the Irish situation over a similar period (McCarthy, 1999; White, 1998a). In fact, prior to Ireland's sovereign independence in 1922, the two countries were economically and politically connected, and as such were also linked culturally and ideologically. Similar to patterns that unfolded in England, was the association of music with social categories and a tradition of antiquarian scholarship that later came to be transformed and appropriated by revivalist interests (White, 1998a: 53–73, 1998b: 27–32). Yet, social stratification in Ireland over this period differed in a number of respects. First, Ireland would remain a predominantly (though not exclusively) rural society well into the twentieth century (Tovey and Share, 2000: 41). Second, antiquarian interests in Irish culture were mediated through parallel processes of social differentiation and colonization. The first collections of Irish folk music by Anglo-Irish scholars represented an attraction to a cultural other, or a fetishization of 'native' Gaelic Irishness, as it were (see White, 1998a: 36–52).[9] A third difference relates to the later folk revival period at the turn of the nineteenth and twentieth centuries. In the case of England, the ideological basis of the folk revival might be interpreted in terms of social stratification, national interests and a counterbalance to the perceived threat of mass culture. However, if we consider Ireland as a British colony during this time, then such an ideological convergence falls apart. In fact, the revival of Irish culture was symbolically appropriated by separatist-nationalist interests and as such became a site of opposition and struggle (White, 1998a: 56).

Perceived differences between Irishness and Britishness often came to be conflated with socio-economic categories and distinctions of musical style. Under this way of thinking, non-traditional musical forms might be regarded as un-Irish. Thus, Irish classical music was often associated with an Anglo-Irish ascendancy comprising the merchant and upper classes while popular music was simultaneously regarded as 'vulgar' and 'foreign'. As Townshend (1999: 34) describes, this 'vocabulary of contamination' assumed the existence of 'an original, organic Irish

---

challenged as it is argued that there are countertendencies in both cases (see Middleton, 1990: 135–9).

[9] The term 'Gaelic' primarily refers to a group of Celtic languages spoken in parts of Ireland, Scotland and the Isle of Man. English is now the first language spoken by most Irish people although a significant number also speak Irish (Gaelic/*Gaeilge*).

culture'.[10] And yet, nationalist propaganda and romantic ideology notwithstanding, the material conditions under which Irish people lived and under which music was produced and consumed were specific to Ireland during the period in question. Counter to trends in the industrialized regions of Europe, a substantial majority of Irish people remained in rural communities and their musical practices were quite distinct from, though by no means unrelated to, music outside of those communities (McCarthy, 1999: 45–51).[11] In other words, I propose that whatever ideological constructions and struggles there may have been, traditional music as a practice or, to borrow Theodor Adorno's term, as a 'living musical collective consciousness', did actually exist (Adorno, 1976: 163, 165).[12] More to the point and as will become apparent throughout the book, traditional music continues to constitute a distinct category in the experiences and beliefs of rural- as well as urban-based people in Ireland today. This is not to idealize the past or to deny the ideological underpinning and political overtones of contemporary 'folk values'. As Coulter (2003: 27) reminds us: 'There are few things as modern as tradition.'

I should emphasize that my use of each of the terms 'traditional', 'popular', and 'classical' is both pragmatic and strategic, and I agree with those writers who point to the contingent nature and the ideological bases of all such generic distinctions (Green, 1999; Manuel, 1988; Martin, 1995; Middleton, 1990; Walser, 1993). As we shall see, these distinctions not only affect what is said and written about music but also have consequences for actual musical practices and for everyday attitudes to particular styles of music (Chambers, 1985: 26; Green, 1988: 5–6; Martin, 1995: 17). At the same time, the construction of commonsense meanings can also be seen as 'the result of a perpetual process of collaborative definition rather than a passive acceptance of received wisdom' (Martin, 1995: 29–30). Style categorizations are used by producers and consumers of music alike. They are also central to mediating processes such as marketing or 'labelling'. It should not be assumed however, as H.S. Bennett (1980: xi–xii) reminds us, that the discourses of producers, consumers and distributors will necessarily correspond with one another or, for that matter, with a defined set of musical practices. Thus, for example, if a label such as 'Irish hip-hop' comes to be assumed by music promoters, journalists or even academics (A. Bennett, 2000: 137; McLaughlin, 1999: 43), it does not

---

[10]   Throughout the twentieth century however, the perceived threat to essential Irishness would gradually shift from a fear of 'Anglicization' to that of 'Los Angelization' (Gibbons, 1996: 3).

[11]   This is not to suggest that Ireland was unique in this respect, as there were other regions in Europe in which a predominantly agrarian base of social organization was retained.

[12]   At the same time, Adorno was scathing in his analysis of classical composers who incorporated folk elements into symphonic music, a tendency he interpreted as an early form of global capitalism through which process 'the qualitative differences between peoples … came to be transformed into commodity brands on the world market' (Adorno, 1976: 163).

necessarily follow that this nation-specific style categorization finds resonance in everyday perceptions about the same general area of musical practice.

National identity and music[13]

The phrase 'national identity and music' is used throughout the book to describe a general process by which individuals and groups may come to perceive, cognize and articulate associations between, on the one hand, specifically musical formations, and on the other hand, wider socio-cultural formations associated with the nation state. While a distinction can be made between the construction of individual and collective musical identities, these are never separable in actual experience (Frith, 1996a: 109). Another way of looking at this is to differentiate between unique moments of musical experience and fixed positions in relation to particular styles and genres (Frith, 1996a: 122). However, it does not follow that an aesthetic experience of music will necessarily negate or transcend essentialist beliefs about the same music. As I have argued elsewhere (O'Flynn, 2007: 24–5), if we accept that commonsense views pertaining to essence and identity in music actually occur, then these commonsense views must be considered to be at least partly constitutive of holistic musical experience(s). Thus, if for some people, specifically Irish associations arise from listening to certain types of music, these associations are neither 'fixed' nor do they occur in isolation. Rather, we need to recognize the links between, on the one hand, essentialist notions about Irish music or any other kind of music and, on the other hand, the unique and contingent nature of all conceptions arising from individual experiences or 'identifications' (Hall, 1996: 2–3) of the same music. Related to this, though perhaps obvious, it is also worth noting that 'national identity' does not equal the sum total of identities or identifications within a bounded nation state. As Brian Graham (1997) argues, criteria of inclusion/exclusion other than those dictated by nationalist agendas are likely to obtain in the modern nation state, and indeed there is often a tendency for the national level to obscure social complexities that emerge in the areas of class, geographical location, gender, race and ethnicity.[14] Furthermore, even in situations where some ideologies appear to dominate, the possibility also exists for the rejection, subversion and/or appropriation of homogenous narratives of national identity, whether in music (O'Flynn, 2007: 25) or in other cultural fields (C. Graham, 1999, 2001: 132–52).

While it may not be feasible to pinpoint exactly what constitutes national identity at either theoretical or concrete levels, it is possible to delineate parameters through which national identity, or identifications connected to concepts of 'nation',

---

[13]   Some of the arguments put forward in this section appear in an earlier essay (O'Flynn, 2007).

[14]   A number of these themes are explored in Nabeel Zuberi's (2001) study of Englishness and popular music.

may obtain. Miller (1995: 22–5) outlines five key areas that characterize national identity: shared beliefs, historical continuity, symbolic activity (a striking musical example would be the Eurovision Song Contest[15]), geographical association and the assumption of common characteristics. To a large degree, it can and often has been argued that nations are 'imagined communities' (Anderson, 1991). Furthermore, terms such as 'nation' and 'national' offer a multiplicity of interpretations, the category of 'nation' often being conflated with those of 'ethnicity', 'state' and 'nation-state' or 'nation state' (Connor, 1994).[16] At the same time, imaginings of national identity usually require particular sets of material conditions in addition to purely symbolic resources. Of particular importance in this regard is the role played by communications media in nationally defined territories (Cloonan, 1999, 2007; McLoone, 1991; Malm and Willis, 1992; Miller, 1995; Shuker and Pickering, 1994), a role that comes to be examined in Chapter 3. Thus, national identity is partially framed and symbolically mediated by the various policies, institutional structures and cultural media that obtain in any one nation state. Žižek (1993: 201–2) offers a further perspective by regarding the affective aspects of individuals' and communities' relationship with the real-imagined nation state or 'Nation qua Thing' as central to the construction and maintenance of national identity: 'A nation *exists* only as long as its specific *enjoyment* continues to be materialized in a set of social practices and transmitted through national myths that structure these practices' (ibid: 202). (See also, Anderson, 2002; Biddle and Knights, 2007: 5–12; Zuberi, 2001: 10–15.)

Throughout this book the term 'Irish music' is employed with reference to a relatively distinct society that is bounded by the nation state of Ireland. Having said this, we can consider music in the context of Irish national identity as a 'porous' cultural field, with the maintenance and/or revision of Irishness dialectically related to the increasingly 'transnational flow' of musical identities (Connell and Gibson, 2003: 143). Furthermore, if we regard differentiations of music as partially constitutive of social identities (Martin, 1995: 26), then the various traditions, styles and repertories of Irish-produced music may act to demarcate other identities in addition to those specifically associated with Irishness. Thus, while this book engages with the particular focus of music and national identity, it does so with reference to other foci of potential social relations.

While recognizing that there is no singular conception of national identity, I involve the use of ideal types for this study. First, I adapt the distinction made between ethnic and civic constructs of nationality (Smith, 1991), eschewing any relative valorization that sets civic nationalism ('Western', 'good', 'patriotic') above ethnic nationalism ('Eastern', 'bad', 'fanatical') (see McCrone, 1998: 7–10). Rather, these ideal types are used to interpret a range of contesting theories and/or

---

[15]   See Raykoff and Tobin (2007).

[16]   'Nation-state' is conventionally used to describe independent states with some degree of ethnic and/or cultural homogeneity whereas 'nation state' suggests a more civically oriented conception of statehood (McCrone, 1998: 85–7).

everyday beliefs about Irish national identity. As we shall see in Chapter 3 and elsewhere, a civic/ethnic dualism can be interpreted in statutory cultural policy, where a clear distinction between 'high art' and 'traditional arts' is made. Indeed, the argument that nationalism has perpetuated a deception through which 'native traditions' are employed in its rhetoric while simultaneously imposing the values of high art/modernity on society (Gellner, 1983: 57) is to some extent reflected in the cultural policy of the Irish state. It could equally be said though that, increasingly, advocates of traditional arts in Ireland have come to renegotiate the terms and values by which national culture is defined. A third ideal-type construction relevant to the discussion is that of economic national identity (McCrone, 1998: 174), an interpretive tool that is particularly apt at a time when, in some quarters, Irish society and culture are primarily regarded in terms of a 'Celtic Tiger' economy. Throughout this book, I regard the three ideal types of civic, ethnic and economic national identity as contesting yet related forms of discourse pervading much of the literature on Irish culture and Irish music. These in turn come to be examined in the light of people's actual experiences of particular types of Irish-produced music.

Comparative perspectives

If 'Irish music' can be considered as a cross-cultural field, then its study requires as much breadth in critical perspectives as it does in musical content. While the analysis of Irish music texts might well tell us something about Irish cultural identities, it would be erroneous to assume that Irish music or styles of Irish music are representative of an Irish nation or of social structures within that nation. I therefore avoid any one-sided culturalist interpretation of identity in Irish music, and accordingly concur with the critique of homology theories made by Middleton (1990: 127–71), Frith (1996a: 108) and Wade (1998: 4). On a number of counts, it is questionable whether the relationship between Irish music and an Irish nation can be reduced to the idea of 'expressive fit'. First, this does not take account of the complex nature of mediation in the wider nexus of social relations that includes a diversity of musical genres and practices. Second, reducing the idea of Irish music to the reproduction of Irish culture denies the potential that music holds for individual development, cultural renewal and social change (Swanwick, 1999: 25). Furthermore, if, as happens with traditional and other Irish genres, the music associated with a particular socio-cultural group comes to be appropriated and integrated by groups external to it (Middleton, 1990: 152–3; Slobin, 1993: 61–82), then any assumed homology between Irish music and an Irish nation is no longer tenable.

Conversely, it can be argued that music is constitutive, rather than reflective of identity (Stokes, 1994; Wade, 1998). Indeed, music is often a primary agent in the construction and maintenance of national identity (Connell and Gibson, 2003: 118). However, even in cases where music does appear to be an active agent in the (re-)construction of national identity (for example, Baily, 1994; Bohlman, 2004; Hudson, 2007; Manuel, 1998; Slobin, 1996), we can never wholly interpret the processes of musical-national identification in unidirectional terms. Rather, the relationship between music and national identity needs to be considered as an interpenetrative process. A useful concept here is what Folkestad (2002: 155) describes as a continuum of insider/outsider perspectives. This not only refers to the potential interface of emic and etic[17] views of particular cultures, but also to possibly distinct functions of music identity within cultural groupings. Thus, in the case of Ireland, a distinction can be drawn between domestic-produced music that may be employed emblematically (external identity) and that which serves to promote group cohesiveness and belongingness (internal identity). The first of these ideas brings to mind the more obvious cultural flags such as national anthems, but it could also describe a process whereby traditional or 'ethnic specific' music is directed outwards to embody symbolic meanings of nation (Folkestad, 2002: 156). Later, it will be shown the extent to which traditional music is often regarded as synonymous with Irish music, both at an institutional level and at the level of individual beliefs.

Of course, the construction and negotiation of internal collective identities within nation states involve more than imaginings of 'nationalness' in music since interrelated ideas of 'foreignness' are often involved in such processes (Magaldi, 1999: 324–6). Moreover, as useful as distinctions such as internal/external, national/cultural or emblematic/catalytic might be, it cannot be assumed that these dualistic concepts are realized in contexts of one 'function' or another. As I set out to show throughout this book, the same piece of music can lead to different types of identity, just as each individual's experience of music may reveal a unique spectrum of musical identifications.

Mediation and hegemony

Insofar as no musical object or musical practice can be regarded as wholly autonomous or *immediate*, it follows that all aspects of music production and consumption are socially mediated (Adorno, 1976: 194–218). There are a number of ways that the concept of mediation is applied in this book. First, I regard the intermediary action of particular individuals and groups in Irish culture- and industry-oriented organizations (Negus, 1996: 66; Sanjek, 1999). This idea of mediation also extends to other social actors such as musicians (in terms of musical reinterpretations and/or modes of presentation – see especially Chapter 4), fan clubs, music societies, teachers, academics, politicians and lobby groups. Particularly active in this regard are those individuals described as 'moral entrepreneurs' (Becker, 1963), people whose intermediary actions exert significant influence on the beliefs and practices of others (see pp. 27–8 for a discussion on composer Seán Ó Riada's missionary quest to forge an Irish musical identity during the 1960s).

---

[17] Terms used to distinguish the perspectives of those directly involved in particular cultural contexts and/or practices from the perspectives of those who observe and analyze the same contexts and/or practices.

The idea of mediation also refers to processes of cultural transmission afforded by technological media (Martin, 1995: 7; McCarthy, 1999: 26–8; Negus, 1996: 68), and this perspective will be used in Chapter 3 and elsewhere to examine aspects of mass-mediated cultural production in Ireland. In yet another application the term can be employed to regard all musical products and experiences as mediated by social relationships (Negus, 1996: 69). This comes close to the concept of hegemony discussed below and suggests some key areas for interpreting the relationships between Irish national identity and people's experience of Irish-produced music. Among these are: the consequences of nationalist and other ideological movements, the cultural and economic policies of the Irish state, and the relative status enjoyed by various socio-economic and/or cultural groups in Ireland at any one time.

If perceptions and theories of Irishness and music at once reveal patterns of similarity and difference, then we need to regard the (Irish) nation as a field of meaning that revolves around a contested concept of that entity (Connell and Gibson, 2003: 123). Rather than capitulating to a wholly relativist interpretation of what Irish music is and how it is perceived, we can adapt the Gramscian perspective of hegemony to the analysis (Dasilva et al., 1984: 95–6; Middleton, 1990: 7–10). Under this view 'disparate cultural and ideological elements are nevertheless held together by an articulating principle or set of central values' (Wade, 1998: 4). The idea of hegemony suggests an approach whereby the workings of major institutions in Irish society can be seen to promote contesting yet potentially interlacing views of dominant groups within that same society (Forgacs, 1988: 224, 230–31).

A broader conception of hegemony extends to all asymmetrical relations of power, and Diamond (1994: 9–11) suggests three levels of hegemony, each of which is applicable to the case of music in Ireland. At a macro level we can examine the governing forces in Irish society and those who are governed by them. Throughout the book it shall be seen how, at both symbolic and material levels, two major groupings involved respectively in the promotion of classical music and traditional music in Ireland often contest the national-cultural field. It will also be shown how some economic interests can radically interrupt the political and cultural basis (and arguably, stasis) of this high art versus traditional arts dichotomy. At the same time, all three types of national identity – ethnic, civic and economic – share a central set of 'Irish' values that may serve to marginalize local and/or individual musical differences. However, the homogenizing tendency of national-musical articulations does not necessarily obliterate opposition and/or heterogeneity in the discourses and practices of domestic-produced music; rather, these two sides can be regarded as dialectically linked (Wade, 1998).

A second hegemonic dimension is concerned with the relationship between hierarchically equal groups who regard themselves as distinct, and it offers a critical perspective for examining the ideological and mythological contexts in which the dominant forces of some societies can come to construct ideas of otherness. This is relevant to the analysis of both colonial and nationalist imaginings of Irish history, both of which types can be found in some contemporary views about Irishness and music. Of course, what is considered 'other' depends on the social experience and subject position of each commentator. Thus, for example, some Irish musicologists distinguish traditional music from other Irish music by designating it 'ethnic', while a number of traditional music's advocates consider non-traditional music as 'foreign'. A different sense of otherness comes to be interpreted towards the end of the book, where it will be argued that, paradoxically, nostalgic imaginings of Irish music and culture suggest a phenomenon whereby musical-national identifications may be realized through the construction of an 'absent national other'.

The idea of hegemony also helps interpret the relationship between musical products and 'representors' or mediators of the same entities. This is a hegemonic level that is critically involved with contesting representations and articulations of cultural distinctiveness that Diamond (1994: 11) describes as 'the point of contact between an art and its languaging, between creators/consumers of expressive culture and the individuals who write about or otherwise represent that expressive culture through interpretations, translations'. In succeeding chapters, it will be shown how some musical texts are represented as authentically Irish whereas others are not. At the same time, it will be revealed how the same musical products and events can lead to different and sometimes opposing conceptions of Irishness between and among various groups of producers, consumers and cultural commentators.

Theorizing Irishness and music

The general area of Irish Studies has traditionally been framed by historical interpretations and/or by cultural studies of Irish literature and other artistic forms. More recently, issues pertaining to national identity have also come under the purview of the academic fields of sociology, cultural geography, economics and media studies. Much of the recent scholarship has questioned the trope of nationalist and essentialist accounts of Irish cultural history, characterized by Brian Graham (1997: 9) as 'the seamless integration of virtually all exogenous influences within a supposedly stable and continuous Gaelic identity'. Critical theories of Irish identity have focused on the dialectical relationship between colonialism and nationalism, and, as these recent titles would suggest – *Writing Ireland* (Cairns, 1988), *Representing Ireland* (Bradshaw et al., 1993), *Translating Ireland* (Cronin, 1996), *Inventing Ireland* (Kiberd, 1996), *In Search of Ireland* (B. Graham, 1997), *Deconstructing Ireland* (C. Graham, 2001), and *Reinventing Ireland* (Kirby et al., 2002) – among some quarters, it seems taken for granted that the very idea of Ireland is itself a social construction (Maley, 1999: 24). However, it cannot be assumed that anti-essentialist positions are any less ideological than the particular constructions of Irish identity that they challenge. Nor should it be taken as axiomatic that sets of values regarding Irishness as the main collective identity are inevitably repressive ones (Richards, 1999: xiii). Broadly speaking, it could be said that cultural theories of Irish music are characterized by an anti-essentialist outlook, but throughout the book it will be shown that this tendency is not replicated in everyday definitions and conceptions. With this in mind, my overall approach is to interrogate essentialist as well as anti-essentialist views of Irishness and music.[18]

The past two decades have seen the emergence of a significant corpus of Irish musical studies encompassing various analytical perspectives on a broad range of domestic-produced music.[19] Common to much of this work is a reflexive awareness of the role that ideology can play in constructions of national identity and music. From some musicological perspectives the dominant ideologies of nationalism and colonialism come to be regarded as inhibiting factors in the development of music in Ireland. Alternative perspectives, particularly those drawn from popular music studies, interpret other sites of contemporary music production, consumption and distribution where national identity may be articulated or contested in more complex ways.

Throughout his substantial contribution to Irish musical studies, Harry White (1995, 1998a and 1998b, 2001, 2003, 2005, 2007) argues that the emblematic status of Ireland's traditional music has actually impeded the development of music (by which White means classical or art music) in the country. While this presents an original and compelling ideology-critique of revivalist and other cultural-political movements, White does not apply a similar critique to the underlying assumptions and institutional structures of classical music practices in Ireland and elsewhere (for example, the ideological construct of musical autonomy). Arguably, White's work reads more as a cultural theory than as a cultural history, since his analysis does not deal in any comprehensive manner with the material aspects of musical life in Ireland over the period surveyed.[20] Post-colonial and revisionist approaches also feature in the theories of others writing with what might be described as classical music sensibilities, notably, Axel Klein (1997, 2003), Richard Pine (1998, 2002, 2005) and Joseph Ryan (1995, 2001). Collectively, these writers can be said to contribute to an overarching modernist critique of 'national' (and by implication, 'traditional') conceptions of Irish music.

It is somewhat ironic that, in spite of these and other musicologists' shared critique of nationalist ideology it seems that the greatest level of engagement with 'national' music occurs in the classical sphere. For example, I have on several occasions witnessed the playing/singing of the national anthem at classical music concerts, Wexford Festival Opera being a high-profile example, whereas this is something I have yet to experience at a traditional or popular music event. The engagement of classical music interests with national issues is perhaps most vividly displayed in advocacy for music education, through publications, symposia and other forms of debate. At no time was this more apparent than at the Music

---

[18]   This follows a strategy employed by McLaughlin (1999).

[19]   At the same time, and as both White (1998a and 1998b, 2003, 2005) and Smyth (2004a, 2005, 2007) have argued, by comparison with other cultural areas, music does not generally feature in the mainstream of Irish Studies.

[20]   Zuk (2004) questions White's rather pessimistic portrayal of classical music production in Ireland over the past two centuries.

Education National Debate (MEND) hosted by the Dublin Institute of Technology in 1995–96. Seemingly pluralist in its brief, the ensuing MEND report (Heneghan, 2001, 2002) would propose a dual content of classical and traditional music, with the latter clearly in the role of second fiddle to the interests of a conservatoire-led conception of Irish music education.

In another history of Irish music, Marie McCarthy (1999) maps the relationships between different modes of music transmission amongst various 'subcultures' in Irish society (see also McCarthy, 1995, 1997, 1998, 2004). In taking this approach she avoids a tendency amongst some Irish musicologists to reify musical-national ideologies without due regard to the complexity of socio-historical factors involved. McCarthy's work presents a balanced evaluation of the contesting claims of folk and high art ideologies in the evolution of Irish musical and national identities, although her analysis for the most part does not address the potential significance of popular music practices and subcultures. Indeed, a general tendency in Irish musicological studies can be noted whereby the idea of popular music as a distinct category appears to be omitted from grand historical narratives (Smyth, 2005: 2–3). While Ireland of the nineteenth and most of the twentieth century could be described as more agrarian and by extension less industrialized than other parts of Western Europe, it nonetheless contained socially stratified urban populations that were not cut off from the successive, international popular culture movements afforded through technologies of mass mediation.[21] And yet, there is to date no comprehensive history of popular music in Ireland that deals with any period prior to the country's economic expansion from the 1960s onwards. Even where the focus is on the last 50 years or so, most musicological studies purporting to engage with Irish musical identities either ignore domestic popular music or at best regard a limited number of artists as a phenomenon of international success. Related to this, while virtually all critical studies of Irish musical culture to date have either explicitly or implicitly employed the ideal-type constructions of civic and ethnic national identities, the bulk of this literature has not considered more recent ideological expressions of economic national identity and the implications that these may have for all types of music produced in Ireland.

In his study of popular music and national identity in Ireland, Noel McLaughlin (1999) discusses the interplay between, on one side, the ideological underpinnings of international rock and pop genres and, on the other side, the cultural-national milieux in which domestic music production takes place. Similar to White's analysis of the ideological struggles facing the development of Irish classical music, McLaughlin problematizes the emblematic status of traditional music and, related to this, the 'burden of representation' (1999: 103) that is often carried by

---

[21]   Prior to the 1960s, the broadcasting of popular music was actively discouraged and in some instances censored by state authorities (Gibbons, 1996: 70–81). While this obviously curtailed the extent to which international popular music was transmitted, many sectors of the population would have had access to external broadcasts, recordings and publications (sheet music).

Irish popular musicians.[22] While McLaughlin draws attention to the dominant homogenizing discourses of music journalism in Ireland, primarily those of rock music and traditional music, the greater part of his discussion is based on a cultural analysis of internationally known Irish music acts and associated musical texts (see also McLaughlin and McLoone, 2000).

Gerry Smyth (2005) also adopts a cultural studies approach in his history of Irish popular music, his perspective departing somewhat from that of McLaughlin insofar as it offers a more localized and detailed view of the genres, musicians and subcultures that obtained from the 1960s to the present day (see also Campbell and Smyth, 2005). Smyth (2005: 7) argues that, given the extent of popular music production and consumption in the country, it is a phenomenon that deserves to be regarded as the most actively negotiated area of modern Irish identity. In contrast to previous studies on the topic, his work suggests potential signifiers of identification with domestic-produced music other than those arising from overt nationalist ideologies. Smyth proposes a focus on the dialectics of space, time and social being, and within this framework makes some speculations about the potential for localized 'sounds' shared by clusters of rock musicians (see also Hogan, 2007).[23] However, while Smyth's theorization of local rock music production presents us with an interesting hypothesis, especially as it interrupts homogenizing discourses of Irishness, questions remain as to how local music 'sounds' are heard by musicians and listeners alike. Smyth (2005: 91–4; 133–6) also discusses the relationship between culture and industry as it might apply to music in Ireland (and its reception abroad), and in doing so highlights an important plane of identity for all genres of Irish-produced music. This can be related to the growing sense of economic Irish identity whereby domestic musical practices and products can come to be regarded equally in terms of economic and cultural capital. Barra Ó Cinnéide's entrepreneurial view of the *Riverdance* phenomenon has arguably been the most celebratory and uncritical articulation of this position to date (Ó Cinnéide, 2002).

An alternative approach to Irish musical identities is presented by Mícheál Ó Súilleabháin (1994, 1998) who draws on Jungian theory to present the idea of an Irish psyche as it might be applied to Irish composers and performers. Adopting a mainly anthropological perspective, he addresses the notion of musical mediation in Irish cultural history, and employs the idea of 'bridge' or transition in his interpretation of the careers of selected musicians, in relatively autonomous musical fields as well as in wider cultural contexts. Much as Ó Súilleabháin employs the term 'psyche' in the case of individual musicians, and much as these may be linked by the idea of crossing musical and/or cultural boundaries, it is

---

[22]   This is of course not unique to the Irish situation. See, for example, Hyder (2004: Chapter 6) on similar issues regarding Asianness and South Asian popular musicians in the UK.

[23]   Beliefs about regionalism and style variation in Irish music are already well documented in the traditional sphere (for example, Corcoran, 1997; Keegan, 1997).

never stated what exactly is meant by 'Irish psyche' in its specific relation to Irish music. However, we get some sense of Ó Súilleabháin's musical-cultural mediation when he employs the concepts of hybridity and syncretism. These terms are also explored in the analyses of McCarthy (1999) and McLaughlin (1999), and in many respects present attractive, alternative ways of interpreting Irish musical identities, particularly when compared with the rigid ideologies and essentialist positions of conservative music interest groups. Yet, as McLaughlin (1999: 34) argues, a key question regarding hybridity and, by extension, syncretism is how it is actually heard, and this returns me to the argument that theories of Irishness and music need to be examined in the light of actual musical practices.

A number of ideas from the existing literature on Irish musical identities are adapted at the end of this chapter when I propose a list of possible associations between Irishness and music. However, *The Irishness of Irish Music* departs from previous studies in two major respects. First, and as argued above, it regards the areas of traditional, popular and classical music as belonging to one interrelated field of cultural production and consumption. In calling for a similar approach, Smyth (2007: 203) suggests that these diverse manifestations of Irish musical life 'are all locked together in a critical matrix in which the stakes are the meaning and the limits of a modern Irish identity'. The wide-lens approach that I take to some extent also reflects a recent and welcome reappraisal of what counts as Irish music in academic circles and among some sectors of the public (Ó Laoire, 2005: 281). For example, a symposium entitled 'Music and Identity in Ireland' held at the National University of Ireland, Maynooth in December 2006 included presentations and discussions that dealt in fairly equal measure with aspects of classical, traditional and popular music produced in Ireland. The second way in which this book differs from previous critical studies of Irish musical identities is that it includes a materialist dimension by seeking original data on people's perceptions of music in actual performance settings. Some valuable insights into the beliefs of Irish performers and/or composers regarding identity issues can already be gleaned from the numerous interviews published in newspapers, specialist magazines and on websites, as well as through a number of dedicated publications (see for example, Contemporary Music Centre, 1991–2004; Harper and Hodgett, 2004; Swan, 2003), although there is as yet no substantial work that interprets this data within a framework of cultural and national identity perspectives. While Višnja Cogan's book on U2 (2006) includes an epilogue with appraisals of the band by Irish and other fans, the opinions of these participants do not otherwise feature in the various themes explored in her work.

General approach and structure

The Irishness of Irish Music juxtaposes established theories of Irishness and music with everyday assumptions and beliefs, a central tenet being that any investigation of ideology about music needs to be grounded in the views of a wide range of social actors (Green, 1999: 10–11). If we wish to understand national identity and music in the general sense, then we must seek out the opinions of producers, consumers and mediators alike; we also need to interpret these perspectives in relation to the range of cultural practices and products from which they arise in the first place. Additionally, as much as cultural and historical analyses may inform an interpretation of residual ideologies, theories and assumptions about Irishness and music also need to be interpreted in the light of the differentiated modern society that Ireland has now become. This book therefore investigates everyday identifications and/or rejections of Irishness in music as much as it interrogates grand narratives of national identity and music. This follows a number of approaches that suggest a more dynamic role for consumers in the arrangement and understanding of their musical 'worlds' (Bennett, 2000: 67; Hesmondhalgh, 2002; Zuberi, 2001: 12).

Associations between Irishness and Irish music are regarded throughout the book as a phenomenon of perception rather than as a definable set of essential meanings. As beliefs and assumptions arise out of perceptions, I also explore people's spoken beliefs and unspoken assumptions about Irish music. A critical focus here is the apparently prevalent and 'commonsense' view of Irish music as synonymous with traditional music and/or traditional-derived music. In the first instance, I set out to ascertain the extent of such a belief among people living in Ireland and, predictably perhaps, a tendency towards this view is confirmed in interviews, though not in every individual case. More specifically, the *Irishness of Irish Music* aims to discover why some conceptions are more dominant than others, and how these and alternative assumptions and/or imaginings of Irishness and music come to be apprehended, articulated and negotiated.

Three interrelated strands extend from the book's theme. First, I examine in what ways Irishness might be perceived in sound. To this end, and insofar as beliefs and assumptions about music are to varying degrees linked to what happens 'inside' the music, to its intra-musical content and structure, I also engage with a range of selected musical practices and products. Second, I consider how Irishness in music might be apprehended differentially according to the various styles of Irish-produced music. A third strand is based on the likelihood that perceptions of Irishness will vary across different musical events and genres, as well as between and among different interest groups and listening subjects. Accordingly, the book also investigates in what contexts and with what values Irishness may or may not be perceived in Irish music.

Mapping the field

Aspects of music production and consumption in Ireland are recorded and interpreted at different points in the book. This draws on Bourdieu's concept of the cultural field of practice (1993) and follows approaches suggested by Cloonan (1999), Kruse (1998: 187–90), and Martin (1995: 26–32). The field identified for this study comprises: recent historical contexts and contemporary musical practices; statutory policy and provision and the agency of non-governmental cultural organizations; and economic aspects of production, distribution and consumption. This set of 'national' data functions less as a survey than as an 'aerial photograph' (Blaukopf, 1992: 228) that places in context a more detailed analysis of events and products, and the perceptions, beliefs and assumptions that emerge from these. A critical perspective on potential associations between Irishness and Irish music requires the identification and interpretation of the specific material conditions that might render phenomena of musical-national expression in the first instance. In turn, we also need to recognize the agency that these potential articulations and identifications hold in (re-)constituting both material and symbolic aspects of the national cultural field. Arguably, then, all such negotiations around the idea of Irishness and Irish music can be viewed as an interplay between structural, cultural and experiential levels of identity and meaning (Kirschner, 1998: 257–8; Shepherd and Giles-Davis, 2000: 219; Walser, 1993: xiii).

Chapter 2 presents a brief and recent history of Irish music, and this is followed by an overview of the national field of music production and consumption in Chapter 3. In keeping with the photographic analogy, Chapter 4 offers some 'snapshots' of musical life in Ireland by taking a closer look at a number of selected music events. These events provide specific contexts in which to interpret people's views about Irish music; at the same time, they constitute part of the 'grand text' of Irish musical life. By this, I refer not only to the sounds that are played, sung and heard, but also to the modes of presentation and other ways in which music comes to be mediated.

Data for *The Irishness of Irish Music* came from two principal sources: first, a selection of published, recorded and broadcast material gathered between 1995–2006 and, second, transcripts of fieldwork carried out at various music events between 1999–2001. My main reason for seeking the latter type of information was that the discussion would become grounded in everyday musical practices and beliefs. The events were selected on the basis of general patterns identified in national listings across the categories of traditional, classical and popular music, and the fieldwork for each event involved two interrelated processes. First, I set out to interview groups of audience members during or after each concert, gig or session. This yielded 28 interviews with a total of 67 attendees across the various events. Second, I recorded my own observations on each event under the broad categories of venues, audiences, sounds, atmosphere, musicians, modes of presentation, and any publicity/paraphernalia pertaining to the acts in question. This was critical since I wished to explore the potential relationships between, on the one hand, musical texts and contexts as observable by myself-as-researcher, and on the other hand, people's beliefs pertaining to the same texts and contexts.

The people who kindly agreed to be interviewed were not approached on the basis of their constituting a representative sample among various sectors of the Irish population or, for that matter, on the basis that they were members of particular subcultures within Irish society. Rather, they were approached because they had chosen to attend certain types of music events. In other words, and following Blacking (1995: 234) as well as studies carried out by Bennett (1997,

2000), Björnberg and Stockfelt (1996), and Van De Port (1999), it was these specific musical-social contexts as opposed to social categories that had been the organizing principle in gathering people's opinions. Combined, the interviews and observations revealed findings that in the first instance emerged from individual voices, in particular situations, at specific times. In addition to providing vignettes of the musical-cultural field, they also presented a set of grounded reflections on conceptions of identity, value and space (Feld, 1994: 93).

The interviews inquired into four general areas. First, I chatted with respondents about their musical preferences. This was followed by a number of general questions dealing with the music heard at each particular event. I next asked interviewees for their views about the potential Irishness of the same music. Lastly, I sought out people's opinions in relation to a number of well-known Irish musicians. Some initial observations and findings from these interviews are described in a more extensive account of the fieldwork in Chapter 4. The responses of the 67 interviewees at these events are then woven into the discussion and analysis throughout the remainder of the book.[24] Indeed, the themes for Chapters 5, 6, 7 and 8 in large part emerge from issues raised by the interview respondents themselves. The views of other social actors are also considered at particular stages in these chapters, and here I draw from the categories of musician, journalist, politician, entrepreneur and academic. Chapter 5 assesses the extent to which perceptions of Irish music are linked to articulations of Irish cultural and national identity. Critically, I examine the emblematic significance that traditional music appears to hold for many Irish people. Chapter 6 looks to alternative conceptions and formulations of national identity in the context of contemporary Irish society. This includes a critique of entrepreneurial perspectives on Irishness and music. At the same time, other opinions and experiences regarding music and contemporary Irish society emerge from interviews, and these are contrasted with the homogenizing and celebratory discourse of economic national identity.

Chapter 7 is concerned with how Irish music comes to be apprehended by listeners, a particular focus being how Irishness in music might or might not be heard in particular configurations and patterns of sound. Significant categories are interpreted from the responses, and these are interspersed and compared with musicological theories and other beliefs about inherent Irishness and Irish music. In Chapter 8, I discuss a number of interrelated themes that find resonance in both literature and data. As many appraisals of Irishness and Irish music appear to be predicated on notions of cultural authenticity, this articulatory principle is theorized and applied to the analysis of a number of dualistic conceptions that emerge from scholarly, journalistic and everyday opinions. The book concludes by reflecting on the dialectical relationship between identity and difference in perceptions and articulations of Irishness in music.

---

[24]   For accuracy, transcripts of recorded interviews were made available to respondents. Approximately one fifth viewed transcripts of the interviews in which they participated.

Possible associations between Irishness and music

I now adapt key ideas from the literature to present a speculative set of associations regarding how Irishness in various types of domestic-produced music may (or may not) be perceived and/or cognized. At various stages throughout the book, these potential associations between Irishness and music are returned to and examined in the light of issues emerging from the fieldwork and from other data.

Essential Irishness and music

As numerous commentators have observed (Acton, 1978; Corcoran, 1982; Deane, 1995; Dillane, 2005; McCarthy, 1997, 1999; McLaughlin, 1999; McLaughlin and McLoone, 2000; White, 1998a and 1998b, 2001, 2003, 2005; Smyth, 1992, 2004a, 2007), notions equating 'Irish traditional music' with 'Irish music' appear to prevail. Clearly, this suggests an essentialist position, but it could also be speculated that for many people, while the Irish = traditional view is acknowledged as culturally embedded, it is not uncritically received.

Irish sound

The assumption or aspiration that Irish rock (and/or other 'non-traditional' styles practised in Ireland) constitutes a distinct sound comes not only from an Irish national perspective, but also echoes the conflation of the concepts of 'local' and 'authentic' within rock ideology (McLaughlin, 1999; McLoughlin and McLoone, 2000).[25] At least two distinct concepts can be involved in claims to an Irish sound. The first of these relates to the essentialist conception of Irish music as synonymous with traditional music. The second and arguably more open concept of an Irish sound refers to local adaptations of international genres that are articulated through accents, narratives and other 'para-musical' aspects. This idea of 'sound' may also be considered in regional terms, for example, 'Limerick tenors' in the case of light opera or 'local rock sounds' in the manner suggested by Smyth (2005).

Cultural Irishness and music

What is meant by cultural Irishness will very much depend on the conception of culture that is involved, and here I draw on Terry Eagleton's monograph identifying three distinct yet interrelated ideals suggested by the term, namely, civil society and the secular state, traditional ways of life and/or heritage, and the 'masterworks' of artistic and intellectual endeavour (Eagleton, 2000). In its loosest sense, the recognition of cultural Irishness might simply refer to the nationality of musicians or to other general 'civic facts'. In a more specific sense, certain music repertoires and practices become invested with heritage and associated with 'Irish

---

[25] See also Regev (1992, 1996) in relation to similar ideas about Israeli rock music.

ways', and what is identified with here is not the music per se, but rather the belief that (some types of) Irish music constitutes a vital part of 'our culture' or 'our way of life' (Žižek, 1993: 201).[26] Cultural Irishness could also refer to conceptions of an Irish 'high culture', specifically relating to musical compositions that draw inspiration from Irish literary and/or mythological sources (White, 2003: 16). This form of cultural Irishness might also lead to a civic sense of pride in musical products that achieve widespread artistic acclaim.

Irish soul

Overlapping with some conceptions of cultural Irishness is a belief in the presence of 'Irish soul' among composers and/or musicians. In some cases, this may arise from perceived continuities between local producers and Afro-American soul music (see McLaughlin and McLoone, 2000; Onkey, 2006). More often though, the idea comes to be associated with non-specific articulations of a generic 'Irish sound', and is in some ways similar to Ó Súilleabháin's speculation about an 'Irish psyche' (1994).

Irishness and inherent musicality

This refers to an assumption that the Irish, in comparison to other peoples, are musically gifted, notably in the area of song. As other writers have commented, such a view arose from anthropological-colonial constructions of Irishness that date as far back as the twelfth century,[27] and were later appropriated in nationalist imaginings of Irishness (McCarthy, 1999; McLaughlin, 1999; McLaughlin and McLoone, 2000; Strachan and Leonard, 2004; White, 1998a). Notions of Irishness and inherent musicality continue to be endorsed, both implicitly and explicitly, and to some degree impact on national policy and provision in cultural, educational and industrial fields.

Economic Irishness and music

The category of economic Irishness and music describes a range of perceptions in which the international commercial success of all forms of Irish music is celebrated. There is a tendency, however, to privilege traditional-derived musical genres, the most notable case being the production of *Riverdance*. At one level, this relates to a growing sense of economic national identity in Ireland whereby domestic musical practices and products come to be regarded equally in terms of economic and cultural capital. However, as with other possible perceptions

---

[26]   According to Žižek (1993: 201), national identities are constructed around such ideas as a means of self-protection against the 'menace' of the Other.

[27]   Brewer (2000: 12) interprets these writings as an early form of colonial ethnography (see also p. 73).

of Irishness in music, it needs to be established whether the much publicized and celebrated international 'success' of Irish musical culture is reflected in the opinions of people living in Ireland.

Mythical Irishness and music

The idea of mythical Irishness and music is closely related to that of 'Irish soul'. In one sense, mythical Irishness is even less specific than 'Irish soul' insofar as it can be related to more nebulous conceptions of Celtic music that transcend national boundaries and/or fixed notions of ethnicity. Ideas of alterity and Irish music might also be conceived by the 'Irish-living-in-Ireland' in regard to shared imaginings of an ancient Celtic culture. Or, at a more mundane level, it is possible that some forms of Irish-produced music will engender feelings of nostalgia for an idealized and undifferentiated Irish society of the not-so-distant past (see Gibbons, 1996: 37–43; Graham, 2001: 61–80).

It needs to be stated that all of these ideas pertaining to Irishness and music may interrelate in various ways. The potential complexity of such interrelated thinking is heightened when we consider that each of these associations or definitions can also be conceived or perceived negatively. For example, traditional sounds might be identified as both Irish and 'twee', or the economic success of some Irish music might be celebrated or, alternatively, equated with undesirable values of modern Irish society. Furthermore, the dialectical relationship between insider and outsider identifications needs to be considered in the case of each potential association between Irishness and Irish music.

Chapter 2
A brief and recent history of Irish music

This chapter sets out some key and recent historical contexts, and interprets the various interrelationships between traditional, popular and classical styles of Irish music in the light of contemporary musical practices. In the previous chapter I argued that there were specific historical and material reasons for considering these as three distinct categories. That said, I acknowledge the inherent difficulties of applying 'universal' stylistic or generic labels to certain types and practices of Irish music.

To begin with, and notwithstanding my strategic approach in retaining a popular/traditional distinction, there are many musical-cultural instances that suggest multiple ways of interpreting the relation between these two 'musical vernaculars'.[1] In this chapter I consider the term 'popular' in two quite different ways: first, to describe any type of music that is enjoyed and supported by many people, and here I agree with Smyth (2004a: 9) who interprets the recent 'emergence of Irish traditional music as a genuinely youth-oriented "popular" music'; second, as the combined repertoires and practices of Anglo-American and Afro-American popular music. While the former affords an inclusive definition, the latter suggests some problems for the interpretation of domestic popular music. There is first the question of whether to regard Irish popular music as a regional articulation of international popular music,[2] as a distinct field of popular music practice, or as a combination of both. Hill (2007: 189–208), discusses the same issues in relation to Welsh popular music, and proposes the notion of 'that in-between space' as a way of negotiating sameness and difference. This is similar to my own dialectical approach. But other, technical difficulties can arise when applying the terms of a discourse grounded in the mainstream of Anglo-American and Afro-American practices (as set out, for example, in Borthwick and Moy, 2004) to specifically Irish expressions of contemporary popular music. Accordingly, my approach is to adapt and modify, where appropriate, these general stylistic and generic codes to the particularities of domestic music practices and discourses. The case of Irish classical music is perhaps more clear cut but, as we shall see towards the end of the chapter and again in more detail in Chapter 4, some contemporary genres of Irish classical music include resources and practices from the traditional sphere as

---

[1]   I have argued elsewhere (O'Flynn, 2006a) on the advantages of viewing traditional and popular music as a combined vernacular field, particularly with reference to the practice of music education.

[2]   This was the way that Irish rock music tended to be represented in earlier popular music studies (for example, in Frith, 1991 and Laing, 1992).

well as drawing on presentation modes normally associated with popular music performance.

The beginnings of a popular music culture and the 'renaissance' of traditional music

One of the first popular music phenomena in Ireland was the folk-inspired 'ballad boom' of the 1960s.[3] Ireland would have been particularly receptive to this transatlantic genre, given the country's own tradition of balladry and with the presence of a significant Irish Diaspora in North America where a contemporary folk movement had gathered ground in the 1950s. Indeed, as O'Connor (1991: 103–4) reports, the re-emergence of the traditional ballad as a nationally popular genre in Ireland owed much to its high-profile reception among North American audiences of this time, evidence of an insider–outsider continuum that, arguably, was to become increasingly significant in the interface between Irish identity and music. As much as the Irish ballad genre might be conceived of as indigenous and traditional, the social origins of its late-twentieth-century incarnation were based more in the urban folk clubs that had become popular in Britain and elsewhere (Brocken, 2003: 34–8, 60–64; Curran, 1999: 59; O'Connor, 1991: 104; Smith, 2003: 36–7). Folk musicians, particularly those who performed in groups, were among the first recording stars in an emergent local production base. Notable among these were The McPeake family,[4] The Clancy Brothers, The Dubliners and The Johnstons. The revival of instrumental traditional music in the 1960s was also influenced by some of the 'international' factors outlined above, but efforts to 'preserve' this music had a much longer history (see Breathnach, 1977; O'Brien Moran, 2007; Ó Canainn, 1978; O'Connor, 1991; Ó hAllmhuráin, 1998; Shields and Gershen, 2000: 390–94). Moreover, successive broadcasting policies of the independent Irish state had privileged traditional music over other vernacular forms (Gibbons, 1996: 75, McCarthy, 1999: 108–16; Pine, 2005: 324–30). Traditional music was further boosted at local and national levels by the establishment of the voluntary organization *Comhaltas Ceoltóirí Éireann* in 1951 (see pp. 49–50). The second half of the twentieth century, however, was to bring about very different ways of conceiving and experiencing traditional music.

---

[3]   As argued in the previous chapter, the history of Irish popular music predates the second half of the twentieth century. However, widespread popular music phenomena such as those experienced in the US and UK following World War II did not reach Ireland until the 1960s.

[4]   The McPeake family in Belfast are regarded as the first group of Irish balladeers who performed and recorded in 'modern' folk style, and are credited with introducing the *uileann* [elbow] pipes, harp, banjo and vocal harmonies to the arrangement of traditional ballads (Wilgus, 1965).

First, from the 1960s onwards, traditional music and the associated 'ballad boom' presented a new type of popular culture that, while retaining much of traditional music's community and/or organizational base, also comprised new social contexts for performance and reception. Among these were the production and consumption of recordings and broadcasts, the accommodation of performance space for traditional music in pubs throughout the country, a more visible division of labour between performers and audiences, and an increased mobility on the part of musicians and punters alike (Curran, 1999; Ó hAllmhuráin, 1998: 127–30). For some people, the first incidents of mass musical culture in Ireland were experienced at the annual *fleadhanna ceoil* (traditional music festivals) in towns and villages throughout the country; later, renowned centres of traditional music would double up as 'happening places' for the influx of young independent tourists from the 1970s onwards (Ó hAllmhuráin, 1998: 141–2). As shall become evident at various points in the book, the appropriation of what had once been considered to be a closed musical (and social) system continues to result in tensions between and among different 'sound groups' and different social groups in Ireland.[5] The second major change in the way that traditional music was conceived and experienced was far more spectacular, particularly at the level of national visibility.

The 'moment' of Seán Ó Riada

If general patterns in the popularization of culture aided the resurgence of some traditional music practices, the moment of its 'renaissance' emerged from a more classically orientated conception of indigenous Irish music. This cultural watershed was the brainchild of Seán Ó Riada (1931–71), an avant-garde classical composer who in his experimentation with musical style had strived for meaningful artistic links between the folk music traditions of Ireland and those of European art music (White, 1998a: 139). As it happened, Ó Riada's greatest popular success came in 1959 with his traditional-classical score to *Mise Éire*, a state-funded film documenting the birth of the Irish state earlier in the century. *Mise Éire*, which was first screened in Irish cinemas and later broadcast on national TV, proffered the Irish public a way of imagining Irish culture that had not been hitherto possible.[6] Given the scale of reception of this cultural product and in particular of Ó Riada's film score, we could interpret *Mise Éire* as a precursor to the *Riverdance* phenomenon that was to occur more than three decades later.

At the end of a relatively fruitful compositional career, Ó Riada abandoned his idea of forging a new classical music from traditional Irish sources on the grounds that the two musical systems were artistically and conceptually incompatible: 'The first thing to note, obviously enough, is that Irish music is not European' (Ó Riada,

---

[5]   The distinction between 'sound groups' and 'social groups' is adapted from Blacking (1995: 232).

[6]   For an in-depth analysis of this cultural product see O'Brien (2004: 101–25).

1982: 21).[7] By focusing on the technical differences of (traditional) Irish music and by declaring it to be closer to more ancient and peripheral musical cultures than to the aesthetic of contemporaneous movements in European classical music, Ó Riada articulated a theory that been foreshadowed in earlier cultural commentary (White, 1998a: 136–7). As will later be revealed, the perceived otherness of traditional and traditional-derived genres of Irish music continues to influence many people's beliefs about Irish music.

Ó Riada can be credited with 'creating' new social contexts and performance practices for traditional music (McCarthy, 1999: 141). He formed and directed *Ceoltóirí Chualann*, an ensemble of traditional musicians who presented in a semi-formal style. This mode of collective performance and presentation differed greatly from the popular *céilí* bands[8] of earlier decades insofar as Ó Riada's music was performed for attentive listening rather than for communal dancing. Paradoxically, this departure was more in keeping with the concert hall tradition of European classical music than with existing vernacular practices of music making. Other changes advocated by Ó Riada and acted upon by *Ceoltóirí Chualann* (and later by The Chieftains) brought about new forms of instrumental practice in traditional music.[9] All in all, and in a manner unprecedented, Ó Riada had managed to elevate the status of traditional music to a type of folk-art hybrid, imagined somewhere between the court music of a mythical Gaelic civilization and a modern, national ensemble of folk musicians.

Popular music

The Irish state's first economic boom in the 1960s facilitated a level of exposure to international popular forms that not been previously possible. Showbands, which had emerged in the late 1950s, heralded the first popular music phenomena in Ireland. These were cover bands that adapted and reproduced Anglo-American popular musical genres (swing, country and rock 'n' roll) and were hugely popular throughout the country. This popular movement continued to thrive until the mid-1970s, and its resilience and success owed much to the showbands' capacity to fulfil a dance-oriented entertainment function in rural and urban locations alike, and to absorb and replicate various genres of international popular music (McLaughlin,

---

[7]   As McLaughlin (1999: 91) suggests, to a large extent Ó Riada's theory of Irishness and music was based on what it was not insofar as he proclaimed Irish musical culture to be non-European, non-classical and pre-modern.

[8]   'A group of musicians organised together either on a permanent, professional or an *ad hoc* basis, in order to provide music for céilí (Irish) social dancing …' (Vallely, 1999a: 60).

[9]   Primarily, this involved replacing the even-tempered piano (generally used as accompaniment texture by the *céilí* bands) with the Irish harp and/or harpsichord. Ó Riada also (re-)introduced the *bodhrán* (a hand-held drum) and bones as appropriate percussion instruments for traditional music ensembles.

1999: 82–4; Power, 2000, Smyth, 2005: 11–17). Though less nationally visible than the showband phenomenon, the mid-1960s also saw beat groups and guitar groups establish 'alternative' music scenes in urban clubs, primarily in Belfast and Dublin (O'Flynn, 2005b: 206; Prendergast, 1987: 12–14). Indeed, the Dublin beat scene would have represented the first identifiable music-based subculture in the Republic (O'Flynn, 2005b: 214). Initially, the state broadcasting authority *Raidió Teilifís Éireann* (RTÉ) appeared to play little attention to these newer domestic-based genres. However, from the mid-1960s RTÉ would broadcast *Like Now*, a TV series that featured local beat groups. The state broadcasting authority gave further endorsement to the idea of an Irish popular music culture in 1965 through participation in the Eurovision Song Contest. Here, perhaps for the first time, was a musical event in which the whole nation could be imagined by proxy, and this would become an important showcase for an evolving domestic music scene that, as yet, had few outlets for commercial production and distribution.[10]

Two significant developments in Irish popular music can be interpreted from the late 1960s. The first of these was situated in a transnational 'folk into rock' movement (Prendergast, 1987: 58) of which Irish band Sweeny's Men played a central role (see Brocken, 2003: 96–7; Harper and Hodgett, 2005: 11-33). This predated the idea of Celtic rock as a distinct genre, the 'invention' of which Prendergast (1987: 79) attributes to the band Horslips following their electric rendition of the traditional reel 'Johnny's Wedding' in 1972. The second significant development in Irish popular music from 1967 through to the mid-1970s was the emergence of guitar-based blues-rock. Notable in this regard were guitar virtuoso Rory Gallagher and the band Thin Lizzy. While the music of Horslips involved a fusion of Irish traditional materials and psychedelic rock, there were no such obvious markers of Irishness in the sounds produced by Rory Gallagher[11] or, for that matter, Thin Lizzy.[12] In spite of the levels of talent, creativity and international success of these musicians and others at that time, their combined achievements did not culminate in a sustained indigenous rock scene. Indeed, it was only in

---

[10]   It has been argued that the high level of success enjoyed by Ireland in this competition over several decades has impacted both on national confidence and on popular music production standards. Ireland won the Eurovision Song Contest in 1970, 1980, 1987, 1992, 1993, 1994 and 1996 (Ó Cinnéide, 2002: 58, 60). However, this success was not repeated in the decade following Ireland's last win in 1996.

[11]   In fact, Gallagher's style of playing, notwithstanding his unique improvisatory approach, was firmly based in Anglo- and Afro-American blues-rock. At the same time, he retained a broad interest in various acoustic traditions, and in this respect can be said to have interacted with the 'Celtic' styles of playing that many folk-rock guitarists had begun to develop around this time (see Smith, 2003: 39–40).

[12]   A major exception here would be Thin Lizzy's earliest hit, a rock version of the traditional ballad 'Whiskey in the jar', which was released in 1973. Gerry Smyth (2005: 40) suggests that a further sense of Irishness ('a note of Celtic mysticism') emanates from some of the lyrics penned by the band's lead singer Phil Lynott.

the following decade that an infrastructure for popular music in Ireland would be consolidated (McLaughlin, 1999: 100). More disruptive and arguably more influential in the development of domestic popular music were the 'punk years' of 1977–80 in which a proliferation of 'new wave' political bands would emerge (Clayton-Lea and Taylor, 1992: 17). Among their number were The Boomtown Rats, The Radiators from Space and The Virgin Prunes (see Smyth, 2005: 51-61).

By the mid-1980s and shortly after the meteoric rise of U2, one cultural critic would observe: 'So far, the more successful the popular music that comes out of Ireland, the less Irish it is' (Vignoles, 1984: 72). Leaving aside the implied assumptions of authenticity and essence here, it is not difficult to understand how, at the level of sound, Vignoles found no apparent differences between well-known Irish rock acts and the general corpus of international rock music. (However, as we shall later see in regard to some of the more recent successes of Irish-produced popular acts, the very opposite of 'Vignoles's law' might now obtain: the more 'Irishy' that the music sounds, the more likely it is to be successful in international markets.)

The status of Irish-produced rock was to improve considerably during the last two decades of the twentieth century (McLaughlin, 1999: 100–01; Stokes, 2000: 5), and, arguably, much of this arose from the unique position of the rock group U2. Not only did U2 become the most internationally successful band ever to originate in Ireland; their decision in the early 1980s to base production in Ireland has been interpreted as a watershed event in the development of domestic music industries (Hot Press, 1998: 37).[13] Thus, Ireland now came to be perceived not only as a country that produced musicians for export; it could also be a place where contemporary popular forms could evolve and where local scenes could flourish.[14] This is not to say that a wholly independent production base had emerged or that pop/rock musicians did not continue to produce and perform elsewhere, but, rather, that there was a growing consciousness of rock and pop industries and subcultures that were domestic-based. That said, in the next chapter I will argue that demarcations of a 'national' popular music industry are problematic, particularly in the light of increasingly globalized patterns of production, consumption and distribution.

Overall, it could be said that popular musical genres, especially rock, gained in audibility and visibility in Ireland during the 1980s and 1990s. Whether or not these developments led to a distinctly Irish rock 'sound' is a matter for further consideration. What can be said for now, though, is that this later period of rock music in Ireland evidenced a wide range of genres that would call into question any simple dichotomy between mainstream Anglo-American rock and localized

---

[13]   It is worth noting, however, that as far back as the 1970s Horslips emerged as the first successful rock group to base their production in Ireland.

[14]   In particular, Dublin became a point of interest in international rock/pop scenes as manifested by its inclusion in mainstream 'world' tours, by the use of its recording facilities and by a growing number of international artists who chose to take up residence there. This international dimension was particularly underlined in 1999 when the city played host to the MTV Europe music awards.

hybrids of the same musical forms. For example, while the 1990s productions of solo performer Sinéad O'Connor and Dolores O'Riordan of The Cranberries could both be labelled under mainstream Anglo-American rock, various aspects of each singer's vocal style (timbre, ornamentation, urban/rural accent, tessitura, etc.) could be interpreted as rock, Irish or individualized, or as combinations of these. Furthermore, the singers themselves projected contrasting images (in O'Connor's case, constantly changing images) that were appropriated from conventional markers of Irish identity, notably, from Roman Catholicism.

The 1990s were also the years that saw a proliferation of pop artists emerging in Ireland. This was the moment of the Irish boy band or girl band, a phenomenon that appeared to mirror patterns established earlier in British and American popular music industries. From the mid-1990s onwards, manager Louis Walsh reworked this type of formula using Irish artists and made significant inroads into mainstream chart sales in Ireland, Britain and beyond. This list included the groups Boyzone, B*witched and Westlife (who continued to enjoy phenomenal success in the first decade of the twenty-first century) as well as the solo artists Ronan Keating (formerly of Boyzone) and Samantha Mumba. By the beginning of the twenty-first century, home-produced commercial pop appeared to have become an established element of Irish media culture, as evidenced by the number of domestic-produced 'reality' TV series with such predictable titles as *Popstars* and *You're a Star*,[15] and through the concomitant emergence of virtual communities and localized articulations of 'celebrity' (Kuhling and Keohane, 2002).

More than any other genre in Irish popular music, the output from Walsh's 'stable' has been interpreted almost exclusively as an economic phenomenon. In the late 1990s, a commentary in the music magazine *Hot Press* ran as follows: 'Although Ireland has enjoyed considerable international success on the rock, classical and folk music fronts, it took Louis Walsh and Boyzone to show us how to crack the lucrative pop market' (Hot Press, 1998: 52). This lucrative pop market, of course, involves the consumption of such music within national boundaries as well as in international markets. As such, the national-cultural impact of the newly established production base for Irish pop also needs to be considered. At a wider level, it is also worth reflecting on what Irish pop has not yet achieved, first, when compared with the national and global visibility of Irish rock, and second, when compared with the more considerable presence of pop in England over the past few decades. Significantly, the cultural impact of 'new pop' and synthpop in the 1980s and, later, Britpop in the 1990s[16] was not matched by any similar phenomena

---

[15] In its original conception, *You're a Star* ('Euro Star') co-functioned as a selection process for Ireland's annual entry to the Eurovision Song Contest. However, this policy was dropped by RTÉ in 2006 following relatively poor outcomes at the event in 2004 and 2005.

[16] For a discussion on Englishness and pop genres see Cloonan (1997) and Zuberi (2001: Chapters 1 and 2).

in Ireland over the same period.[17] Related to this, McLaughlin (1999: 140) notes that there has been no substantial engagement with ironic and camp identities in Irish-produced popular music, whereas such identities are long embedded in English popular culture. McLaughlin goes on to interpret this absence by arguing that the values associated with pop were largely incompatible with 'pre-existing representations of Ireland and the Irish ... . In short, the sound of Ireland was to become much more homogeneously rock centred than in Britain' (1999: 165).

The arrival of rave and club culture in the mid-1990s led to the establishment of a distinct dance scene later in the decade with the emergence of high-profile DJs, notably, David Holmes, Mark Kavanagh, Glen Brady, Johnny Moy and Mark McCabe (see McLaughlin, 1999: 196–8, 2004). While the urban dance scene has undoubtedly had its impact on Irish popular culture, there is no evidence to support the view that other forms of popular music events have suffered in the long term, at least quantitatively. From an ideological perspective, however, McLaughlin (1999: 198) argues that the initial emergence of club culture did serve to fracture the dominant canon of Irish popular music, namely, rock. During the first decade of the twenty-first century, the domestic rock scene appears to have consolidated somewhat, a pattern that is evidenced both by the sustained reception of 'veteran' acts from the 1980s and early 1990s – for example, the groups Aslan, The Frank and Walters, and The Hothouse Flowers – and the increasing number of newer bands, among which are The Revs, JJ72, The Walls, Ruby Horse, BellX1 and The Thrills.[18] At a more localized level, tribute band and college circuit scenes also appear to be on the increase.[19]

A plurality of popular genres

As is the case in other nation states, much popular music activity in Ireland defies notions of a rock/pop dichotomy (Guilbault, 1993: 14–18; Manuel, 1988). Although rarely if ever celebrated in a national sense, domestic adaptations and variations of country and western music ('country and Irish') can be heard on local radio stations, on the Irish-language television channel TG4,[20] and in many venues throughout the country (Mac Laughlin, 1997a; see also McGlynn, 2006). Arguably, this is one of the most popular forms of music in Ireland, with many of its artists, notably, the singer Daniel O'Donnell, enjoying sustained success at

---

[17]   On the other hand, it could be argued that many Irish popular musicians have been influenced by these genres, particularly when considering the proliferation of domestic 'indie' bands from the mid-1990s onwards.

[18]   This assertion is based on listings for Irish popular bands and musicians in yearbooks of *Hot Press* magazine between the years 1996 and 2006.

[19]   See www.irishbandslist.com.

[20]   One series to feature on an annual basis was *Ceol Tíre* ['Country Music' – in another context the same term translates as 'Folk Music'].

home and amongst the Irish Diaspora.[21] The singer/songwriter genre is another significant subcategory of Irish popular music that has been well established since the 1970s. Its repertoire and presentation style involves strong continuities with the Irish ballad tradition, along with other aspects drawn from international folk and rock genres (see Smyth, 2004b: 89–91). Singer/songwriters Jimmy MacCarthy and Paul Brady, as well as song interpreters Dolores Keane, Christy Moore and Mary Black are among the most experienced and well known in this field. Indeed, commenting over two decades ago, Prendergast (1987: 103) argued that Mary Black's eponymous debut album in 1983 signalled 'another new direction for Irish folk-rock – that of the adult-oriented market', and, indeed, this market has proved to be a resilient one.

The past decade has witnessed the emergence of a second wave of singer/ songwriters, and by comparison with most of the artists listed just above, the output of these composer/performers could generally be said to engage more with individual and contemporary perspectives and less with traditional and/or folk themes. Their number includes David Kitt, Eoin Coughlan, Juliet Turner, Jack L, Declan O'Rourke, Paddy Casey, Mundy, Gemma Hayes, Julie Feeney (who also composes and performs in the classical sphere) and Damien Rice, whose debut album *O* featured in the soundtrack to the film *Closer*. Not unrelated to this subcategory of singer/songwriters is the significant number of Irish-based bands who combine rock/pop conventions and acoustic-oriented practices (from traditional, folk, country, and blues), and who also display a range of local sensibilities in stylistic traits and/or in modes of interaction with audiences. Two well-known bands in this regard are The Saw Doctors from East Galway and The Frames from Dublin. The year 2008 brought international attention to The Frames when front man Glen Hansard along with singer/songwriter Markéta Irglová achieved the 'best original song' Oscar award for their composition 'Falling Slowly'. This was one of a number of Frames songs to feature in the soundtrack to the film *Once*, a contemporary, 'low key' drama set in Dublin, with Hansard and Irglová also taking lead acting roles.

As popular musical practices in Ireland and elsewhere become more and more diverse, the labelling of various sounds and practices becomes increasingly problematic. Rock and pop can absorb elements from hip-hop and dance while folk/blues genres may engage with sophisticated levels of pre- and post-production. Thus, as would be the case with any music in any other society or national entity, there is no clear way of ring-fencing a definition of Irish popular music, except perhaps to recognize, where possible, a distinction between domestic popular music that is more local-oriented and domestic popular music that has clearer continuities with international genres. Either way, we are often speaking of hybrid musical forms, particularly when we consider the simultaneous separateness

---

[21]   O'Donnell's music has been derided in much discourse about Irish music (see Bradby, 1994; Mac Laughlin, 1997a; Smyth, 2004a).

Illustration 2.1   The Frames © Friction PR

(at least in people's minds) and the potential fusion of popular music and traditional music.

The interface between traditional and popular genres gained momentum throughout the 1990s. The most famous group in this respect have been The Corrs, whose musical output could be characterized as a blend of traditional style phrases and riffs with radio-friendly pop-rock music. A different type of pop-traditional sound was produced by B*witched in the late 1990s. In the recordings of this group, the digital sequencing of 'girl power' chants, hip-hop grooves and traditional reels combined to produce some unusual polyrhythmic textures. At this juncture, a few patterns of pop-traditional genres of Irish music can be identified, and these include the boy band/girl band format (for example, the groups B*witched, Switch and Reel), 'ethnotechno' hybrids[22] (for example, Hyperborea,

---

[22]   See Björnberg (2007: 19–22); Taylor (1997: 185, 195).

Afro-Celt Sound System and Metisse), and New Age/Celtic (for example, solo artist Enya and traditional group Clannad since their 'rediscovery' as world music artists). Indeed, looking back at the various engagements of international popular genres with Irish traditional music over the past four decades, it could be noted that earlier articulations of folk-rock and Celtic rock have gradually given way to a contemporary batch of 'ethno pop/dance' hybrids.

The popularization of traditional music

A wave of traditional supergroups from the early 1970s onwards included such artists as Planxty, The Bothy Band, Dé Dannan, Patrick Street and, later, Altan and Dervish (Curran, 1999: 62; Ó hAllmhuráin, 1998: 137–40). These groups owed much to the Ó Riada construct of traditional ensemble that began with *Ceoltóirí Chualann*, to the early output of The Chieftains who had recorded their first album as early as 1961 (Meek, 1987) and continued to prominence as 'world music' artists in succeeding decades (Taylor, 1997: 214, 220, 222), and to the innovations of Sweeney's Men in the late 1960s (Prendergast, 1987: 58).[23]

Although collectively the supergroups could be said to have contributed to a new type of generic traditional sound, some were particularly innovative. This was manifested through experimentation with the tempi of traditional dance tunes, through the integration of 'new' acoustic instruments into the musical texture (including guitar, bouzouki, mandolin, clavinet and double bass) and through engagement with the materials and/or stylistic conventions of other musical cultures. This became a particular hallmark of Planxty's music, most noticeably through their adaptation of asymmetric Balkan rhythms following extensive travels in Bulgaria, Romania and (former) Yugoslavia by some band members (primarily, Andy Irvine, who had earlier been a member of Sweeney's Men). Arguably, this would inspire many of the 'intercultural Irish music' projects that would follow in succeeding decades, including, folk-rock band Moving Hearts in the early 1980s, *Riverdance* in the 1990s and, more recently, Mosaik, an international acoustic band with Dónal Lunny and Andy Irvine, who in common with Paul Brady and Christy Moore were onetime members of Planxty (1971–76, 1978–82).[24] The folk-trad groups of the 1970s and 1980s represented a highly innovative and in some respects, avant-garde movement in recent Irish music history. As Smyth (2004b: 93) observes: 'in some ways, punk's relationship with classic rock mirrored the relationship between bands such as Planxty and the traditional music with which (according to some) they played so fast and loose'. Also of note was the manner

---

[23]   See Smyth (2004b) for a discussion on the interface of Irish traditional and international folk genres.

[24]   Lunny and Moore later became members of Moving Hearts (1981–84, 1987). Both Planxty and Moving Hearts staged successful comebacks in the first decade of the twenty-first century, Planxty in 2004 and Moving Hearts in 2007.

Illustration 2.2   Altan © Plankton

in which the musical interests and travels of some of the folk-trad 'pioneers' led to early forms of cross-cultural hybrids, long before the ideas of globalization or world music had consciously taken root.

Throughout the 1970s and 1980s the popularity of some traditional and newly composed political ballads owed much to a heightened sense of nationalism that followed the outbreak of civil strife and political violence across the border in Northern Ireland. The rebel song was (and remains) a particular specialization of overtly republican[25] ballad groups such as The Wolfe Tones, but during the years of the conflict in the 1970s and 1980s, nationalist sentiment also found a place within the repertoire of more mainstream artists such as Christy Moore

---

[25]   The term 'republican' is used in a narrow sense here, and refers to a particular expression of Irish nationalism.

and Moving Hearts (see Denselow, 1989: 156–72; Smyth, 2004a: 94–5).[26] At the same time, alternative perspectives on Ireland's 'troubles' would also feature occasionally in popular music recorded south of the border. Notable in this regard was the song 'Sunday, Bloody Sunday' an early hit from the U2 album *War*.[27] Explicit engagement with domestic political issues, at least among high-profile musicians, appeared to wane in the 1990s and in the early years of the twenty-first century. That said, a small but not insignificant number of artists, including Sinéad O'Connor and, more recently, the singer/songwriter Damien Dempsey, continue to foreground Irish political issues in their work.

Traditional (as distinct from folk-trad) groups of the 1980s also included ballads and other song forms in their repertoire but, in contrast to contemporary ballad groups, folk-trad groups and singer/songwriters, musical acts in this category were more likely to include songs with Irish-language texts. This was particularly the case with The Bothy Band and Clannad, and can still be observed in the contemporary practices of the groups Altan, Dervish and Kila. It is worth observing at this point, however, that the Irish language (*Gaeilge*) does not feature in the mainstream of domestic popular genres in the way that the Welsh language is centrally involved in debates about the Welshness of Welsh popular music (see Hill, 2007: 25–6). Arguably, though, the idea of the Irish language continues to exert influence on what is imagined to be unique about Irish culture. A key term in the discourse of Irish music is that of *sean nós* [old style] singing, a genre that is normally associated with traditional singers in the Irish language but, amongst some performers, can also translate into Irish song traditions in the English language. As shall become apparent at various points throughout the book, *sean nós* is an idea that assumes many different qualities, depending on the musical contexts involved and on the perceptions of different listeners. In this way, it is a cultural term that is comparable with the various articulations of the term *flamenco* (Biddle and Knights, 2007: 13–14; Zaplana and Biddle, 2000).

Riverdance

Ireland's most spectacular cultural event of the 1990s was *Riverdance*, a dance show that had originated as an interval piece during the 1994 Eurovision Song Contest held in Dublin. In broad cultural terms, the music of *Riverdance* was to have a similar impact on the national imagination as Ó Riada's *Mise Éire* did some thirty-five years earlier. The composer of *Riverdance*, Bill Whelan, had been a member of Planxty for a brief while and certainly, elements of that group's Irish-Balkan hybrid could be heard in the use of *uileann* pipes[28] and in the asymmetric

---

[26]   However, the political views and activities of these musicians were not limited to nationalist issues alone. For example, Christy Moore fronted three anti-nuclear festivals at Carnsore Point, Co. Wexford in 1979, 1980 and 1981.

[27]   See Bradby and Torode (1984) for a detailed textual analysis of this song.

[28]   Irish bagpipes worked by squeezing bellows under the arm.

Illustration 2.3   Bill Whelan © BillWhelan.com

beat patterns in some sections of the piece. However, *Riverdance* differed from the music of the traditional supergroups in a number of fundamental ways. First, it involved substantial orchestral and choral resources and, as such, suggested crossovers with classical music. Second, traditional music and dance came to be recontextualized in a theatrical setting (Brocken, 1997: 19), though this was not without its precedents in the folk theatre idiom (Ó Cinnéide, 2002: 48–50). Most significantly, perhaps, *Riverdance* went on to enjoy unparalleled popular and commercial success (and in some quarters, critical acclaim) in Ireland and beyond. It is arguable then, that *Riverdance* has impacted on practices in all three major style categories of Irish music, classical, traditional and popular.

In order to understand *Riverdance* as a cultural phenomenon, we need to go beyond its specific music/dance aspects, whether in its original form or in subsequent productions. First of all, the premiere was highly significant insofar as it was transmitted to a mass international TV audience. Symbolically, this was an event for consumption at both national and international levels, and it is arguable that any perceived Irishness of *Riverdance* occurred with a mutual awareness of these two levels. What I suggest here is that the positive sense of national identity experienced by the domestic audience – as suggested by the frequency of radio play, record sales and the number of commentaries, reviews and documentaries that followed the event – was not unrelated to that audience's consciousness of a (mass) outsider perspective. Although a dialectic between internal and external senses of Irish identity and music had been manifested on previous occasions, the particular case of the *Riverdance* premiere was unprecedented in terms of the scale at which the nation was imagined, not only to itself, but to other national groupings.

It is plausible that *Riverdance* would have appealed to many people simply because there was much to enjoy in it regardless of national identity and related issues. However, for Irish TV viewers of the 1994 Eurovision Song Contest, it would be very difficult to disassociate this enjoyment from the knowledge that a mass international audience would also be watching this event, and that they too would probably appraise it in similar, positive terms. Not only would there be some level of pride in the fact that Ireland was symbolically represented by this kind of slick presentation, but also because Irishness itself came to be represented by a combination of sounds, images and movements that were at once contemporary, uniquely Irish and self-confident (see Ó Cinnéide, 2002: 105–15).[29] This could glibly be described as a kind of Irishness-in-your-face.

The phenomenal reception of *Riverdance* was followed by *Riverdance – The Show*, a music/dance production with musical-type vignettes based on Irish folk history. This is turn led to a range of audio and video products. At its peak, the international show was so successful that four separate production companies were needed to exploit its worldwide market (Ó Cinnéide, 2002: 88). Thus, *Riverdance* not only became a marker of a new kind of Irishness at the national level, but also projected images of Irishness, both old and new, to global audiences. *Riverdance* was certainly not the first of its kind. It did, however, more than any cultural product before it, suggest an explicit link between ethnic and economic ideas of Irish national identity, signalling an era in which Irishness could (unashamedly) be regarded as an exportable form of cultural and economic capital.

By the mid-1990s the modern 'renaissance' of Irish traditional music had already spanned a number of decades, and this process had gradually brought about increases in the areas of amateur participation, institutional formation and professional activity. Thus, rather than representing a unitary socio-cultural movement, the late-twentieth-century 'renaissance' of Irish traditional music can be seen as a conduit through which both community and industry interests would be articulated and negotiated, and through which various facets of musical activity would interact and develop. Arguably, the moment of *Riverdance* was to interrupt that delicate equilibrium insofar as the perceived Irishness of traditional music would now be openly traded and, arguably, in many cases exploited. This was a time, as Brocken (1997: 179) remarks, when there was a great interest in all things Irish. The launch in 1995 of *Irish Music*, the first industry-oriented magazine for traditional music was evidence of the growing professional and commercial nature of the field. Yet, the self-conscious celebration of Irish music would not be confined to traditional genres alone. For example, in 2006 and again in 2007 RTÉ

---

[29]   The experience of the insider/outsider showcasing of Irishness was repeated at the official opening to the Special Olympics, which took place at Croke Park Stadium in Dublin on 21 June, 2003. The televised ceremony and ensuing party included performances from Irish music acts The Corrs, U2, Ronan Keating, Samantha Mumba – and *Riverdance*.

broadcast a TV series entitled *Celebrity Jigs and Reels*, the very title of which suggested an accommodation of traditional forms within a mainstream formula of popular entertainment. However, while the very idea and choreographic aesthetic of *Celebrity Jigs and Reels* was clearly *Riverdance*-inspired, the selection of Irish-produced music for the various acts proved to more eclectic in nature, incorporating as it did a range of (Irish) rock, pop and other contemporary genres. Furthermore, as we shall see below, the sounds, movements and images of *Riverdance* were to afford a range of marketing possibilities for 'classical crossovers' of Irish music.

Classical music

The rise of classical music in Ireland in recent decades has not been as spectacular as in the other two major style categories, particularly when measured in terms of national recognition and/or success. However, there is much evidence of a significantly increased level of activity at local and amateur levels in addition to the phenomenal rise in the number of Irish composers during this period (Hoctor, 1998; Keogan, 2000; O'Leary, 1996). The international continuities that had been established in previous decades were reinforced through increased movement in and out of the country by composers, performers, students and pedagogues, as well as through the foundation of international events (Klein, 1996; McCarthy, 1999: 154–72). Similar to the status negotiated by Irish rock over much the same period, it could be said that these developments for the first time marked Ireland out as a place for classical music.

In regard to overall domestic production of classical music, a general distinction can be made between classical music that is Irish composed, and Irish-performed classical music that is composed elsewhere. This leads me to note two forms of imbalance in the national context. First, the proportion of domestic-composed material is relatively small – a comparative scale of measure here would be the much higher proportion of domestic-composed music within the classical musical repertory of European countries such as England and Hungary.[30] Second, within the category of Irish-composed music, a high proportion of concert programming features contemporary works. (This assertion is based on patterns noted in programme lists for the state-funded classical music station Lyric FM and in the 'Composers' News' section of the magazine *New Music News* between the years 1996 and 2004.[31]) Arguably, this proportion of contemporary against standard repertoire is unusual by comparison with other European countries. Performances

---

[30]   I choose England and Hungary to substantiate this comparison since, having spent significant periods of my life in both countries, I attended numerous classical concerts as well as being a frequent listener to classical music radio broadcasts.

[31]   *New Music News* was published by the Contemporary Music Centre (CMC), Dublin between the years 1991 and 2004. Since 2004, information on new Irish classical music has been available online at the CMC's website www.cmc.ie.

by living Irish (and international) composers are further promoted through the activities of two specialist groups, Concorde, since 1976, and The Crash Ensemble, established in 1997. The second of these groups not only brings together a critical mass of young composers and performers initially inspired by the New York ensemble, Bang on a Can All-Stars (see Gilmore, 2005); of equal significance is that Crash attracts new audiences, and in so doing sustains a 'downtown' scene for the performance and reception of 'new' music.

Much of the programming in the category of 'old' Irish classical music is largely nineteenth century or early twentieth century in origin and is sometimes labelled as 'Anglo-Irish' insofar as the Irish-born composers of these works had strong cultural ties with English music and for the most part lived and worked outside of Ireland. Among their ranks are such names as John Field, William Wallace, Michael Balfe and Charles Villiers Stanford. Selected pieces from this repertoire continue to enjoy modest popularity among choral societies in cities and larger towns, and, as will later be shown, some of this music has come to be clearly labeled, if not identified with, as Irish. Folk-inspired compositions from the early to mid-twentieth century provide another source of 'old' Irish classical music, and here I refer to works by composers such as E.J. Moeran[32] and Joan Trimble. In more recent decades, a number of composers, performers, academics and ideologues hearkened back to Irish musical traditions of the eighteenth century, an era when the high musical culture of a vanishing Gaelic aristocracy hybridized with the new fashion for Baroque music among the settler gentry.[33] Whether we regard this kind of music as hybrid or pastiche, it is a conception of Irish classical music that has influenced a number of composers including Seán Ó Riada, Thomas C. Kelly and, more recently, Mícheál Ó Súilleabháin.

Compared to previous decades and centuries, there is much more to choose from mid-twentieth-century Irish classical music, by composers such as Frederick May and Brian Boydell, but perhaps because of the prevailing modernist and avant-garde compositional styles of that epoch this music seldom features in standard concert repertoire.[34] In fact, it could be said that most programming time for modern Irish classical music is dedicated to 'new' music, that is to say, music composed in the past 20 years or so, and in this sense, the perceived problem of sourcing 'old' music that is at once Irish and classical presents many opportunities for living Irish composers. It should be remembered though that Irish-composed music constitutes a small part of the overall concert repertoire. For example, the brochure for the 2003–04 season of the National Symphony Orchestra of Ireland listed a total of 80 major symphonic works, just three of which were written by

---

[32] For a discussion on Moeran's nationality, see pp. 74, 87.

[33] In particular, composers have looked for inspiration to the music of the harpist Turlough O'Carolan (1670–1738).

[34] Works by these composers do, however, feature in some chamber recitals or at specialist music festivals.

Irish composers. Significantly, each of these 'Irish' listings involved the première of a work commissioned by the national broadcaster RTÉ.[35]

Irish-composed contemporary classical music can be divided into two principal types, namely, works that have links with international modernist genres and works that retain strong, audible associations with Irish traditional music (White, 2003). Prominent composers writing in the first subcategory include Gerald Barry, Roger Doyle, John Buckley, Deirdre Gribbin, Raymond Deane, Eibhlís Farrell, Jane O'Leary, Eric Sweeney, and Kevin Volans.[36] The second subcategory would include the Gaelic–Baroque hybrid described above as well as more contemporary-oriented works by Shaun Davey, Bill Whelan, Michael McGlynn, Patrick Cassidy and Mícheál Ó Súilleabháin. I would add, however, that there are countertendencies and subtleties within both of these putative subcategories. For example, the output of both Whelan and Ó Súilleabháin includes music with no obvious sonic markers of Irishness. On the other hand, a small number of composers whose works are generally associated with international genres will at times look to musical ideas from the traditional sphere. For example, Donncha Dennehy's *Aisling Gheal* ['Bright Vision/Dream'] and *Grá agus Bás* ['Love and Death'] are inspired by the *aisling* form[37] and *sean nós* style of Gaelic song. Both pieces were performed at The Crash Ensemble's tenth anniversary 'Shindig' in October 2007, and featured *sean nós* singer Iarla Ó Lionaird (whose voice is perhaps best known through his work with the Afro-Celt Sound System).[38]

In proposing these two 'ideal types' of Irish contemporary composition, White (2003: 16) notes a quantitative disproportion in terms of composition and performance/reception:[39] while works in the modernist category are by far more numerous, the smaller corpus of traditional-derived pieces enjoy much higher levels of audibility and national recognition. Among composers in the latter category, Mícheál Ó Súilleabháin is perhaps best known, not only for his compositional output, but also arising from his profile as an academic and performer, and through regular exposure in national broadcast media. In some respects, Ó Súilleabháin's entrepreneurial vision can be compared to that of Seán Ó Riada (who was one of Ó Súilleabháin's music tutors at University College Cork) insofar as both in

---

[35]   The pieces in question were Raymond Deane's *Concerto for Violin* (24 October 2003), *Mystic Nativity* by Philip Martin (7 November 2003) and Stephen Gardner's *Concerto for Orchestra* (6 February 2004).

[36]   US-born Jane O'Leary has lived and worked in Ireland since 1972. Kevin Volans was born in South Africa, and has lived in Dublin since becoming an Irish citizen in 1986.

[37]   See Keohane (1997: 301–2) for a discussion on ex-Pogues singer Shane McGowan's appropriation of *aisling* imagery and form.

[38]   'Shindig' involved a two-day marathon performance of works by Irish and international composers.

[39]   In the same article and elsewhere, White also makes a qualitative distinction between the two, broadly regarding 'European/modern' music in aesthetic terms, and 'Irish/ ethnic' music in ideological terms.

different ways and with different degrees of success have endeavoured to elevate the status of traditional music in Irish culture. Another field in which Ó Súilleabháin has followed his former lecturer is that of film scoring: in 1997–98 he wrote and directed music to accompany the reworking of the 1926 silent film *Irish Destiny*.[40]

Crossover genres and mega-productions of Irishness

The 1994 success of *Riverdance* led to a growth in both the number and scale of Irish-produced musical shows. It set a precedent for spectacular presentations of Irish music, song and dance that could at once be consumed by Irish and international audiences. These shows were themed, as was the case with *Riverdance – The Show* and *Lord of the Dance*, and were often centred on particular star performers. Of recent note was the staging of *Celtic Tiger* by dancer/producer Michael Flatley in 2006. In both its title and storyline, this production appropriated a metaphor that was originally coined to describe the Irish economy's meteoric expansion from the mid-1990s, and retrospectively reworked it into a narrative of Irish nationalist identity. Indeed, a unifying element to all of these mega-productions was and continues to be an association with a real or imagined Irish past, in what might be described as the wholescale presentation of (Irish) nostalgia. For example, one of these themed shows, *Faith of Our Fathers* (1996–97) comprised a concert performance of traditional Catholic hymns involving several operatic singers, a *sean nós* singer, a symphony orchestra and a chorus.

The second type of mega-show to develop was based around the personae of popular operatic singers and classical crossover repertoire. This Irish appropriation of the 'three tenors' formula[41] continues to be clearly manifested through such group titles as The Three Irish Tenors, The Irish Tenors and The Celtic Tenors.[42] As with the themed shows, the genre of Irish tenor shows has developed into a transnational industry. What once might have been considered as parlour music and/or the concert ballad genre is now closer in presentation mode to the Andrew Lloyd Webber musical. In saying this, I refer not only to the size of venues, but also to the star presentation, choreographed movements, electro-acoustic accompaniments, and saleable products along with other paraphernalia that these productions entail (see pp. 85–6).

---

[40]   Ó Súilleabháin's score to *Irish Destiny* is included in the album *Becoming*, and was most recently performed under his direction by the RTÉ Concert Orchestra on 16 March 2006 at a gala screening of the film in the National Concert Hall, Dublin. *Irish Destiny* was originally produced in 1926 to mark the tenth anniversary of the Easter Rising, an event that precipitated the advent of Irish national sovereignty (see Barton, 2004: 42–4, 53–4).

[41]   This format was 'patented' by Pavarotti, Domingo and Carreras at the opening of the World Cup soccer tournament in Italy, 1990.

[42]   These confusingly similar names give an indication of the level of competition involved in this form of cultural production.

Celtic genres

Unpacking the range of meanings and identities suggested by the category of Celtic music is beyond the scope of this book;[43] at the same, and as will now already be apparent, it is difficult to avoid this term when negotiating the various discourses of Irish music (Reiss, 2003: 146). Associations between Irish music and Celtic music emerge from a range of ideological and economic strategies (Chapman, 1994; Mathieson, 2001; Stokes and Bohlman, 2003), but what I wish to discuss for now are the various genres and contemporary musical practices that attract the Celtic apposition. By comparison with 'Irish music', 'Celtic music' connotes an area of cultural production that is (even) more imagined than real. However, it could also be argued that, irrespective of the moment and arbitrariness of its 'invention', there are instances where the Celtic label describes relatively distinct sets of musical elements and practices. 'Celtic rock', as a local articulation of folk-rock, is actually more sound-specific than the overall category of Irish rock, while 'Celtic guitar' suggests particular forms of string tuning,[44] modality and accompaniment practices (Smith, 2003). The term 'Celtic school' is generally understood to describe continuities in the works of some British and Irish composers of the early twentieth century, which might include, amongst other stylistic traits, the adaptation of folksongs to symphonic forms and the use of 'natural', modal tonalities.

Less clear but in some way tangible are those practices and products collectively categorized as New Age/Celtic and which typically involve some form of 'minimalist' choral arrangement. Articulations of the genre can include combinations of materials and performance practices drawn from vocal styles in English- and Irish-language song traditions, modal harmonies in *a cappella* settings, and synthesized or 'techno-acoustic' instrumental resources. Arguably, the group Clannad were among the earliest pioneers of New Age/Celtic music in the early 1980s, and this '*Urtext*' has since come to be adapted (and at times replicated) by a considerable number or artists. The most recent, high-profile ensemble to emerge in this category is (the appropriately named) Celtic Woman, which, as already noted, has already achieved considerable success in world music rankings. However, in contrast to the more low-key presentation modes of the New Age/Celtic artists of the 1980s and early 1990s, performances and products promoted by Celtic Woman appear to be more self-consciously Irish, and in this regard have much more in common with the '*Riverdance*/Three Tenors' formula of Irish mega-production.

---

[43]   I have previously explored the idea of Celtic music as a distinct focus within Irish popular music studies (O'Flynn, 2006b).

[44]   The most widely used tuning is D-A-D-G-A-D.

Chapter 3
Mapping the field

Statutory policy, national agency and music

By comparison with more 'regional' nations such as Scotland, nation states such as Ireland are theoretically in a stronger position to develop cohesive policy and planning strategies for music (Frith, 1996b: 102). Indeed, compared with most other member states in the European Union (EU), Ireland has a highly centralized system of arts and culture organizations (Klamer et al., 2006: 11, 29). However, as will be shown in the discussion that follows, policies for music in Ireland are articulated through a variety of government departments and other statutory agencies that do not necessarily share the same conceptions, interests and goals.

National arts policy in Ireland has been under government ministerial control since the 1980s. From 2002 onwards, the arts have been under the remit of the Department of Arts, Sport and Tourism (DAST). Although starting from a relatively low base, statutory investment in the arts rose steeply in the late 1990s until 2001 (Department of Arts, Sport and Tourism, 2003). However, this rate of increase did not match the economic growth of 'Celtic Tiger' Ireland over the same period or in the years immediately following; when measured as a percentage of gross domestic product, Ireland continued to be at the bottom of the EU 'league' in terms of per capita arts expenditure (The International Arts Bureau, 2000: 5; Klamer et al., 2006: 28). Furthermore, by comparison with other arts areas, funding for music was proportionally low. For example, in 1998, out of the €33.14 million Arts Council funding budget, just over €4 million was allocated to music projects, most of which were opera productions and other classical musical performances (Dungan, 1999: 9). This funding policy endured a constant stream of criticism from two principal sources. First, it was argued that the development of original classical music in Ireland had suffered as a result.[1] Second, statutory arts policy was criticized in regard to a lack of direct subventions for traditional music.[2] The years 2005–07 saw significant increases in statutory investment. By 2007 the arts council budget had risen to €80 million (Department of Arts, Sport and Tourism, 2006), thereby bringing the proportion of Irish public expenditure in arts and culture closer to EU averages. Furthermore, since 2001 DAST has made additional long-term investments through its Arts and Culture Capital Enhancement Support Scheme.

---

[1] For example, by the electroacoustic composer Roger Doyle (2002: 24).

[2] Such criticisms were voiced by members of the traditional group Dervish (Laffey, 2001: 13) and by music and film producer Philip King (Murphy, 1998: 32–3).

The Arts Act, 2003[3]

In 2002 a new Arts Bill was introduced to the *Dáil* (the Irish parliament). This was arguably long overdue given the cultural and broader socio-economic changes undergone in Ireland since the last arts legislation enacted in 1973. However, the bill brought about much controversy, particularly in relation to its proposal of three standing committees to advise the Arts Council, namely, a committee for innovation in the arts, a traditional arts committee and a local government arts committee. The first two of these were redolent of the differing conceptions of culture explored at the end of the Chapter 1 insofar as tradition/heritage and high art were put forward as relatively distinct aspects of national culture. A central theme to the Arts Bill debate arose from the explicit distinction made between tradition and innovation, not only in regard to ideology and identity issues, but in material terms also, since the original bill distinguished the traditional arts advisory body from the other two by empowering it with a funding brief. Throughout the latter months of 2002, these issues were discussed in the national press and debated on radio and TV. Most of this discussion centred on the implied dichotomy between, on the one hand, culture that was Irish and traditional and, on the other hand, culture that was international and innovative. Not surprisingly, perhaps, this dualistic conception came to be rejected by many practitioners and critics. For example, journalist Arminta Wallace (2002: 12) wrote:

> Is a saxophone player any less Irish than a fiddle player? As the dissenting murmurs over the new Arts Bill 2002 heat into howls of protest, the debate over the distinctions between 'tradition' and 'innovation' – if indeed there are any – begs the question about the 'Irishness' of the arts.

While many individuals and organizations (including The Irish Traditional Music Archive and The Contemporary Music Centre) voiced their opposition to such cultural stratification, *Comhaltas Ceoltóirí Éireann* (CCÉ), representing the largest network of amateur traditional musicians, welcomed the new proposals. One reason for CCÉ's support for the bill came from the observation that, hitherto, traditional music had not been recognized in any arts legislation (Comhaltas Ceoltóirí Éireann, 2002). Another possible reason for the organization's support was that under existing legislation CCÉ did not receive any direct arts funding; however, the organization had up to this time been grant-aided through the government's Irish language budget (Vallely, 1999b: 78). Other musicians voiced their concerns about Irish traditional music being treated as a separate category. This group included the well-known figures of Christy Moore, Paul Brady and Paddy Moloney of The Chieftains (Hot Press Newsdesk, 2002). In early 2003 the proposal for a separate traditional arts committee was withdrawn from the final stages of the bill. The DAST minister of the time, John O'Donoghue, justified

---

[3]   Office of the Attorney General (2003).

this removal on the grounds that traditional arts might be 'ghettoized'. However, he also signalled that a greater level of recognition and increased funding for traditional arts would be made possible by the amended legislation (Kelly, 2002).

The debate that surrounded the Arts Bill echoes many of the themes that arise in this book, not least, the seemingly oppositional terms of tradition and innovation, an issue to which I return in Chapter 8. More significantly, perhaps, the debate highlighted the ongoing contestation of national patronage in both emblematic and material terms, since it not only proposed (and exposed) opposing definitions of art, culture and Irishness, but also represented a struggle for financial resources. This represents an arena that is very much concerned with the negotiation of cultural capital and cultural power. However, in this instance the articulation of different musical interests was not reducible to the delineation of broad style categorizations since part of the debate involved different interest groups within the traditional music world. It is arguable that the Arts Council distinction between professional and amateur musicians (in favour of the former category) needs to be considered in any interpretation of such 'internal' contestations.

As already stated, revenue grants for arts organizations and activities were to increase substantially between the years 2005–07. In 2007, €5.13 million was allocated to 'music', €3.15 million to opera companies,[4] and a further €1.87 million of revenue funding was directed towards 'traditional arts'.[5] These figures (which are exclusive of capital investment) are detailed here to illustrate a significant shift in arts funding policy since the 2003 act. While opera is still privileged above any other type of music production, its proportion of overall music funding has actually decreased since 1998. Meanwhile, funding for traditional arts (which in large part feature music activities) has substantially increased over the same period, and has been further augmented by additional subsidies which in 2007 alone amounted to just under €3 million.[6] Another significant aspect of the Arts Bill debate and its ensuing legislation was, and remains, the complete absence of any reference to, or for that matter, lobbying for subventions in respect of popular music. Thus, in contrast to both classical music and traditional music, it would appear that domestic popular music activities have yet to be afforded any potential artistic recognition in official conceptions of Irish culture. The corollary of this is that the state and other national agencies actively appraise the popular field in economic terms.

---

[4] These figures are calculated on the basis of information received through email correspondence with Kate Jameson, The Arts Council in February 2008.

[5] This information was provided via email by Paul Flynn, Head of Traditional Arts, The Arts Council in February 2008.

[6] Flynn (2008). See note 5 above.

Popular music policy and investment

Throughout the 1990s a number of music industry agencies advocated the economic potential of Irish popular music (IBEC Music Industry Group, 1998; Music Industry Group, 1995; Simpson Xavier Horwath Consulting, 1994). In 2001 the Music Board of Ireland (MBI), composed of DAST and music industry representatives, was established. MBI-commissioned publications outlining a strategic plan and highlighting the economic significance of 'the Irish music industry' (Goodbody Economic Consultants, 2003; Music Board of Ireland, 2003) did not lead to any substantial policy change and investment, and the MBI itself was disestablished in 2004. This decision by the Irish state to postpone the formulation of a cohesive, long-term strategy for the development of popular music will be commented on later. For now, I wish to interpret two problems emerging from the joint governmental and industrial approaches to date. First, the policy discussions appear to be premised on the idea that culture is there to produce exports, without considering the role that industry can and does play in re-shaping and 'producing' culture (Negus, 1999: 14). Second, to speak of *the* Irish music industry is to ignore the multiplicity and complexity of socioeconomic relationships that obtain in domestic as well as in internationally oriented music production enterprises (on this point, see Williamson and Cloonan, 2007). [7]

An indirect state subvention for all types of music comes from the artists' tax exemption provision of the Finance Act, 1969.[8] Arguably, this has influenced successful Irish-born musicians to conduct their business at home while at the same time attracting several international musicians to base aspects of their production in Ireland (Clancy and Twomey, 1997: 30). In 2006 this exemption was capped to earnings of €250,000 or less;[9] shortly afterwards, U2 would move their multi-million business out of Ireland into a more favourable tax regime in The Netherlands (McConnell, 2006). A further incentive for small to medium scale production enterprises has been facilitated through the Business Expansion Scheme for Music.[10] And, representing another of the state's interests in cultural matters, the Department of Foreign Affairs Cultural Relations Committee has provided financial assistance for exhibitions and performances that 'are likely to promote a knowledge and appreciation of Ireland's cultural life in other countries' (Keogan, 2000: 5). Since 2005 this brief has been for the most part taken over by DAST with the establishment of Culture Ireland, a statutory agency that 'promotes the best of Ireland's arts and culture internationally and assists in the development of Ireland's international cultural relations' (Culture Ireland, n.d.). Later in Chapter 6

---

[7]   The idea of a singular Irish popular music industry also appears in scholarly discourse, for example, in Burke (1995), Clancy and Twomey (1997) and Strachan and Leonard (2004).

[8]   Office of the Attorney General (1969).

[9]   Office of the Attorney General (2006).

[10]   Department of Arts, Sport and Tourism (n.d.).

I examine a number of music productions and tours that have benefited from the various funding schemes enabled by these agencies (pp. 127–8).

Representative bodies and support agencies

A wide range of statutory-based and voluntary organizations supporting music provides evidence of a developing and increasingly diverse cultural field. Established by the Arts Council in 1986, the organization Music Network supports live music and music development throughout the country.[11] The all-island Contemporary Music Centre (CMC) promotes living classical composers and is grant aided by the arts councils of both the Republic and Northern Ireland, with The Irish Traditional Music Archive receiving funding on a similar basis. Other organizations dedicated to traditional music include the extensive national and local operations of *Comhaltas Ceoltóirí Éireann* (CCÉ) whose Irish-based membership alone runs into tens of thousands, and the more scholarly oriented Folk Music Society of Ireland and the Irish Council for Traditional Music. The Society for Musicology in Ireland (SMI) brings together a wide range of academic interests in all types of music, though it would be fair to say that most of that organization's output to date has featured scholarship in classical music.[12] Coalitions of music interest groups have come together in recent years, notably, the Music Education National Debate, 1995–96 (see pp. 14–15), and The Forum for Music in Ireland (FMI), established in 1999.[13] The FMI continues to lobby for a greater proportion of national funds allotted to music, primarily through submissions to the Department of Education and Science (DES) and to DAST. A considerable number of national voluntary organizations exist to promote structures and activities in music education (see McCarthy, 1999: 150–71).

While there are a number of smaller organizations servicing the interests of professional musicians, the greatest levels of membership are to be found in associations representing amateur activities. Chief among these are the Association of Irish Musical Societies, *Cumann Náisiúnta na gCór* [Association of Irish Choirs] and Create, an umbrella group for community-based arts activities, including music. Although there are a number of agencies dedicated to aspects of popular music production (see below), there is no nationwide association for popular musicians in the way that classical and traditional musicians are represented. However, amateur

---

[11] To date, Music Network has promoted national tours/ensembles in the areas of classical music and traditional music and, to a lesser extent, jazz. Popular music has not been included in the organization's activities thus far.

[12] SMI activities include the convening of annual conferences, the publication of an ongoing book series entitled *Irish Musical Studies*, and the online publication *Journal of the Society for Musicology in Ireland*.

[13] By and large, these umbrella groups do not include the interests of popular musicians.

and semi-professional popular musicians are to some degree supported by the Federation of Music Collectives, an amalgamation of local network groups. With the exception of professional orchestral players, there has been no longstanding tradition of Irish musicians belonging to trade union organizations. This pattern changed, however, with the establishment in 2003 of the Musicians' Union of Ireland, reflecting perhaps the increasing number of professional musicians practising in a wide range of contexts and styles. Furthermore, Recorded Artists and Performers (RAAP) was established in 2001 to administer the rights of all Irish-based musicians to receive fees in respect of broadcasts and other public uses of their recorded work in Ireland and abroad.

Other forms of organization to impact on the domestic musical field are major events such as festivals, competitions and national award ceremonies, and the growing number of specialized cultural centres throughout the country (see p. 128).[14] There are close to 250 annual festivals in Ireland that are either dedicated to music or feature music events in their programmes.[15] Perhaps the most unique of all Irish music festivals is the annual *Fleadh Cheoil* organized by CCÉ. Each year since the organization's establishment in 1951, the *fleadh* (pronounced 'flaa') has taken place in a different location (usually a large provincial town) and has included various levels of formal competition along with informal sessions.[16] This is by far the largest of the traditional music festivals having an estimated participation rate (that is, the number of musicians) running into thousands[17], and anecdotal claims of attendance rates in excess of 200,000. Many other traditional music festivals are organized on a more local basis, and normally take place during the summer months or at holiday weekends.

Rock festivals have been established for several decades now with the largest 'one-off' events taking place at the outdoor venues of Slane Castle in Meath and Croke Park in Dublin. The biggest outdoor music festivals in recent years have been Oxegen and Electric Picnic.[18] In Dublin, the annual Heineken Green Energy Festival features music in mostly rock genres, and presents a mixture of domestic and international acts. The apposition of the Heineken brand with this particular event reflects an emerging national pattern in which a significant proportion of festivals, competitions and other major events receive sponsorship

---

[14]   As Sanjek (1999) argues, all such competitions, awards, events and centres can be regarded as processes of music institutionalization.

[15]   This estimate is based on listings in the *Irish Music Handbook* (Keogan, 2000: 220–49) and in the *Hot Press Yearbook* for the years 2001–06.

[16]   See Chapter 4, pp. 67–8 for a discussion on traditional music sessions.

[17]   Observations following the *fleadh* in 2002 suggested a participation rate in the region of 5,000 musicians. However, with the inclusion of preliminary festivals at county and provincial levels the annual number of participants was calculated to be in and around 20,000 (Comhaltas Ceoltóirí Éireann, 2003).

[18]   Oxegen takes place during July in Punchestown, Co. Kildare. The more eclectic Electric Picnic is held in Stradbally, Co. Laois during August/September.

from multinational alcohol companies (Courtney, 1999).[19] Meanwhile, classical music festivals in Ireland tend to specialize in one genre or another, some of the higher profile events being Wexford Festival Opera, which in addition to receiving substantial Arts Council funding is sponsored by Guinness, and the Cork International Choral Festival, which is funded on a similar basis. Music that does not fall into the major style categories of classical, popular and traditional is also celebrated in events such as these. It could be argued that jazz, for example, receives more exposure in major festivals (primarily Cork and Dublin) than it does in regular listings, radio play and other contexts of production and distribution. Intercultural music festivals were first organized on a small scale in the 1990s, but this is an area that has noticeably expanded in the early years of the twenty-first century. Since its establishment in 2000 the numbers attending the annual Festival of World Cultures at the Dublin coastal suburb of Dún Laoghaire have increased, with estimates of attendance similar to those observed for the national *Fleadh Cheoil*. A number of music festivals co-function as competitions, for example, the multi-stage *Fleadh Cheoil* and the many choral and other classical music festivals. As McCarthy (1999: 190–91) has observed, the canon of music competition is an inheritance from late Victorian times, and is one that has been adopted by classical and traditional music organizations alike. It is noteworthy that many of these national and regional competitions continue to thrive, notable instances being the *Feis Ceoil* and *Oireachtas na Gaeilge*.

Unlike classical and traditional music, popular music has no longstanding culture of amateur-led organizations ('societies'), festivals or competitions. Rock and pop music sung in the Irish language does however feature in the annual heats and finals of *Slógadh*, a national youth talent competition organized by the cultural agency *Gael Linn*. Recent years have witnessed an industry- and media-driven promotion of popular music acts through competition. There is, of course, the annual selection for Eurovision, and related to this, a number of song contests that are held at various locations around the country. In a relatively short time, two other types of industry-oriented talent competitions have become established in Ireland. First, there are what might be termed the 'grassroots' competitions that, while depending on sponsorship from commercial companies and media organizations, are based on pre-existing amateur or semi-professional bands and their specific audiences (at schools, in local communities, or on the university gig circuit).[20] At the other end of the scale, the reality TV approach has more

---

[19]   See Duffett (2000) for a discussion on the relationships between popular music, national identity and alcohol company sponsorship in Canada.

[20]   Major competitions in the early 2000s were the Bacardi/Hot Press Unplugged Band of the Year Competition and the Wella Shockwaves Unsigned New Music Competition. More recent years have seen the promotion of Coca-Cola Blastbeat, an all-island juvenile band competition with an interactive website for schools, and the similarly organized RTÉ 2FM School of Rock.

spectacularly presented aspiring popular musicians, predominantly young singers, to a mass national audience (see p. 31).

Education

As noted in the opening chapter, education is often invoked in debates about the role of music in Irish society and about Irish identity in general. A generally critical stance towards music education policy and provision emerges not only from classical music perspectives (for example, Heneghan, 1995, 2001, 2002; Pine, 2002; Ryan, 2001; White, 1998c, 2005: 121–40) but also from the vantage points of traditional music and ethnomusicology (Mac Aoidh, 1999; Ó Súilleabháin, 1982b, 1985; Smith, 2001; Vallely, 2002, 2004b) and of music industry interests (KPMG Stokes Kennedy Crowley, 1994; Music Board of Ireland, 2003; Simpson Xavier Horwath Consulting, 1994). Whatever particular interests these sectors may represent, there are certainly grounds for critiquing the as yet insubstantial infrastructures for formal music education in Ireland. Yet it is also worth noting that very little attention has been directed towards informal and community-based learning, and towards how such phenomena might inform future strategies. This is all the more surprising given the assumptions of inherent musicality amongst Irish people that lie behind so many official reports. As Strachan and Leonard (2004: 47) note: 'The fact that Ireland is *unquestionably* a musical nation is not merely an argument made by representatives for the industry but a premise upon which future plans are built.' While little or no research has been carried out exploring the acquired musicality of Irish popular musicians, studies by both Veblen (1994) and Waldron (2006) provide some insights into informal practices of traditional music learning.

In theory, music education is available to all children attending state-supported primary schools under specific provisions of the 1998 Education Act,[21] though the extent to which this policy has been realized remains to be investigated.[22] Formal music education in post-primary schools is an elective area and, traditionally, the proportion of students taking music as an examination subject has been low (McCarthy, 1999: 161). This may have been due to the fact that, prior to the mid-1990s, the post-primary music curriculum was modelled on a narrow conception of conservatoire education. The current syllabus for the Leaving Certificate examination[23] (Department of Education, 1996) is clearly based on a broader view of music education. Preliminary reports released by the DES in the years following its publication indicate a higher rate of participation overall, and

---

[21]   Office of the Attorney General (1998).

[22]   Earlier surveys at best suggest a haphazard delivery of music education in primary schools (see McCarthy, 1999: 148–54).

[23]   The examination taken at the end of the senior cycle of post-primary education in Ireland.

concomitant increases in the numbers practising traditional music and popular music (State Examinations Commission, 2003). However, a closer examination of music provision in secondary schools reveals a 'hidden curriculum' (Bernstein, 1997) whereby, although students may elect to perform in any musical style for the purpose of state examinations, instrumental tuition is not made available to the majority of those attending state schools (Music Network, 2003: 7). Existing provision, such as it is, privileges the performance of classical music, and the pervasive influence of the classical canon is further reflected in syllabuses that continue to emphasize notation-centred and analytic approaches, along with similar tendencies in the professional preparation of post-primary music teachers.[24] It may seem facetious to interpret these lacunae as further proof of assumptions regarding inherent musicality among Irish people, and yet this does present a plausible explanation, especially where young traditional and young popular musicians are concerned. In short, it would appear that the state's education authority deigns to appraise what it is not yet prepared to support.

Related to the above point, it has been consistently reported how Ireland falls behind many other European countries in the statutory provision of municipal or local music schools (Heneghan, 2002; Music Network, 2003: 8). However, various centres for formal music learning can now be found in most of the larger urban centres. While some of these are established on a local authority basis, the majority are only partially subsidized by public monies or rely wholly on endowments and/or tuition fees. In the year 2000, there were just over 60 such music schools registered in the Republic of Ireland with the majority of these primarily addressed to education in classical music (Keogan, 2000: 67–83).[25] At the same time, the past decade has witnessed a greater variety in the type of instrumental schools available, a notable example being *Maoin Cheoil an Chláir* in Co. Clare, which affords equal status to classical and traditional styles. Traditional music is further supported by a voluntary education infrastructure, mainly through the extensive national network of CCÉ branches. Indeed, the organization of teaching facilities has been one of CCÉ's primary aims since its establishment (Vallely, 1999b: 77). At one level, the collective music sessions at local CCÉ branches can be seen to promote informal methods of music teaching and learning. At another level, CCÉ embraces more formal ideas of music education through its highly organized merit structures (co-functioning as festivals or *fleadhanna*) and since 1998, by a graded examination system. Along with CCÉ's other activities, these structures 'have contributed to a professionalism throughout traditional music which is its major visible evidence today' (Vallely, 1999b: 79). Contemporary education practices in traditional music can also include the use of online databases (for example, Irish

[24] The relative merits of these approaches are not under question here; rather, I wish to highlight the absence of alternative strategies and methods that may be more suited to education in popular music and in traditional music.

[25] The actual number of music schools in Ireland at the time of writing is likely to be much greater.

Traditional Music Archive, n.d.), interactive websites and other multimedia forms. At the same time, traditional music to a large extent continues to be learnt through family connections and/or from master instrumentalist/singer to learner (Veblen, 1994; Waldron, 2006).[26]

Undergraduate music degrees may be pursued at four of Ireland's seven universities, as well as in two institutes of technology and at three music academies.[27] Additionally, music is offered as part of an overall arts degree in most universities, in three higher colleges of education and in several institutes of technology. The majority of these third-level courses present a traditional view of music scholarship insofar as they are structured around conventional principles of (classical) music history and analysis. However, rather like the Leaving Certificate syllabus referred to above, most university music courses contain at least one module addressed to Irish traditional music,[28] and there are now two undergraduate degrees dedicated to traditional music performance.[29] Although general modules on popular music are found in most degree programmes, the overall status of music outside classical and traditional canons remains peripheral, with the first lectureship in popular and jazz music established only as recently as 2001 at University College Cork. Indeed, the resilience of the Oxbridge model of third-level music education in Ireland leads jazz composer/performer Ronan Guilfoyle to comment paradoxically that the 'Eurocentricity' of university music departments in Ireland is no longer reflected in many other European states where a greater proportion of 'non-classical' programmes of higher level music education are made available (Dungan, 2001: 11). However, over the past few years, more comprehensive undergraduate programmes for popular music studies have been established at some institutes of technology.[30]

With the exception of a small number of private music schools in large urban centres and the newer degree programmes offered by a few third-level institutions, formal education in popular music is unavailable to the vast majority of Irish people. This is in stark contrast to the visibility and audibility of Ireland's numerous popular musicians. A small number of vocational courses are available at post-

---

[26]   While this suggests a predominantly aural form of transmission, literacy also plays a key role (see Keegan, 1996).

[27]   Two of these, the Dublin Conservatory of Music and Drama, and the Cork School of Music, are academically and administratively linked to larger institutes of technology.

[28]   Traditional music studies were first included in the music programmes of University College Cork (where Seán Ó Riada and later Mícheál Ó Súilleabháin had lectured).

[29]   These undergraduate programmes are available at the Irish World Academy of Music and Dance at the University of Limerick and at the Conservatory of Music and Drama, Dublin Institute of Technology.

[30]   Dundalk Institute of Technology runs degree programmes in applied music and in music production/recording, while Waterford Institute of Technology offers a specialized popular music and jazz stream in its music degree.

Leaving Certificate level,[31] with similar initiatives organized from time to time by the labour training agency FÁS (*Foras Áiseanna Saothair*) or by local music collectives (IBEC Music Industry Group, n.d.). There are also some state-funded vocational courses in sound engineering, although these are outnumbered, both in terms of the quantity and the range of courses offered, by studio-based training enterprises. Most of these courses, it can be noted, are addressed to employment and industry needs, rather than to the teaching and learning of popular music per se. Once again, a pattern can be observed whereby the combined musical talent and creativity of young Irish people are assumed to be natural and unlimited. This assumption, in turn, facilitates the view that statutory and/or commercial investment should focus mainly on industrial, rather than on educational or artistic aspects of popular music production.[32]

Comment

A two-tiered system is implied by existing infrastructures for music and for music education in Ireland. On the one hand, traditional music and classical music are valued, albeit to varying degrees, on broad educational and artistic/ cultural grounds. On the other hand, popular music is not valued in terms of Irish national culture and, accordingly, is generally not accommodated in conceptions and configurations of arts education. However, vocational training in aspects of popular music production is considered to have some value, at least from the perspective of industry interests. Such a dualistic approach fails to acknowledge any potential educational and indeed cultural value to non-commodity popular musical practices. Conversely, it serves to ignore the increasingly professional and commodity-oriented aspects of traditional and classical music production.

From the discussion thus far, it could be argued that inconsistencies in statutory policy and provision for music in artistic, industrial and educational fields reflect a national level of hegemony in which civic, ethnic and economic conceptions of Irish music are contested. This has as much to do with the distribution of material resources as is does with the relative status (including the perceived degree of Irishness) afforded to traditional, classical and popular music. However, across all musical styles, statutory investment in music and in music education falls short of what might be expected from a comparatively wealthy country. In spite of these contradictions and shortfalls, and as already suggested in Chapter 2 and in the section above, there would appear to be a considerable and diverse range of musical activity in contemporary Irish society. Once again, it could be speculated

---

[31] One of these runs at the Ballyfermot Rock School in Dublin, and comprises a two-year programme in rock performance and management. Two other state-funded vocational courses, one each in Cork and in Enniscorthy, Co. Wexford, offer programmes of study in music management.

[32] Burke (1995) draws such a conclusion in his statistical analysis of employment prospects in 'the Irish popular music industry'.

that the Irish nation state assumes inherent musicality among its people and for this reason does not adopt a coordinated approach to policy and provision. However, as we shall now see, data pertaining to other strata of the national-musical field give cause to question any assumptions about the musicality of, or for that matter, the uniqueness or 'Irishness' of Irish people.

Production, distribution, consumption

The Irish Recorded Music Association (IRMA) represents the interests of Irish recording companies, and is affiliated to the International Federation of the Phonographic Industry (IFPI). A more broad-based consultative body is the Music Industry Group (MIG) of IBEC, the Irish Business and Employers Confederation, and it was this group that sat with government-appointed personnel in the Music Board of Ireland between 2001 and 2004. Several agencies are involved in the collection and distribution of royalties, namely, Phonographic Performance Ireland (PPI), which is closely linked to IRMA, the Irish Music Rights Organization (IMRO), which actively promotes composers/performers and publishers, and the above-mentioned RAAP.

Looked at globally and in crude monetary terms, Irish-produced music would appear to have substantial economic value relative to the Republic of Ireland's population of 4.2 million. This is certainly the case if domestic production is measured according to the international market share of some Irish-based artists (Strachan and Leonard, 2004: 39–40).[33] Other Irish successes may be less spectacular but nonetheless demonstrate how traditional and/or traditional-derived genres have consistently found a niche in global markets since the 1970s (see Taylor, 1997: 225–30). Given this disproportionate share of international music markets, it is perhaps not surprising that Irish popular and Irish traditional music often come to be described in celebratory terms. However, these 'successes' become problematic when measured in specific relation to domestic production and consumption. On the production side, internationally successful Irish artists are usually signed to divisions of global corporations located outside of Ireland (primarily in the UK and in the US) and, accordingly, the monies earned by these companies do not directly benefit domestic recording activities (Frith, 1996b: 101). As Strachan and Leonard (2004: 42) put it: 'Whilst the appeal of Irish music is certainly linked to locality, the manufacture, promotion and financial flows related

---

[33]   To present one example, sales of albums by Irish artists represented 8 per cent of all album sales in the UK during the year 2000 (British Phonographic Industry, 2001). In the same year, two Irish popular bands, U2 and Westlife, were among the top ten earners of all acts in the UK and Ireland combined. U2, earning STG £50 million were second only to The Beatles and were significantly ahead of Elton John, The Rolling Stones and David Bowie (Sullivan, 2001).

to the realization of that music as a commercial cultural commodity are generally happening away from the country of origin'.

Looking at patterns of consumption at the turn of the twenty-first century, of particular note is the small market share enjoyed by Irish-produced music within the domestic recorded music market. Indeed, the market share of indigenous products can be seen as particularly low when compared with equivalent data from other countries. In other words, relative to populations in other nation states, it appears that people in Ireland spend far less money on 'domestic' products than they do on 'international' products. These are the terms applied to statistics published by the IFPI on record sales throughout the world. 'Domestic' in this case would include all genres of Irish-produced music, whereas 'international' and 'classical' refer to music produced outside of Ireland. As can be seen from Table 3.1, the market share of domestic products in Ireland decreased overall between the years 1997 and 2006:

Table 3.1   Percentage share of record sales by repertoire in Ireland 1997–2006

Year	Domestic (%)	International (%)	Classical (%)
1997	28	67	5
1998	26	69	5
1999	27	71	2
2000	26	72	2
2001	22	78	—
2002	19	81	—
2003	19	81	—
2004	25	75	—
2005	22	78	—
2006	21	79	—

Source: International Federation of the Phonographic Industry (1998, 1999, 2000, 2001, 2002, 2003, 2004, 2005, 2006, 2007a).

Before commenting further on this breakdown of domestic market share, it is worth looking at comparative data for other national markets in the year 2001 (Table 3.2).

The comparatively low share of Irish-produced music in the domestic market for the period 1997–2006 is consistent with similar findings in respect of the early 1990s (Clancy and Twomey, 1997: 37). Although the proportion of classical music sales in Ireland increased steadily increased between 1994 and 1998, this had actually decreased to 2 per cent in 1999 and 2000 (with further decreases in

Table 3.2   Comparison of sales by repertoire between Ireland and a selection
             of other countries for the year 2001

Country	Domestic (%)	International (%)	Classical (%)
Ireland	22	78	—
UK	43	48	9
France	59	36	5
Germany	40	52	7
Japan	76	24	—
Greece	54	42	4
Denmark	32	68	—

Source: International Federation of the Phonographic Industry (2002).

the early years of the twenty-first century).[34] Furthermore, by cross-referencing
Tables 3.1 and 3.2 above it can be observed that the market share of classical
music recordings in Ireland is generally well below that obtaining in other parts
of Western Europe.

There are a number of factors that might explain the overwhelming dominance
of international (popular) recordings in the Irish market. First, although all the
major multinational record labels have subsidiaries in Ireland, distribution for the
Irish market is centred in the UK. In Ireland, as in other countries, the marketing
of international popular music is the predominant activity of these multinational
enterprises. Second, if it is accepted that international popular music industries
are dominated by Anglo-American music, this partially explains why the market
share of domestic music products for the UK is almost twice that which obtains
in Ireland (by definition, 'Anglo' is domestic in a British context). Related to this
it could be argued that, since English is the first language spoken by most Irish
people, Ireland is more receptive to mainstream popular products than countries
such as France, Greece and Japan where there is a greater demand for repertoire
in national languages other than English and hence for indigenous products. Of
course, the corollary of this is that the predominant use of the English language
in Ireland presents a potential advantage for Irish music exports (Clancy and
Twomey, 1997: 7; Strachan and Leonard, 2004: 40).

Overall, the 1990s and early years of the twenty-first century witnessed a
steady and substantial increase in the consumption of recorded music products in
Ireland, as Table 3.3 shows.

---

[34]   Since the year 2000, classical music sales within Ireland have not been included as
a separate category in IFPI annual overviews. However, the market share of classical music
is included in calculation of sales by genre, and this has remained consistently low (between
1 and 3 per cent) up to the time of writing.

Table 3.3   Per capita recorded music sales in Ireland 1989–2006 (in US$)

1989	1995	2001	2006
10	22	33	36

Sources: Clancy and Twomey (1997: 34); International Federation of the Phonographic Industry (2002); Irish Recorded Music Association (Bindl, 2008).

This rise in the amount of money spent by Irish people on music commodities provides evidence of a growing consumer society, a theme that comes to be considered later in Chapter 6.[35] To put this increase in perspective, in 2006 Ireland registered the fourth highest per capita CD sales in the world (International Federation of the Phonographic Industry, n.d.). In terms of actual market size, Ireland is now ranked twenty-first,[36] and as such is significantly 'ahead' of many countries with larger populations.[37] Yet, in spite of consumer confidence and a seemingly buoyant music industry, the data presented in Table 3.1 above suggests that the growth in Ireland's market size has not led to any significant concomitant increase in the sale of domestic products over the same period; in fact, domestic share of the total market has actually decreased over the past two decades. Furthermore, if the category of domestic recorded products is broken down into 'multi' (released by the major record companies) and 'non-multi' or 'indie' (released by local independent labels) then the proportion of Irish-produced music becomes even lower.[38] This low proportion of non-multi domestic sales is further divided if we consider that production for this sector includes foreign-owned as well as local-owned independent labels. For example, in the year 2006, just one out of the five highest earning independent labels, Dolphin Records, was Irish-owned (International Federation of the Phonographic Industry, 2007a: 31). The contradictions implied by the poor performance of indigenous industries compared to the disproportionate success of national-based artists in international markets is consistent with the designation of Ireland as one of the most globalized states in the world.[39] And I would argue that 'globalized' in this sense applies as much to issues of cultural identity as it does to the economic domain. As Fagan

[35]   Against this trend, the years 2002 and 2003 showed a decline in recorded music sales in Ireland, reflecting a general global reduction in CD purchases at that time, and coinciding with a growth in digital music downloads.

[36]   This information was provided via email by Daniela Bindl, IRMA in January 2008.

[37]   This still represents less than 1 per cent of combined global sales (International Federation of the Phonographic Industry, 2006: 45).

[38]   Significantly, neither the IFPI nor IRMA publishes information on the proportion of multi to non-multi sales within the sphere of indigenous production.

[39]   Ireland was ranked as the most 'globalized' of 62 states included in the annual A.T. Kearney/*Foreign Policy* magazine survey in the years 2000 and 2001 (Taylor, 2003).

(2003: 110) writes: 'Perhaps culture cannot be measured in the same way as GDP [gross domestic product] but it is arguably a central element in the globalization process, and thus a vital element in any critical analysis of its impact.'

How do the above industry statistics compare with chart information? The following general tendencies can be observed in a selection of national chart data from the period 1996–2006: first, international repertoire is dominant; second, Irish popular artists who feature in singles charts are usually also internationally successful (for example, U2, The Corrs, The Thrills, Westlife); third, while domestic artists of all genres generally fare better in album charts than in singles charts,[40] international popular repertoire still dominates both categories.[41] Thus, not surprisingly, chart data is generally consistent with the industry statistics presented in Table 3.1. From a positivist perspective, these sets of data and observed tendencies do not say much for any uniqueness and/or diversity of musical tastes in Ireland. In particular, they present a stark contrast between, on the one hand, the celebratory discourse of Irishness and Irish music, and, on the other hand, the reality that, proportionally, Irish people appear to engage with more international music and less domestic music than populations in other states. Related to this observation, both Hamilton (2001) and Mac Aoidh (2006) question claims concerning the widespread popularity of Irish traditional music.

It needs to be stated, however, that charts and other music industry statistics present an incomplete picture of music production and consumption in any nation state (see Malm and Wallis, 1992; Manuel, 1988). For a country of its size and population, Ireland has a disproportionately high number of recording studios spread across urban and rural locations (Laing, 1996; O'Flynn, 2005b: 208). Live music events, including festivals, have been on the increase in recent years, and the quantity and quality of venues have greatly improved (see pp. 67–70). Whatever relationship successful artists may or may not have with global economic interests, the majority of music production in contemporary Ireland could be described as a 'low-profile hive of activity' (Duffy, 2006). Furthermore, and as shall be illustrated below, the range of music broadcast on national and local radio stations suggests more variety in the listening habits of the Irish public, even if the overall proportion of domestic-produced music broadcast on radio remains comparatively low. Moreover, findings of a comprehensive survey published by the Arts Council in 2006 indicate a greater diversity in patterns of music consumption amongst the Irish public than those suggested by industry statistics; the same survey also finds a considerable percentage of respondents involved in various forms of music making

---

It has continued to be ranked high in the same index up to the time of writing (A.T. Kearney/ Foreign Policy Magazine, 2006).

[40]   Burke (1995: 99) noted a similar pattern in regard to Irish artists' penetration of UK charts in the early 1990s.

[41]   Primary sources included *Hot Press* magazine and various 'top thirty' or 'top forty' shows broadcast on radio and TV. A valuable archival source is provided through the website www.irishcharts.ie (Irish Recorded Music Association, 2006–08).

(Hibernian Consulting et al., 2006). Even if we do limit the discussion to recorded products, it should be borne in mind that the sale and purchase (not to mention the illegal copying) of many items falls outside the purview of industry figures. The actual amount of CDs sold by domestic artists is likely to be underrepresented by statistical data since many transactions take place during discrete events and/or national tours. (This was my experience at four out of 15 events observed when carrying out fieldwork.) Additionally, there are several local and genre-specific music scenes that can lead to small-scale CD industries, and that are unlikely to be included in national and international surveys. Lastly, music industry statistics cannot fully account for the recent global phenomenon of digital music downloads and peer-to-peer file sharing (Cloonan, 2007: 3).[42]

Domestic recording activity

It is perhaps noteworthy that the majority of record labels and distributors listed in annual music industry directories (for example, Hot Press, 2007) are not members of IRMA, whose respective board is for the most part constituted by representatives of the multinational subsidiaries. Many nationally recognized acts, for example the traditional groups Dervish and Kila, are released through their own labels. The most successful of the independent labels are those supporting folk and traditional genres, and it has been argued that their market resilience may arise from such factors as: (a) the relatively low cost of acoustic production; (b) the ongoing popularity of such music in local markets; (c) the potential for 'niche' export markets (Clancy and Twomey, 1997: 60). Examples in this category include the Dolphin/Dara, Gael Linn and Tara labels. However, from the mid-1990s onwards, as traditional and traditional-derived music became reinvented as a category of world music, quite a number of artists signed up with specialized outlets for the major multinational labels. Prime examples here would be the groups Altan and Afro-Celt Sound System, who have both released through Real World/Virgin/EMI. At the other end of the scale, the archiving/recording of amateur traditional music practices has been subsidized and subsequently released through a number of cultural institutions (for example, *Raidió Teilifís Éireann* (RTÉ) and The Irish Traditional Music Archive).

Up until the 1990s there were relatively few commercial recordings of Irish-performed classical music apart from the releases of RTÉ Music, a division of the national broadcaster whose resources include the National Symphony Orchestra (NSO) and the RTÉ Concert Orchestra.[43] Over the past two decades both of these orchestras have recorded a number of classical standards for the Naxos label, with some recent titles specializing in Irish-composed repertoire under its subsidiary,

---

[42] Digital music sales have recently figured in IFPI statistics (see International Federation of the Phonographic Industry, 2007b).

[43] See Klein (2001) for a comprehensive discography of Irish classical recordings throughout the twentieth century.

Marco Polo. Irish contemporary classical music has also been recorded through the British independent label, Black Box. Many of these recordings of contemporary works have received financial support from the Arts Council. Other works by living Irish composers have been included in a series of promotional albums produced by the Contemporary Music Centre in Dublin.[44] Meanwhile, performances of 'traditional-inspired' contemporary compositions tend to be recorded on labels catering for a popular-traditional niche (for example Shaun Davey with Tara and Mícheál Ó Súilleabháin with Virgin). A significant development in the past decade has been the production of compilation disks in various genres of Irish music; while there have been numerous compilations of folk, traditional and 'Celtic' music from the 1970s onwards, the emergence of such 'non-traditional' titles as *Classical Ireland, Louis Walsh's History of Irish Pop, Irish Dance Anthems* and *Tom Dunne's 30 Best Irish Hits* is a fairly recent phenomenon.

Broadcast music

There are three major broadcasting organizations in Ireland. There is first the state-funded national broadcaster, RTÉ, which provides three TV channels, four national radio channels and a number of local TV and radio services. The second organization, the Broadcasting Commission of Ireland (BCI) is also state-funded and exists to license the independent broadcast sector as well as regulating many aspects of public broadcasting in general. The independent sector is directly represented through the recently established Independent Broadcasters in Ireland (IBI), an association comprising one TV channel, two national radio channels and just under 30 regional and local radio stations. Radio listening is one of the primary sites of music consumption in Ireland, with an estimated 85 per cent of the adult population tuning in to national and/or local stations daily (Broadcasting Commission of Ireland, 2007). Predictably, many of the country's local commercial stations follow a pattern in which chart music is favoured although it would be erroneous to assume that these are the same in every respect.[45] For example, it can be observed that country and western (or 'country and Irish') tends to be broadcast more from rural-based stations whereas rock, pop, dance, hip-hop and r 'n' b feature more in the programming of urban-based stations. A greater diversity can be found among the community stations, which, as the designation implies are geared towards specific localities (or 'communities of interest').

Radio play can be considered as an important factor in shaping national imaginings of Irish popular music. It has been argued that influential DJs helped maintain the dominance of rock in domestic popular production and consumption

---

[44] At the time of writing, CMC had commissioned a feasibility study into the establishment of a domestic recording label for 'non-commercial' genres.

[45] A number of the independent stations serving the cities of Cork, Dublin, Galway and Limerick could not be characterized in this way since they cater for 'niche' markets.

throughout the early 1990s (Clancy and Twomey, 1997: 38). Certainly, in the first decade of the twenty-first century, rock and pop remain at the core of Irish popular repertoire selected by radio DJs,[46] although the selection of domestic material has recently broadened to include acts that cross over into singer/songwriter, folk and other genres. The greater tendency, however, is to play international chart music, one obvious consequence of this being that much Irish-produced music has relatively low exposure. For example, estimates of the domestic share of national music airtime for the year 2002 were as low as 10 per cent (Stokes, 2003). Not surprisingly, perhaps, during the same year the combined broadcasts of the four RTÉ stations afforded more airtime to Irish-produced music, but even here the proportion was just under 25 per cent (ibid.). These low figures are somewhat surprising given that since 1994 a 30 per cent quota of 'Irish music' has been recommended for all applicant radio licenses.[47] However, this domestic music quota has tended to be 'negotiated down' by radio stations and in any case cannot be enforced on a statutory basis. These problems are further exacerbated by varying interpretations of how Irish music is defined – whether by genre, production base, repertoire, musicians' residence, nationality or combinations of these.[48] This lack of any statutory legislation with explicit guidelines makes it extremely difficult for the BCI to monitor the enforcement of existing self-declared quotas. Effectively, this means that there is little or no positive discrimination in respect of domestic-produced music and, in this regard, the general category of Irish music compares unfavourably with equivalent repertoire in many other nation states where promotional policies are both enacted and maintained (see Cloonan, 1999, 2007; Connell and Gibson, 2003: 118–19; Malm and Willis, 1992; Shuker and Pickering, 1994). Given this state of affairs, it is somewhat surprising that, with the exception of a few lobby groups, notably, the music magazine *Hot Press*, issues surrounding broadcasting quotas have largely not featured in Irish cultural debate.

The ubiquity of international popular forms on many of Ireland's commercial channels is to some degree countered by the RTÉ specialist stations RnaG and Lyric FM, which could be said to privilege, respectively, the interests of Gaelic culture and classical music tastes, although both stations have to some extent developed more eclectic programming strategies over the past decade. In their study of music policy and music activity in a number of nation states, Malm and Wallis (1992: 250) observe that larger national radio stations tend only to broadcast music that exists in commercial, 'mediaized' forms, whereas specialist channels are more likely to reflect live music activities that are based in the community at large. It is certainly the case that RnaG and Lyric FM broadcast more live music than the

---

[46] A prime example here is the show 'Pet Sounds' presented each weekday night by Tom Dunne on the national independent Today FM.

[47] This recommendation was originally made by the Independent Radio and Television Commission (1988–2001) which was subsequently reconstituted as the BCI.

[48] This assessment was given by the BCI Broadcasting Standards Officer, Dermot McLoughlin during a telephone interview carried out in March 2003.

other national stations. Also, to varying degrees, both channels are involved in the sustenance, development and even construction of particular sound groups. For example, RnaG was to contribute to an increased awareness of traditional singing in the Irish language (including *sean nós*) as a distinct genre (Henigan, 1999: 338). Arguably, these are positive developments, although it should be noted that there are many other communities and types of live music practices in Ireland that are not serviced in a similar way. This facilitation of some special interests over others can be interpreted as a sign of the power that minority (national) elites may hold in aspects of media policy (Malm and Wallis, 1992: 250). Of note here is how such specialized broadcasting is mirrored in arts-funding policies that support classical and traditional music activities (and to a lesser extent, jazz and world music), but fail to acknowledge the cultural significance of domestic popular music performance and reception.

All in all, the extent and diversity of musical activity across the national-musical field does not appear to be reflected in the consumption of recorded and broadcast music products where international popular forms can be said to dominate. Additionally, while media policy tends to favour some kinds of music over others (including selected domestic genres), the overall effect of market deregulation is for domestic-produced music, in both commercial and non-commercial forms, to be underrepresented in national and local broadcasts.

Chapter 4
Snapshots

This chapter describes a selection of music events and interviews that took place at various venues in Dublin, Limerick, Kerry and Meath between the years 1999 and 2001. These events were chosen because they featured domestic-based producers and, in a few cases, because they were nationally themed productions. The narrative built around this fieldwork is offered to give some 'close up' insights into patterns of live music production and consumption across the national-cultural field. The chapter in turn interprets comparative observations that were made in respect of venues, producers, audience groups, modes of performer presentation, and, where relevant, promotional materials that were produced in conjunction with the events. Finally, it records and discusses the stated music preferences and other musical interests of the 67 audience members interviewed at different concerts, gigs and sessions.

Participatory and performance music

In the opening chapter I argued for the use of style categorizations in delineating different types of Irish music, and this strategy continued into Chapters 2 and 3 where I took a macro view of music production, consumption and distribution. Consistent with that approach, I now look at three relatively distinct types of music events, namely, classical, traditional and popular, and interpret these within a broad and interrelated conception of the national-musical field. Additionally, while the main focus at this juncture is on the music events themselves, the discussion here and in later chapters also extends to include a range of related products – primarily, recordings and broadcasts of Irish music. To accommodate such a wide lens view of this differentiated musical field, I first set out a framework that maps the potential connections between categories of style, and between events and products (Figure 4.1 below). Here I employ the complementary ideas of participatory music and performance music (Blaukopf, 1992: 193).[1] These terms are not necessarily concerned with musical style but rather with how music is produced and consumed (Blaukopf, 1992: 194–5). Viewed this way, the model enables us not only to interpret the potential interrelations between the practices and products of traditional, popular and classical music in Ireland; it also suggests ways of comparing and contrasting the social contexts in which various aspects of production and consumption can take place.

---

[1]   Blaukopf (1992: 193–5) adapts the terms originally coined by Heinrich Besseler and later developed in Vladimir Karbusický's theory of empirical musicology.

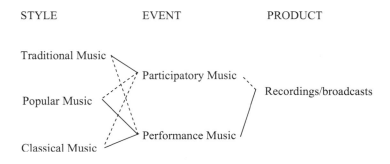

Key: Continuous lines denote strong associations.
      Broken lines suggest the possibility of other ties.

Figure 4.1   Style categorizations and production modes of music in Ireland

Figure 4.1 above illustrates how events, broadcasts and recordings can all be considered as part of music's overall production. It further accommodates the possibility of both commodity and non-commodity forms and practices across all musical styles. 'Commodity' here is used to refer to events and products that involve some form of commercial exchange, whereas non-commodity musical practices generally refer to informal and/or amateur activities. The distinction between participatory and performance modes of production also suggests different forms of social organization at music events. Thus, Figure 4.1 acknowledges the 'secondary' culture of all music types in addition to those commercially successful and/or publicly acclaimed forms that in various ways come to be known as 'the Music' (Bennett, 1980: 112–13). Even within this latter category, artists will at different stages occupy different positions along the 'continuum of success' of the broader musical field (Kirschner, 1998: 249–50). Accordingly, there are different levels of 'visibility' and audibility for Irish-produced music, ranging from the local through to the national and the transnational (Slobin, 1993: 17–23). For this reason, my investigation into live music practices in Ireland is not confined to high-profile producers inasmuch as it considers performances by amateur as well as by professional musicians. This is particularly pertinent to the traditional sphere where both participatory and performance modes of production can be seen to occur with some frequency. Furthermore, as much as it recognizes three relatively distinct musical styles, Figure 4.1 above also allows for the possibility of musical crossovers, not only in respect of intra-musical elements but also, as we shall see, with regard to modes of production and musical-social contexts.

Events and venues

One of the most immediate observations to be made by looking at live music listings in Ireland[2] is that the range of music available does not reflect the dominance of international chart repertoire as suggested by the music industry statistics presented in the previous chapter. Although some international acts do reach many of the larger and mid-size venues, the vast majority of live music produced in Ireland is by Irish-based artists. Furthermore, the chart dominance of international pop and rock, and, more recently, dance and hip-hop genres is not reflected in the totality of domestic gigs, though it should be borne in mind that such music is produced and consumed in the various clubbing scenes that abound in cities and larger towns.[3]

Many popular and traditional music events in Ireland take place in pubs. Indeed, from the ballad boom of the 1960s onwards, the pub was to become a typical venue for many traditional/folk and popular genres. In the first decade of the twenty-first century, pubs and extended lounge bars continue to provide venues for such music acts although the establishment of dedicated performance spaces for popular and traditional gigs is on the increase. The local pub continues to provide a space for many informal traditional sessions and, as shall be illustrated later in the chapter, the pub session is believed by many people to be the 'natural' context for traditional music performance, this in spite of the pub session's relatively short history (Hamilton, 1999a: 345; McCann, 2001; O'Connor, 1999: 172–3). Before discussing this matter further, I now present one brief description of what a traditional music session or *seisiún* might entail.[4]

> Session. A loose association of musicians who meet, generally, but not always, in a pub to play an unpredetermined selection, mainly of dance music, but sometimes with solo pieces such as slow airs or songs. There will be one or more 'core' musicians, and others who are less regular. (Hamilton, 1999a: 345)

The magazine *Irish Music* lists an average of over 300 traditional music sessions taking place on a weekly basis. These are not evenly distributed around the country, with most being concentrated in southern, western, and north-western counties and in Dublin. It should be noted, however, that traditional music sessions are not solely the preserve of pubs; it has already been reported how the voluntary organization CCÉ promotes traditional music performance in a number of alternative settings. However, in terms of the interface between the community

---

[2]   See, for example, www.entertainment.ie.

[3]   'Production' here includes a range of DJ activities, from the selection and playback of recordings to more creative processes of mixing and turntabling.

[4]   For rich narratives of traditional music sessions see Carson (1996) and Foy (1999). O'Shea (2006–07), meanwhile, presents a more critical ethnography of session 'dynamics'.

of traditional musicians and the public at large, the pub would appear to have become established as the primary venue for the performance and reception of traditional music (McCann, 2001: 91).

Two traditional sessions in different Dublin pubs are among the featured events of this study (see Table 4.1 below). In both venues it was relatively easy to conduct interviews with listeners since there were regular opportunities to talk when musicians took breaks between the various instrumental sets and/or sung pieces. At the session in one of the pubs, Noone's, it was also possible to conduct interviews while the music was still playing, as this seemed to be acceptable behaviour for musicians and punters alike. However, this would not have been appropriate at the other session in Hughes's pub, where customers were generally more engaged with the music being played. The evening at Noone's yielded an additional (unstructured) interview with a group of musicians. This was not part of my original plan since my goal was to interview customers at the pub; however, it appeared that these musicians expected that I would talk with them!

Table 4.1   Traditional music events

Date	Venue	Musical act	Genres
April 1999	Hughes' pub, Dublin	Five amateur instrumentalists	Traditional
March 2000	Noone's pub, Dublin	Six amateur instrumentalists, two amateur singers	Traditional
August 2000	St John's Centre, Listowel, Co. Kerry	Martin Hayes (fiddle) and Denis Cahill (guitar)	Contemporary/ Traditional
January 2001	Cultúrlann na Cille, Ashbourne, Co.Meath	Martin Hayes (fiddle), Patrick Marsh (bouzouki), Mary MacNamara (concertina), Helen Hayes (singer)	Traditional

I also attended two traditional type events that were in concert rather than session format. I chose these alternative venues because I wished to consider formal as well as informal contexts of traditional music performance and, related to this, because they would give some grounded insights into the professional side of traditional music practices in Ireland. The first such event took place at an arts centre in Listowel, Co. Kerry, while the second was staged in a school community hall in Ashbourne, Co. Meath. Although both venues were relatively small, pick-ups and microphones were used on each occasion. Both of these events had been chosen because they featured the renowned traditional fiddle player, Martin Hayes. There were many points of comparison between the two concerts, not least, those arising from the different musicians performing with Hayes on each occasion and the generic variations following such differing circumstances.

Live popular music events in Ireland typically take place in extended bar premises or in a growing number of dedicated mid-sized venues. A small number of internationally successful artists also perform in larger venues such as the RDS (Royal Dublin Society) and Point Theatre in Dublin, and Millstreet Arena in Co. Cork. For my fieldwork, I decided to focus on domestic popular artists who enjoyed some degree of national visibility and audibility, and who were likely to tour some of the more established mid-sized venues throughout the country (see Table 4.2).

Table 4.2   Popular music events

Date	Venue	Musical act	Genres
November 2000	Temple Bar Music Centre, Dublin	Dara	Rock
November 2000	HQ, Dublin	Jimmy MacCarthy	Singer/songwriter
June 2001	Dolan's, Limerick	Pierce Turner	Singer/songwriter (rock/folk)

One of the selected events in the popular category took place at the extended performance space of Dolan's Pub in Limerick (Pierce Turner), with another two situated in the newer type of dedicated venues that had sprung up in Dublin throughout the 1990s (rock band Dara in the Temple Bar Music Centre, and singer/songwriter Jimmy MacCarthy at HQ).[5] As opposed to lounge bars with extended performance spaces, these were custom-built music venues with café bars attached. My fieldwork around this time further included attendance at other popular and folk/traditional gigs, notably, The Walls (Vicar Street, Dublin), Picture House (Dolan's, Limerick) and Andy Irvine (Whelan's, Dublin). Observations made at these locations were also valuable inasmuch as they contributed to a broader picture of atmosphere, repertoire and artist–audience repartee at popular music events. Each of the 'key' popular acts outlined in Table 4.2 above presented a distinct musical genre. Dara had an eclectic contemporary sound that seemed to range from progressive rock to more laidback soul. Pierce Turner presented as a modern balladeer who adapted aspects of progressive rock and folk to his highly versatile performance. Jimmy MacCarthy's gig was selected on the basis that his song material has been hugely popular in Ireland for some decades, having been covered by such artists as Mary Black and Christy Moore.

As is the case elsewhere, classical music events in Ireland for the most part take place in concert halls or in other formal 'chambers' such as churches and

---

[5]   HQ was opened in 1997 as part of the Hot Press Irish Music Hall of Fame in Abbey Street, Dublin. The Hall of Fame closed down after less than a decade and the venue now hosts Spirit, which at the time of writing was the largest dance club in Dublin.

galleries. Classical musical performances are more differentiated than either traditional or popular type events in two major respects: first, the division between composers and performers tends to be more formally accentuated; second, within performance, there is potential for a wide range of personnel that might include conductors, orchestras, choirs, soloists, accompanists and chamber groups. All of the classical events that I attended were located at acoustic concert venues. It is worth noting that prior to the establishment of the National Concert Hall (NCH), Dublin in 1981 there were virtually no large custom-built performance spaces for classical music in the Republic of Ireland. Since then there have been a number of developments, notably, University Concert Hall (UCH) in Limerick, the Helix Centre in Dublin and, more recently, the refurbishment and substantial extension of the original Theatre Royal in Wexford. While non-classical music is also performed at these venues, they are for the most part associated with symphonic music and opera. The Theatre Royal hosts the annual Wexford Festival Opera, while the NCH, UCH and Helix each provides a home for one of the country's three professional orchestras.

As Table 4.3 illustrates, four of the classical events that I attended took place in large concert halls (three in the main NCH auditorium and one at UCH), with a fifth recital taking place in the more intimate surroundings of the John Field

Illustration 4.1   The National Concert Hall, Dublin © John O'Flynn

Room at the NCH. A broad range of Irish classical genres were represented by these selected concerts. The Gerald Barry/NCH performance comprised avant-garde contemporary works while much of the music at the UCH Limerick event was in the traditional-derived mould of contemporary classical music. Here, I refer to pieces by Mícheál Ó Súilleabháin and Bill Whelan. Meanwhile, programmes for both 'The Irish Ring' concert and the chamber recital of E.J. Moeran's music presented examples of 'old' Irish classical music. Finally, The Celtic Tenors event could be described as a classical crossover mega-show, although there were some stylistic continuities between it and 'The Irish Ring' concert.

Table 4.3   Classical music events

Date	Venue	Musical act	Genres
June 2000	National Concert Hall (NCH), Dublin	Gerald Barry Retrospective performed by the National Symphony Orchestra	Contemporary classical
November 2000	NCH, Dublin	'The Irish Ring' performed by Lyric Opera Orchestra, Dublin County Choir and soloists	Ballad opera (excerpts, scenes)
November 2000	University Concert Hall (UCH), Limerick	Irish Chamber Orchestra performing works by Mícheál Ó Súilleabháin, Bill Whelan and Elaine Agnew	Contemporary classical
December 2000	John Field Room, NCH, Dublin	Chamber concert of E. J. Moeran's music (song cycles and piano pieces)	Classical (chamber music)
December 2000	NCH, Dublin	The Celtic Tenors	Classical crossover

Producers and performances

Traditional

The two traditional music events that took place in Dublin pubs were typical of what might be expected from informal sessions (see Hamilton, 1999a). In both cases the format for instrumentalists was to sit around one or two small tables and play while facing other musicians. There was quite a range of musical talent amongst both groups, and it seemed as though this was not an issue for anyone involved in the sessions; rather, the emphasis was on communal participation (within reasonable musical standards). In this way, both events were participatory rather than performance oriented. The instruments played at Hughes's pub were wooden flute, guitar, *bodhrán*[6] and two fiddles. At Noone's the musical texture comprised three fiddles, *uileann* pipes, banjo and guitar. From time to time (usually in between sets of instrumental dance tunes) pub customers would join the musicians' circle to perform a traditional ballad.

As noted earlier, the fiddler Martin Hayes was involved in two concerts that I attended, respectively, in Listowel, Co. Kerry and Ashbourne, Co. Meath. Hayes, who originally hails from East Clare, mainly divides his professional activities between recordings and performances in the US and Ireland. His collaboration with Chicago-born acoustic guitarist Denis Cahill (the line up for the Listowel concert) could be described as traditional with a decidedly contemporary feel, as much of that performance echoed the spirit of jazz improvisation. Generally speaking, Hayes adhered to the regional style of East Clare playing during the first half of the show, and here the overall sound produced could be characterized as fiddle solo with minimal guitar accompaniment. The second half was more improvisatory in nature, with a greater sense of a musical duo coming through this part of the performance. At the 'Best of Irish' concert in Ashbourne, Co. Meath, Hayes shared the platform with singer Helen Hayes, concertina player Mary MacNamara and bouzouki player Patrick Marsh. In contrast to the regional–international makeup of his collaboration with Denis Cahill, this grouping was more in the line of a regional–national ensemble. All of the performers had grown up and made music together in East Clare, and two were siblings. While the instrumentalists sometimes played together in the style of the modern traditional group, much of the programme was given over to solo melodic performance, East Clare style.

Popular

Based in Dublin, Dara is the name given to both a band and its lead singer Dara O'Toole. This is a relatively large rock act with guitars, bass, drums, male and female vocals and a string quartet, and all of the band's material is written and orchestrated by its lead singer. Dara has been categorized by local rock journalists in terms such as Celtic rock and/or progressive rock.[7] These general labels seemed to make some sense during a number of the pieces that I heard on the night in question, though other sounds made by the band suggested a rock–soul mix, particularly when the vocals of Josie Doherty were added. There was one major similarity between the musical texture of Dara and that used by Pierce Turner insofar as the latter's band also included a string quartet. At different stages of this gig, Turner himself played acoustic and electric guitars, a small Casio keyboard

---

[6]   The *bodhrán* is a hand-held goatskin drum that is typically used by traditional groups.

[7]   During a spoken introduction to one song performed at this event, Dara O'Toole registered his objections to these journalistic labels, and in particular to the 'over the top' connotations of the term 'progressive rock'.

and, during one song, a glockenspiel. Pre-recorded drum 'n' bass sequences were also used, and these appeared to have been sampled by the singer himself. Pierce Turner, originally from Wexford, is a New York based musician who returns to Ireland most years to tour and promote his new recordings. Stylistically, Turner's music is difficult to categorize. The instrumental line-up and highly individualized style might suggest some kind of art band. Then again, there are the sounds of rock/pop, traditional ballad and even plainchant. Arguably though, the overriding sense of Turner's music is derived from its lyric content, more of which later.

Lyric content is also central to the output of Jimmy MacCarthy whose songs, if not his voice, are known to at least two generations of Irish people. More than any other songwriter of recent decades, MacCarthy's narratives have, as it were, been adopted as part of a national musical imagining. To my ear, the musical structures and harmonies of MacCarthy's output have continuities with international singer/songwriter genres, as well as bearing some similarities with ballads penned by other Irish songwriters. At the event in question MacCarthy played piano or acoustic guitar to accompany his own singing.

Classical

The first selected classical event was a concert featuring the music of Gerald Barry, who in terms of international performances, publications and recordings could be described as one of the most successful of Irish-born contemporary composers. The concert that I attended at the NCH in Dublin was the opening of a series celebrating Barry's work. The music was played by the National Symphony Orchestra (NSO) and conducted by Robert Houlihan (Ireland).[8] Both of the Barry pieces performed that night, *The Road* and *The Conquest of Ireland* were in fact Irish premieres of the works.[9] *The Road* is a piece for enlarged orchestra, while *The Conquest of Ireland* is scored for bass solo and orchestra, the soloist on this occasion being Stephen Richardson (England). The context for *The Road* is attributed to the composer's childhood images of a country road in the west of Ireland; *The Conquest of Ireland* is a setting to extracts from the eponymous volume written by the twelfth-century Welsh-Norman scholar Giraldus Cambrensis or Gerald of Wales. (As it happens, Cambrensis is generally regarded as the first recorded commentator to assume inherent musicality amongst the Irish – see p. 22.) However, the parts of this volume that Barry sets to music could be said to be incidental to the grand historical narrative implied by the title. In fact, the text chosen by Barry is a series

---

[8]   By stating the nationality of music producers here, I am observing a convention of classical music programmes (published and/or broadcast) whereby a composer's or performer's country of origin is often indicated.

[9]   *The Road* was originally commissioned by Hessian Radio for the Frankfurt Radio Symphony Orchestra in 1997, while *The Conquest of Ireland* was commissioned by the BBC in 1995.

of descriptions of the physiognomy of individual Norman soldiers, and is scored in dizzying snatches of vocal and orchestral sounds.

If the Barry concert represented all that is new in Irish classical music, 'The Irish Ring' event of November 2000, also at the NCH, brought 'old' Irish classical repertory to the performance platform. The music featured was a selection of arias and choruses from three nineteenth-century ballad operas: *The Bohemian Girl* by Michael Balfe, *The Lily of Killarney* by Julius Benedict and *Maritana* by William Vincent Wallace. Just two of these composers, Balfe and Wallace, were Irish-born. However, Benedict's work has come to be regarded by some groups as Irish (in part arising from its stage-Irish libretto), and this has led to a tradition of association between the three operas in Dublin and in other cities (see White, 2007).[10] The performers at this event included the Dublin County Choir, The Lyric Opera Orchestra and five solo singers. Another type of 'old' Irish classical repertoire was performed one month later in the John Field Room at the NCH. This was a chamber recital of works by E.J. Moeran, and was the second of two concerts commemorating the death of that composer in 1950 in Kenmare, Co. Kerry. The programme comprised a series of piano solos and the setting of seven poems by James Joyce for voice and piano. The performers were Una Hunt on piano and mezzo-soprano Edel O'Brien. Moeran's nationality is one that is up for discussion since he was born in England to an Irish father and English mother, and spent significant periods of his own life living and working in both countries. Broadly speaking, his music could come under the labels of late romantic and/or early twentieth century 'Celtic school'.[11]

The classical concert that I attended at UCH in Limerick featured works by contemporary composers who often adapt aspects of Irish traditional music to their work. The composers in question were Mícheál Ó Súilleabháin and Bill Whelan, although this concert also included a newly commissioned work by Belfast-born Elaine Agnew, whose contemporary writing style would not generally be associated with Irish traditional music. As with the Gerald Barry concert, the works of these Irish composers were interspersed with performances of music by non-Irish composers. The Irish-composed parts of this programme comprised *Hup!* by Ó Súilleabháin, *Inishlacken* by Whelan, and *Wait and See* by Agnew. The works were performed by the Irish Chamber Orchestra (ICO) which was guest conducted on this occasion by Rachel Worby (US). *Hup!* also featured the dance performance of Roisín Ní Mhainnín and two percussion instruments associated with traditional music, the *bodhrán* and bones. The resources for *Inishlacken*, meanwhile, were

---

[10]   This 'trio of inseparable works' was also highly popular among English opera audiences until the 1930s and in that context became known as 'The English Ring' 'which appellation must surely have been applied jocularly, if not derisively, for the three operas are light years removed from the four music dramas that make up Wagner's *Nibelungen Ring* cycle' (John Allen, CD programme notes for a Naxos recording of *Maritana*, 1996).

[11]   See Huss, 2007; Self, 1986.

augmented by the traditional fiddler/classical violinist Zoë Conway[12] who played alongside orchestra leader Fionnuala Hunt. The performance of Agnew's work involved the ICO and a post-primary school choir from Limerick.

A different type of crossover event was observed at The Celtic Tenors performance at the NCH, Dublin in December 2000. I categorize this mainly as a classical event for a number of reasons: (a) the technical musical background of the performers; (b) the orchestrations, which were generally more classical-oriented; (c) the venue and audience; (d) the inclusion of music by The Celtic Tenors in charts compiled by the classical music station, Lyric FM. That said, most of the repertoire sung by The Celtic Tenors that night included material drawn from traditional song (Irish, Scottish, Neapolitan and other), modern ballads and Broadway musical hits. The tenors in question were Matthew Gilsenan, James Nelson and Niall Morris. 'Classical' elements of the orchestration included a concert grand piano and string quartet, whereas the more 'popular' elements included electronic keyboards, guitar, bass and percussion (on the surface, not so different from the orchestration at the rock gig by Dara).

General observations on audience groups

Audience groups at some events appeared more homogenous than those at other events. For example, all interviewees at 'The Irish Ring' operatic concert were in some way connected to the Dublin County Choir who were performing that night, or were themselves members of other choral societies in Dublin. My overall impressions were that the majority of audience members at this concert were either middle-aged or elderly and that most of these had a regular interest in choral and operatic music (or were related to such people). A similar type of audience could be observed at The Celtic Tenors concert. The audience at the classical concert in UCH, Limerick was more mixed in terms of age, and since none of the six people that I interviewed there reported any regular attendance at similar classical events, I had no general insights into any 'typical' groups that might have been associated with this concert. The Gerald Barry concert turned out to be a fairly glamorous event as it was also the launch of a highly publicized festival of Barry's music. Contemporary composers and performers along with music administration personnel could be observed in clusters during the interval and immediately after the concert.[13] The interface of these various groups could be described in terms of

---

[12]   It could be argued that Zoë Conway presents an example of an Irish 'bimusical' musician insofar as she displays proficiency in two distinct musical styles.

[13]   Although I succeeded in gatecrashing a VIP wine reception during the interval (attended by the featured composer, the Head of Lyric FM and other public luminaries), I decided against carrying out interviews until the second half of the programme was performed. Interviews subsequently took place in the bar of a nearby hotel where many performers and audience members had congregated in small groups.

'serious classical meets avant-garde chic'. As with the Limerick classical event, there appeared to be an even age mix at this concert. Meanwhile, it was difficult to regard the ten people who attended the lunchtime recital of music by E.J. Moeran as constituting any particular type of audience. Indeed, this was a surprisingly low turnout, given that the event had been actively promoted by Lyric FM (see below). Among many possible factors for this sparse attendance, not least the fact that it was a bitterly cold day, it could be speculated that Moeran's music is not well known, even to regular Irish concertgoers.

Audience atmosphere was difficult to gauge at the three popular type events where I conducted interviews. This was reflected also in the interview data from these events, which by and large did not suggest any 'profiles' of particular listening groups in the way that identifiable groups emerged at some of the classical and traditional events. However, the three acts in question, Dara, Jimmy MacCarthy and Pierce Turner, had dedicated followers among their general audiences. In the case of Jimmy MacCarthy and Pierce Turner, many people sang along to the various song choruses, indicating that the repertoire was familiar to them. The amplified production qualities of the Dara rock gig did not permit the same level of participation, but it seemed clear to me from the interviews and from my general observations that this band also had a regular following.

The events where I had the greatest opportunity to observe people's behaviour were the two traditional sessions in pubs. I use the term 'people' in the first instance here because the roles of musician and pub customer were not always clearly demarcated. Musicians consumed drinks in between the instrumental sets, and from time to time pub customers known to the musicians were invited into their circle to sing a ballad. At the session in Noone's pub, the core group of instrumentalists did not seem too bothered when one rather inebriated woman added percussion by way of an empty beer glass and a spoon. There were some differences in the overall atmosphere observed respectively at Hughes's and Noone's with the event at the former establishment having a slightly more 'serious' tone than the latter. Related to this perhaps, it appeared that people at Hughes's consumed less alcohol (and/or were less affected by it) than those at Noone's. All the interviewees at Hughes's pub came across as keen followers of traditional music whereas several of the interview participants at Noone's seemed to regard the music more as part of an overall atmosphere. A clear finding to emerge from the interviews was how those attending traditional events tended to ascribe significance to venue and atmosphere whereas those in attendance at classical concerts and popular gigs for the most part did not. Among the groups of people that I interviewed at traditional sessions, it was generally assumed that the pub was the authentic setting for traditional music:

Cameron (Hughes's pub)[14]

I enjoy being in the setting of this traditional music, you know, in a pub or whatever.

Máire (Hughes's pub)

I like the liveliness of it, I mean, it's usually not just music on its own, it's the setting that the music is in, the lively background whether it's people talking or dancing ... .

Eileen (Hughes's pub)

I think another thing distinctively Irish is the setting. I don't know if that's relevant or irrelevant ... but the fact that it's casual, the fact that they're sitting there, whether they've been asked to come here on a Saturday night or whether they have just wandered in ... and everyone else is just sitting around and listening if they feel like it, and they don't if they don't.

Jonathan (Noone's pub)

I like live music of all sorts. This is the type of live music that I like to go to in a casual setting such as this. I also like to attend lots of other types of live music in different settings. I like to go to classical concerts, jazz sessions, world music – stuff like that in different contexts. To me, this is the perfect setting to see music like this.

As it happens, all of the above interviewees had more than a passing interest in traditional music, and this suggests that associating traditional music with 'casual' or 'informal' performance practice does not necessarily represent an indifference to the music per se. For such people, it would appear that the informality and setting is a part of the overall musical experience. Jonathan, in particular, emphasized this by comparing informal traditional sessions with other musical styles and reception contexts. In Eileen's case, the casual setting of traditional music was believed to be uniquely Irish. However, as shall be seen in the next chapter, other interviewees who regarded the pub as the natural setting for traditional music tended to be less attentive to the music for its own sake.

Predictably, perhaps, some of those attending traditional music events in more formal settings had different ideas, not only about the music but also, in some cases, about the context of performance. Eoin and Mick had travelled by public transport from West Dublin to attend a 'sit down' concert of traditional music in Ashbourne, Co. Meath on a particularly icy night. These teenage traditional music enthusiasts appeared to reject any assumptions about the pub being the natural setting for traditional music:

---

[14]   Pseudonyms are used in all interview extracts to ensure anonymity.

Eoin and Mick
J: What sort of things about the music here tonight do you like?
Eoin: Ah, I think your man is a wonderful fiddler, beautiful.
Mick: I like the idea of it being a non-drink event as well, and with kids being involved as well, family tickets and all that. That's nice. It's good to see it.
J: Why, because people aren't talking as they are in the pub?
Eoin: Well, people are listening and families … it's a nice mix.
Mick: And it's good that people are listening to the music, no messing about it.

The views of Eoin and Mick are close to those of many traditional musicians who increasingly are voicing their frustration at indifferent audience behaviours in pubs and similar venues (Hamilton, 2001). At the same time, it could well be argued that many amateur traditional musicians (and some professional musicians also) prefer the more informal setting of the pub; this was the definitely the impression given to me when chatting to the musicians after the event at Noone's. It can also be observed in the body language of many session players, in that the musicians perform to each other in an intimate chamber music fashion, as opposed to presenting outwards to a formal audience.

One final general note on audiences concerns nationality. As might be expected, the various audience groups appeared to be comprised mainly of Irish-born people, and this pattern was reflected amongst the 67 interviewees, of whom there were just five 'non-Irish nationals'. Of these, three were domiciled in Ireland through marriage, one had decided to live and work in the country on a temporary basis, and one was a tourist. There were some differences in the makeup of audiences at the two events featuring the traditional fiddler Martin Hayes. The 'Best of Irish' gig at Ashbourne, Co. Meath was mostly attended by locals, among whose number were members of the local CCÉ branch, and other traditional music practitioners who had travelled from outside the locality. Combined, these various traditional interests constituted an identifiable sound group. There were many traditional aficionados among the 'locals' at the other Hayes event in Listowel, Co. Kerry, but equally significant was the number of tourists who attended this gig. As I shall describe in the next section, these apparent similarities and differences in social groupings across the two events would to some degree impact on the performer's mode of address.

Modes of presentation

In this section I draw comparisons between different events in regard to modes of address and overall performance presentation. Related to this, I describe how in some events and related promotions, particular constructions of or allusions to Irishness are projected through the intermediary agency of individuals and groups. My analysis of presentation modes for traditional sessions is treated differently from those in other contexts, primarily because there were no spoken introductions or printed information pertaining to either of these events. However, since I was given an opportunity to chat with the group of musicians in Noone's pub after other customers had left the premises, summary points from this group interview are now included as a general set of observations.

Traditional

Traditional music sessions are participatory events where performer presentation is typically understated. Generally speaking there is no mode of address, that is to say, performers do not speak to audiences before, during or after the musical sets. However, this does not necessarily mean that musicians do not interact with or are indifferent to other pub customers at traditional music sessions. Furthermore, the level of interaction may differ from session to session, and from player to player. There was considerable variety regarding the individual musical practices among the group of musicians interviewed at the Noone's pub session. Some only played in Noone's once a week whereas others had alternative sessions and venues in which to participate. One or two were occasionally paid to perform gigs but the majority described themselves as strictly amateur. Among the three fiddlers at this session, one young woman spoke about the different atmosphere from venue to venue, and how such changes in contexts might bring about variations in her own style of playing. By coincidence, she mentioned her involvement in a weekly session at the nearby Hughes's pub (though not on the same weekly night nor with the same group of musicians as I had observed). This player suggested that there were different codes for performers and listeners at Hughes's, which she characterized as being 'more formal' than those obtaining in Noone's that night. This was consistent with my own comparative observations of the two locations. I spoke with other members of the group about the ballads that had been sung that evening by members of the core instrumental group as well as by pub customers who had been invited to sing. According to these musicians, the level of participation varied depending on the night of the week and the particular crowd at any one session. They also spoke about their sensitivity to audience interaction, particularly in regard to whether the pub customers were 'local' or 'mixed'. This awareness extended to distinguishing between a mainly Irish cosmopolitan crowd (such as I had witnessed on the night in question) or one with a high proportion of tourists. In any of these scenarios, it seemed, the musicians were prepared to adapt to the situation.[15]

In contrast to the pub sessions, a direct mode of address can often be witnessed at sit-down performances of traditional music where performers make frequent verbal interactions with their audience. Where this occurs, it appears that the formal platform of the performance mode is utilized to recreate the informality of more intimate surroundings. In a way, then, the traditional performer recreates

---

[15] Such a versatile attitude is not dissimilar to that reported by Van De Port (1999) in his description on aspects of performance practices among gypsy musicians in Serbia.

some of the participatory 'aura' of amateur sessions through spoken means. This was observed in the two events featuring Martin Hayes, who on both occasions was the front musician engaging in repartee with audiences. In both of these concerts Hayes was quick to build up a rapport with his audience, albeit in a very understated though humorous fashion, and this served to put people at their ease. Although audience participation was not as involved as it might be in an informal session, Hayes's manner seemed to invite transgressions of the formal distance between audience and performers. Quite often at the Listowel concert, when the tempo became more upbeat and spirits got higher, there were members of the audience who would shout in falsetto, 'Yuh!' or 'Good boy ya!' or exclamations to that effect. Towards the end of that particular evening, Hayes invited audience members to suggest some tunes that he and Denis Cahill might play. There were several suggestions from the crowd but one woman, louder than the rest, was ultimately successful:

> Woman: Play *Paddy Fahy's*!
> Hayes: Oh yeah, we've a whole set beginning with that.
> Woman: Well, play them all.
> Hayes: Right so.

Hayes's spoken introductions referred to the social contexts of traditional music as well as to more general aspects of Irish life, both past and present. While he did refer to the names and/or origins of tunes, this was not done with any emphasis on accuracy. Here it appeared that Hayes was putting a value on not being accurate or precise in his knowledge about the music. At both events, the crowd seemed to empathize with this outlook. For example, when at one stage during the Ashbourne event he said that he had forgotten the name of a tune just played, one member of the audience shouted 'You're fine out!', indicating that the name did not matter, it was the music that mattered.

Hayes addressed several groups within the audiences at both events. First, he spoke to the local musicians by making tongue-in-cheek observations about differences in regional styles of traditional music or about the moral character of known musicians amongst the crowd. At the Listowel event he directed some comments towards tourists and other remarks towards the farming community of North Co. Kerry. Further humorous distinctions were made between, as he caricatured it, an Ireland of the past (turf fires, hardship, magical fairy fields) and contemporary Ireland (communications, comforts, technology). At the Ashbourne concert both he and Mary MacNamara presented vignettes of their own past in East Co. Clare, and while these images were undoubtedly based on fact, it could also be said that the audience was presented with an idealized account of traditional music in a rural community.

A number of tendencies in traditional performance have been adumbrated so far. These I now summarise as: (a) a seemingly informal approach that includes repartee/banter with an audience; (b) understated personality: though never quite the opposite of popular music's star performer, shyness and self-effacement would appear to be desirable qualities even among professional traditional players; (c) a degree of musical introspection, thus maintaining the aesthetic of the informal session; (d) changes in expression are co-produced with the interactive response of listeners; (e) a discursive vagueness that authenticates direct musical experience at the expense of factual knowledge. Generally speaking, the idea of a star performer is anathema to traditional music sensibilities. This is not to suggest a lack of commercial interest on the part of professional traditional musicians and associated promotional agencies (on this point see Mac Aoidh, 2006: 138–9). However, as McCann (2001: 92) observes, while many musicians involved in sessions may also be professionals, 'once embraced by the aura of the session, the hierarchies are of a "traditional" not a commercial nature'. In her research into the 'symbiotic relationship' between traditional musicians and tourists in North Mayo, Kneafsey (2003: 78) finds that the growing number of seated concerts in the area 'do not necessarily replace the sessions, which retain meanings that defy commodification'. Indeed, even within the more formal traditional arena, it can be observed how highly prominent performers such as Donal Lunny and Sharon Shannon carry an introspective trait to the level of shyness and even humility, a communication style that would be alien to the performance norms of most popular and classical musicians. A striking example of this tendency emerged when I attended an Andy Irvine gig at Whelan's pub, Dublin in December 2000. In spite of a sustained critical acclaim that owes no small part to his achievements with Planxty in the 1970s and early 1980s (along with Christy Moore, Donal Lunny, Paul Brady and others), arguably, Irvine does not currently enjoy the same national recognition as that afforded to many other folk and traditional musicians. Towards the end of Irvine's solo gig he was joined on stage by Donal Lunny, much to the surprise and delight of the capacity crowd present. However, contrary to what this audience seemed to expect, Lunny's musical input took nothing away from the particular artistry of Irvine's programme, taking as he did the supportive role of a session musician. On both musical and social levels, this came through as a poignant gesture.

Returning to the Martin Hayes gigs, there were layers of presentation and representation other than those directly involving the musicians. This was obviously the case with the Ashbourne event, itself a part of the 'Best of Irish Traditional Music Tour' promoted by Music Network and which went on to visit 15 venues throughout Ireland over a two-week period. As much as this was billed as a national tour, the events themselves had a decidedly 'local' feel, not only because the performances featured a particular regional style, but also because most of the venues appeared to be chosen on the basis of their community function (school halls, local arts centres, churches). Furthermore, it is also likely that this tour would have held a particular interest for local traditional sound groups such as the group that I witnessed at Ashbourne. Arguably, then, the emblematic status implied by the 'Best of Irish' label was significantly downplayed by the specific musical and social contexts of the events themselves. If the tour had any national dimension, this was achieved through advance advertising and through other forms of promotion (one performance from the tour was broadcast on RTÉ television almost one year later in January 2002).

The promotional material for the Listowel gig (Martin Hayes in concert with Denis Cahill) suggested a more 'international' form of artist representation. The same programme had already been performed to US audiences, the accompanying posters of which were also displayed at the event that I observed in Kerry. These posters, which also functioned to promote a CD of music by Hayes and Cahill, characterized their sound as 'contemporary' and 'minimalist'.[16] (The poster included some comments by US-based music critics, including one that compared the Hayes–Cahill 'minimalist' sound with the music of Philip Glass). The fact that the music of Martin Hayes can simultaneously be represented as local, national and global illustrates the phenomenon of 'level-shifting' for many contemporary Irish musicians (Slobin, 1993: 21), particularly among those practising in traditional and/or traditional-derived genres.

Popular

The rock concerts that I attended bore some similarities with the more formal traditional events insofar as the performers introduced their music by giving the titles and background to particular pieces or by introducing band members. However, in all cases, the leading musicians confined any remarks to their own music and group and avoided verbal interactions with the audience. Common to the Walls, Dara and Picture House events was the dynamic established between star performers and their fans. Unlike any of the other events that I attended, the dimmed house lights at these rock gigs were in contrast to the lighting and other effects on stage. This had the dual effect of rendering the audience anonymous while intensifying the aura of the star performers. A major difference between traditional and rock presentation could also be observed at the level of 'extra-musical' movement. For example, Dara (the singer) introduced a degree of theatricality into his performance by dancing around the stage, and by occasionally hitting the hi-hat of the drum kit in seemingly throwaway but perfectly syncopated gestures.

In some respects, the presentation modes of Jimmy MacCarthy and Pierce Turner bore more resemblance to the style of Martin Hayes or Andy Irvine than they did to those employed by the rock acts. For one thing, the physical arrangements of the venues, while not necessarily smaller, appeared to be more intimate. The rock/pop band Picture House had played in Dolan's, Limerick from a raised platform. In Turner's case, the same platform was gradually tiered downwards to reach audience level and the projection of a short 'catwalk' further helped to remove the distance between the musicians and audience. Turner used this to great advantage, allowing himself to be kissed by one or two women, giving friendly hugs to both men and women, and generally establishing individual eye contact as he moved

---

[16]   *Live in Seattle* (Green Linnet, 1999).

about and sang. In this and in other ways (for example, the singer's use of 'novel instruments') the performance had a level of theatricality verging towards cabaret. The event that I attended was part of a national tour, and it coincided with the launch of a CD, which was enjoying regular radio play on RTÉ Radio 1 during that same summer of 2001. Jimmy MacCarthy's presentation mode was more understated than that of Pierce Turner, and was somewhat akin to the confessional style of a folk singer. His repartee with the audience was intimate, eliciting comments and suggestions in a pattern similar to that observed at the Martin Hayes events.

A strong sense of personal and national narrative came through in the performances of both Jimmy MacCarthy and Pierce Turner, so much so in fact, that at times it was difficult to distinguish between the sung and spoken word. Jimmy MacCarthy spoke extensively about songs of his that had been recorded, about his identity as a person from Cork and about his experience as an Irishman who for many years had lived abroad. At the end of the concert, MacCarthy encouraged people to buy his new songbook, which was due to be published during the same month. Making a parody on an old radio advertising slogan in order to promote his own work he jibed: 'And remember, if you do sing a song, sing one of my songs – and they're all Irish!'[17] Pierce Turner also spoke about musical origins, his hometown of Wexford and his insider/outsider experience of Irishness ('I didn't know I was Irish until I came to America'). A further reference to things Irish was made when he felt a need to work the crowd more during one of his walkabouts – 'Ah come on. Pretend you're Irish!' – a remark seemingly intended to remind those gathered that the Irish had a reputation as responsive audiences. There were some similarities between the constructions of a recent Irish past by Pierce Turner, Jimmy MacCarthy and Martin Hayes, albeit if such imaginings arose from different sets of circumstances. MacCarthy and Turner juxtaposed the sentimental feelings of nationhood and belonging with some degree of social critique on Ireland in the late twentieth century. Hayes, meanwhile, played with some contradicting images of contemporary Ireland, finding, as it were, his own way of negotiating the differences between local, national and international levels of performance and reception.

Classical

The presentation mode at most of the classical concerts that I observed would match what might be expected of classical music events anywhere. In this I refer to the relatively formal nature of these concerts by comparison with popular

---

[17] This was a reference to a commercial radio show sponsored by Waltons, a music publisher and retailer in Dublin, and which featured conservative genres of Irish music. The weekly show, which was broadcast between 1952 and 1981 invariably ended with the advice, 'And remember if you sing a song, do sing an Irish song'. MacCarthy's statement contained a double ironic twist insofar as the same company had just published his songbook (MacCarthy, 2001).

and traditional type events. Such conventions were completely upheld at the two separate concerts celebrating the music of Gerald Barry and E.J. Moeran; in both cases the musical programme was executed without any introductions or other comments. However, this format was modified at the ICO concert at UCH, Limerick and the 'Irish Ring' concert at the NCH, Dublin.

During the ICO concert, American conductor Rachel Worby broke with convention by speaking about the various pieces on the programme that evening. In her introduction to Ó Súilleabháin's work *Hup!* she suggested that the composer was trying to translate the idea of a *seisiún* [traditional music session] to a piece for formal sitting and listening. Worby spoke about the blending of classical traditions with the gestures of *sean nós* [old style] dancing, and her own apprehension of jazz influences in the piece (mainly, Theolonius Monk). This pattern, whereby musical and cultural analysis was accompanied by a revelation of personal musical experience, was followed throughout the concert. Worby's remarks also extended to the performers, and she gave a particular word of praise to the schoolchildren who took part in the performance of Elaine Agnew's commissioned work. The six people that I interviewed during and after the concert appeared to appreciate this community approach to performance presentation and, as already noted, none of these were people who attended classical concerts on a regular basis. Two people were there to support a family member in the choir; the other four interviewees indicated that their initial interest in the concert had been to see how Irish dance and music traditions would 'translate' to the concert platform. It is arguable, then, that just as parts of this music programme were consciously conceived in terms of stylistic translation or syncretism, so too were many aspects in the conductor's (and other artists') mode of presentation, which acted as a bridge between formal and informal contexts of performance and reception.

Another adaptation to the conventions of classical music performance took place at 'The Irish Ring' concert. Rather in the manner of a variety show, the event was compèred by Angela Molloy, a veteran committee member of the Association of Irish Musical Societies. As the concert comprised a series of opera scenes, Molloy introduced each one, adding a personalized commentary on aspects of the different plots. She also made it clear that this was an Irish event with such opening remarks as 'Welcome to this special night of music: an all-Irish night', or by stating that all of the featured operatic singers were 'our own' and/or 'Irish'. The sense of national identity was further underlined by the playing of the national anthem at the start of the concert. This unambiguously emblematic statement of Irishness was the only such one encountered over 15 live music events in the course of my fieldwork. Concerts centring on Irish ballad opera repertoire have become something of a tradition in the choral music scenes of Dublin and other urban areas. The performance and reception of the national anthem, along with the presenter's mode of address that night, suggest that a particular construction of national belonging is facilitated by events like these. It is somewhat ironic, then, that although this concert was presented and advertised in the context of its

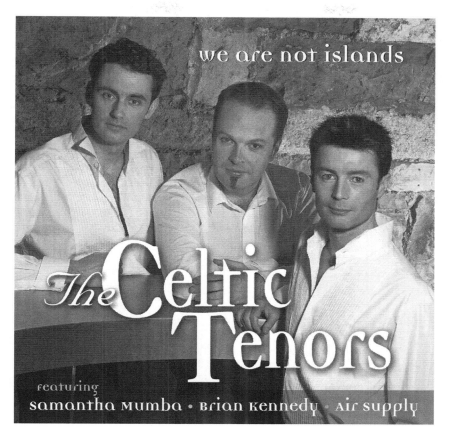

Illustration 4.2   Cover artwork for The Celtic Tenors' *We are not islands* © Dara
Records

Irishness, all six people that I interviewed there were unanimous in rejecting the
notion that the music listened to that night *sounded* Irish (see pp. 96–8).

As described above, The Celtic Tenors concert was a crossover musical event.
This designation arose not only from the musical repertoire and orchestration, but
also from the performers' mode of presentation and from the overall promotion
of this event and its related products. The show began with its nine-piece band
repeatedly playing what could be described as a contemporary 'Celtic' riff: a
heavily amplified drum and bass sound layered with a repeated four-note pattern
played by strings. Over this pattern the voice of the pianist and musical director
announced: 'Ladies and Gentlemen, welcome on stage EMI recording artists, The
Celtic Tenors!' The singers then ran energetically onto the concert platform, and
opened with a performance of 'Ireland's Call', a national rugby anthem composed
by Phil Coulter (a well known personality in Irish musical life who was also
executive producer of The Celtic Tenors' first CD). Each of the tenors in turn

gave some biographical account of themselves, where they were from, musical background, their fondness for Irish song, and so on. Costumes at the beginning of the show were 'smart casual', that is to say, formal wear but without ties or bow ties. These changed throughout the show, with all three tenors wearing black T-shirts and jeans towards the end (at which point they looked more like a boy band and less like a trio of operatic tenors). This change of dress was accompanied by more throwaway theatrical gestures as the show progressed, though it would be accurate to say that all movements had been carefully choreographed from the beginning. As the performers sang 'Spanish Lady', a traditional song made famous by The Dubliners many decades before, one of the tenors, Niall Morris, ran into the audience presenting one woman with a single rose. This Andy Williams-type gesture went down very well with the audience, which mainly comprised middle-aged and elderly people. Indeed, after the show, all three tenors could be observed in the NCH foyer, happily complying with a substantial number of requests to sign the concert programme. I was already familiar with the phenomenon by which some Irish classical performers have crossed over into other musical genres. The major revelation on that night, however, was the extent to which classically trained musicians could be presented as star performers, in addition to the way that Irish, 'Celtic' and other musical material could be formulated into a quasi-narrative show. Furthermore, the blatant and constant references to CD products throughout the concert far exceeded that observed at any of the popular or professional-traditional events. This was also the only event that I attended where performers were publicly associated with their recording company.

Although the performers at the Gerald Barry and E.J. Moeran concerts adopted the norms of classical music production by not directly addressing their audiences, in other ways these events were involved in particular representations of Irish music. The Barry concert was one in a series entitled 'The Lyric FM Gerald Barry Festival'. This was of itself significant in that it represented the first retrospective festival of music by a living Irish composer. The concert series was conterminous with a series of radio broadcasts on Lyric FM that, among other matters, explored the festival theme in the context of contemporary classical composition in Ireland. A more explicit form of national representation followed the Moeran chamber music event when two programmes dealing with the same composer's music were broadcast on Lyric FM. These were presented and produced by Una Hunt, who had also been the pianist at the recital that I attended. Broadcast in December 2000, the programmes offered a number of musicological perspectives on Moeran's work, not least a theory about the Irishness of some of his music. Towards the end of the second broadcast Hunt spoke about the final movement of Moeran's Symphony in G minor, and the composer's musical reference to a rural market fair in the second theme of the movement.[18] The perceived Irishness of this section of the work caused Hunt to reflect: 'and I for one am haunted by that sound'. Speaking in more general terms, she went on to suggest:

---

[18]   The annual Puck Fair in Killorglin, Co. Kerry.

My theory is that Jack Moeran and his music suffers from an identity crisis. In England they think he's Irish while here, we don't claim him at all.

... I firmly believe that the Irish inspiration in his music is, if anything, more marked than most have realized up 'til now.

... I see Moeran as a national hero whose music expresses what Sibelius does for Finland or Grieg for Norway. (Transcribed from a recording of the original broadcast, 2000)

Una Hunt has been working on performances, broadcasts and CDs of twentieth-century Irish music for almost a decade now; as such, she could be regarded as an active cultural mediator. Hunt's genuine engagement with the music of Moeran and other Irish composers such as Joan Trimble and George Alexander Osborne comes through in her own performances, and more recently through historical research (Hunt, 2006). At the same time, the above statements reveal a strong feeling of national identity, a feeling that might equally apply to musical and non-musical contexts alike ('identity crisis', 'national hero', Ireland/England identity relationship, citizenship and nationality, and a comparison with Nordic nation states). However, this is a case of national identity and music where neither side can be seen to be constitutive of the other. Hunt's work not only represents a general feeling of national pride and/or an imagining of collective musical identity; arguably, her active engagement in performing, recording, broadcasting and writing has the effect of contributing towards a particular articulation of Irish national identity and music.

Musical interests of interviewees

My interviews with audience members were generally carried out at interval periods or immediately after the events themselves. They took place in audience seating areas, adjacent bars and cafes, or in outside areas designated for smoking. In order to encourage extended discussions, I interviewed at least two people at a time. As already outlined in the introductory chapter, each interview was structured around the same four general areas (see p. 20). However, because I wished to facilitate an informal, 'chatty' atmosphere, the line of questioning was adapted to each unique situation. I now present summary findings from the first section of the interviews, in which I asked respondents how the live music heard at a particular event might fit into their overall music listening habits and other musical activities. My reason for including this information is in keeping with the 'snapshots' idea that heads this chapter. Critically, it serves to give some insights into the broad range of music enjoyed by audiences at domestic events, as this becomes an important consideration when I later interpret the same people's beliefs and assumptions pertaining to the potential Irishness of Irish music, both in the contexts of the specific events that they attended as well as in relation to a number of well-known musical acts. This information cannot be regarded as a survey, insofar as the sample size is too small, and also because the interviewees already constituted a specialized group by virtue of their attendance as selected music events. Where I do draw implications, these are intended as speculative rather than representative of music listening and music making across the entire national field. As already reported in Chapter 1, the interviewees were approached on the basis of attendance/availability at concerts, and not on the basis of class or other social categories. That said, my interpretation of people's musical 'taste' acknowledges the potential for cultural distinction afforded by the various genres and events in question (Bourdieu, 1984).

When sorting through transcriptions of interviewees' stated musical interests, I distinguished between definite or unqualified statements of preference for a music style and those statements indicating that a certain style of music might be heard or listened to but was not actively sought out. Examples of the latter type included 'half listening' to commercial pop/dance on radio when driving, or traditional music heard as background music in the local pub. As we shall later see, the distinction made between listening/half listening would often impact on how identifications with particular types of music were described. In some cases, interviewees indicated that they liked music in a general style, but only to a certain degree (for example, liking middle-of-the-road rock music but expressing a dislike for 'heavier' genres such as punk and metal). Definite or unqualified statements of musical preference were interpreted when interviewees were unequivocal about their enjoyment of a particular kind of music and/or indicated that they bought recordings, attended live events or sought out broadcasts in the same music style. This is shown in the second column of Table 4.4 below. The third column sets out the sum total of all citations (qualified and unqualified) pertaining to the participants' engagement with a range of styles and sub-styles. A proportion of interviewees also reported participation in music making, and this is recorded in the fourth column of Table 4.4. Indeed, the number who identified a direct engagement with music (other than listening) came somewhat as a revelation. The principal activities cited were choral singing, instrumental playing, teaching, learning and set dancing.[19]

By combining the figures for pop/dance, rock and hip-hop below, the general category of popular is cited more than Irish traditional and classical, though these categories are also high up on the list of preferences for the entire interview group. Table 4.4 also shows how Irish traditional music and classical music are actively engaged in by a significant number of people. Of note, however, is the apparent lack of popular musicians among the interviewees. This absence is significant not only within the group as a whole, but particularly among the subgroup who attended popular type events. This somewhat reflects findings in respect of broader patterns in Irish musical life insofar as structures for education and amateur participation

---

[19]   Set dancing is a type of traditional quadrille practised in many parts of the country. In many instances, the dancing takes place at pub sessions to the accompaniment of traditional musicians.

Table 4.4   Reported music preferences among the entire interview group
              (67 people)

Style	Unqualified preferences	All citations	Participation
Irish Trad.	27	64	11
Classical	22	51	17
World	21	25	1
Jazz	16	33	5
Pop/Dance	14	38	—
Rock	11	37	—
Hip-hop	4	6	—
Blues	4	4	—
Country	3	3	—
Folk	2	2	—

are facilitated for some kinds of music but not in others (see pp. 49–56). Of
course, this is not to say that the country as a whole lacks popular musicians:
according to several reports Ireland compares well with other countries in terms
of the proportion of popular musicians among the general population (Clancy and
Twomey, 1997; Goodbody Economic Consultants, 2003; IBEC Music Industry
Group, 1998; KPMG Stokes Kennedy Crowley, 1994). What the trends outlined
above do suggest is that the relationship between production and consumption
activities may be less integrated in popular music scenes than is the case with the
more readily identifiable sound groups of traditional music and classical music.

Among those who indicated some kind of performance activity, a considerable
number engaged in two or more 'musical pathways' (Finnegan, 1989). For example,
Sophie and Fiona, who had attended the concert of music by contemporary
composer Gerald Barry, were classically trained pianists who also identified
themselves as learners in jazz piano. Tom and Margaret (Hughes's pub traditional
session) practised set dancing and were also members of a choral society. Indeed,
the general music tastes of the interview group could be described as quite broad,
with a high proportion expressing interest in the categories of jazz and world music,
in addition to the three major style categories under review. The identification of
world music as a preferred category is somewhat surprising, particularly when
compared with the category of (international) folk, which, arguably, would have
been a more popular type in the not so distant past.[20] While Table 4.4 above
suggests a low level of interest among the interview group in country music, it
should be noted that this sub-style comes to be cited more frequently than classical
music in the reported listening and purchasing behaviours of a large sample of

[20]   This finding bears some similarity with the emergence of world music as a preferred
category among British music teachers as reported by Green (2002).

the population surveyed by the Arts Council in 2006 (Hibernian Consulting et al., 2006: 14, 18–19).

Overall, and combined with findings from surveys carried out over the past two decades (Clancy et al., 1994; Hibernian Consulting et al., 2006), the patterns emerging in Table 4.4 show how music industry statistics and data on radio listenership present an incomplete picture of music interests in Ireland. When the active agency of consumers is considered, a much more complex picture emerges. In many cases, the activity of listening intersects with other musical behaviours. The interview data also shows the ability of many listening subjects to cross over style boundaries. Of particular note here was the consistent level of popularity enjoyed by traditional music in all of the interview subgroups, a consistency that was maintained on an event-by-event basis.

Chapter 5

Ireland in music?

A number of the possible associations between Irishness and music outlined at the end of Chapter 1 provide sub-themes for this chapter. First, I examine the extent to which people regard Irish music as synonymous with traditional music, and consider how non-traditional styles of domestic-produced music are viewed in the light of this apparent, taken-for-granted reality. Next I explore perceptions of an 'Irish sound' and/or 'Irish soul' in music. Finally, a range of ideas pertaining to 'cultural Irishness' and music are discussed.

Style categorizations and perceptions of Irishness

Traditional music and Irishness

Although I did not directly ask interviewees any question pertaining to the definition of Irish music and/or Irishness, this was a general theme to emerge from the fieldwork. Indeed, at traditional events, references to Irishness and music were usually forthcoming before I had introduced such terms. At all remaining events, the issue did not arise until a direct line of questioning was pursued. Quite often, the question as to whether the music being listened to sounded Irish led to statements and indeed questions about how Irish music is defined. This was also the case when I asked interviewees to rate individual musicians or groups in terms of 'Irish-sounding'. A number of participants had difficulty with or sought clarification on my question about whether certain music was Irish-sounding, be it the live music taking place at an event or in reference to music by well-known performers. In many cases, this was more to do with a reluctance to talk about the music per se, an observation that will be elaborated on later in Chapter 7. But many people also had difficulties or queries with the terms 'Irish' and/or 'Irish-sounding'.

Eileen, an interviewee at the traditional session in Hughes's pub, showed a distinct unease with the question. Eileen liked Irish traditional music very much and was in fact learning to play the fiddle, yet she seemed to regard the label of Irish as problematic:

> *Eileen*
> J: Do you think the music here tonight sounds Irish?
> Eileen: I tend to shy away from … I think a lot of the stuff you see on TV about the Irishness of Irish music is a bit of a turnoff, to be honest. I don't know, I don't really like that. I think it's been over schmalzified – for want of a better word.

J: But the sounds you hear right now, is there something in them that to you
sounds uniquely Irish?
Eileen: Ah yeah, I think it'd be untrue to deny that … .

A number of people asked about or suggested different categories of Irish music:

Elaine (Gerald Barry concert)
What did you mean by Irish: traditional Irish or contemporary Irish?
Anne (UCH Limerick)
Yeah, you see it depends on what you mean by 'sounds Irish'.
Betty (UCH Limerick)
Well, it depends on the Irish you're talking about.

Conversely, it happened quite often at the beginning of interviews when I asked
people about their general tastes in music, that someone would list 'Irish music' as
one of their interests. Invariably, when asked to give examples, they would confirm
that they meant Irish traditional music. For many people, a piece of music, or the
music of a particular performer/group was unambiguously regarded as Irish. In
such responses, the words 'obviously', 'definitely' and 'inherently' were typically
used to underline affirmations of an Irish sound. This occurred several times in
the case of live music at traditional events, just once at a popular event (Jimmy
MacCarthy) and not at any of the classical events. The following statements,
selected from different interviews at traditional events, arose from my question as
to whether the live music we were hearing sounded Irish:

Karl (Hughes's pub)
… this to me seems inherently Irish and it really fits in here. It's what you expect
… I mean, it's always different, every pub's different, every tune … but to me
it's inherently Irish.
Tom (Hughes's pub)
… when you hear Irish music you don't have to think. Instinctively you know.
Jonathan (Noone's pub)
What we heard tonight would be, you know, typically Irish. You wouldn't
associate it with anywhere else … . You'd listen to that and say it was definitely
Irish
Eoin ('Best of Irish')
Well, I think Irish music is very distinct … you can't really mistake it for
anything else, like.

A similar pattern, that is, an unhesitating description of music as Irish-sounding,
happened when I mentioned certain performers. This was the particularly the case
with the traditional group Altan, and with solo performers Dolores Keane and
Christy Moore. In fact, everyone who knew them rated Altan as unequivocally
Irish-sounding. Quite a number of listeners were aware that their responses were

made instinctively, rather than on any particular aspect of the music that they could articulate.

Other responses suggested that, while 'traditional' was closely associated with 'Irish-sounding', the nature of that relationship was considered in more complex ways, as though the listeners themselves were aware that it was indeed an assumption. Stephen, who attended the Pierce Turner gig in Limerick, qualified his 'yes' and 'no' in relation to the perceived Irish sound respectively of Altan and Afro-Celt Sound System. I should add that, as a researcher himself, Stephen was probably more likely than most to take an analytical approach. That said, and in spite of his own wariness of circular definitions, he did associate 'traditional' with 'Irish', at least in terms of an overall sound.

> *Stephen*
> J: In terms of Irish-sounding, how would you describe Altan?
> Stephen: Let me remember now. I think they were ... I mean in my living memory of what Irishness or Irish music is, I think it largely kind of epitomizes it in many ways – the traditional band of the 80s and 90s. Eh, so in terms of that kind of marker, yeah, I'd say they were.
> J: How about the Afro-Celt Sound System?
> Stephen: They base a lot of their sound, developing from the *bodhrán* ... . I mean, it's a fusion type of music, isn't it like the kind of Afro-reggae sound? Is it Irish? Is it traditional music?
> J: Well, my question was just: 'Does it sound Irish?'
> Stephen: Does it sound Irish? There are recognizable aspects to it. Eh ... but that's a problematic question. I mean ... because there are recognizable aspects to it doesn't make it Irish. Does it sound Irish? Does it sound Irish? Eh, not really, no. If you're going to say, if you're going to give me ... you see, what's missing here is a definition of Irish traditional music or what it sounds like.

Traditional sounds without Irishness

Another group of statements suggests that, while listeners can hear what they identify as traditional sounds in the music, and while they tend to regard traditional as synonymous with Irish, some music may *sound* Irish but does not really *feel* Irish, as the following examples illustrate:

> *Cathal* (Noone's pub)
> J: How about The Corrs. Does their music sound Irish to you?
> Cathal: It does in a way, but it's very obvious why it does. They put in a couple of reels that are populist and packaged very well. So yeah, it does sound Irish, but it's one end of a spectrum of Irish music. Maybe there are other bands that are just as good as them. They do sound Irish but they have a certain media package.

Brendan (UCH Limerick)

J: What do you think of B*witched in terms of Irish-sounding?

Brendan: I totally dislike it as well [as the music of The Corrs]. I think it's completely using ... I mean, when you listen to real Irish music you can feel, what they're putting across. And these are just using it, you feel, you just hear it in your ear like, you hear it in your ear but you can't feel it inside you – if that makes any sense.

J: Mm, yes.

Brendan: Well, you can move your feet to it or you can feel a movement coming, but a movement, Jesus, like ... [feigns a vomiting fit].

In the interview extract that follows, Deirdre and Fionnuala express their views about the music of Bill Whelan, in relation to his piece *Inishlacken*, which was heard at the UCH Limerick event, and also in relation to other pieces by the composer that were already known to the interviewees (including *Riverdance*). The implied argument, that the sum of (Irish) musical parts does equal the Irishness of Irish music, echoes the statements of Cathal and Brendan above:

Deirdre and Fionnuala

J: You said you can recognize traditional elements to his music, but do you think Bill Whelan's music has an Irish sound?

Deirdre: I just don't find ... you see, I think that, I get this feeling about Bill Whelan always that he takes a load of notes and a load of rhythms, and that he kind of nearly puts them up on the computer. Now, I might be exaggerating when I'm saying this but he just comes up with a load of possibilities and he takes an idea from here, and one from there, and one from there, and I just don't get the feeling of unity – ever – from any of his work ... . It's a kind of a ... he obviously loves sound ... . I never get carried away with anything he has done.

Fionnuala: Elements of the Bill Whelan sounded Irishy as opposed to Irish, to me.

Thus far, two general patterns can be noted. First of all, the idea of Irish music is broadly equated with Irish traditional music. Second, within this general association, a qualitative distinction is made between, on one side, music that sounds and feels Irish ('Irish'), and, on the other side, music that sounds but does not feel Irish ('Irishy').

Non-traditional styles and Irishness

In some cases, music was negatively associated with Irishness, not only because it didn't sound traditional, but also because it did sound classical. Ann and Tanya, with whom I spoke at the Dara gig in the Temple Bar Music Centre, Dublin, could not have put this across more directly:

Ann and Tanya

J: Do you think The Three Irish Tenors, what they sing and how they sing, sound Irish?

Tanya: They don't sound Irish.

Ann: It's because they sound classical.

Deirdre (UCH Limerick) spoke more specifically about the differences, as she saw them, between traditional music and modern classical music. In the following statement, she assesses the music of Mícheál Ó Súilleabháin and Bill Whelan:

Deirdre

... I didn't feel it was at all Irish. As far as using the modern, say the twentieth-century kind of scales and rhythms and dissonances, they were very strong. I mean, Bill Whelan is particularly strong on that. So is Mícheál's in a sense. I loved the second part of Mícheál's in the *Hup!* ... . It was concentrating mainly on the cello and very kind of, what would you call it, sort of harmonics on the violin. Definitely, the harmonies and that kind of thing were very much twentieth century. I didn't sense anything Irish about it. Maybe I wasn't looking for it, maybe if I heard it a second time I'd notice little influences. But with the very name *Hup!* and the *sean nós* dancing, and a *bodhrán* in the middle of it was ... redundant.

Deirdre not only regards traditional and classical musical idioms as mutually exclusive, but goes on to emphasize this point with particular reference to contemporary genres of Irish music. As such, the musical systems of modern classical and Irish traditional appear to be antithetical, and this is redolent of what Harry White (1998a) considers to have been the dominant ideological position of Irish nationalism towards classical music. Ironically, while White (2003) would characterize this piece of music by Ó Súilleabháin in terms of its 'ethnic Irishness', quite clearly, Deirdre does not regard it so. Nor does she celebrate Ó Súilleabháin's or Whelan's music as a form of contemporary syncretism. However, this is not to say that Deirdre dislikes modern classical music; in her own words, she actually loved what she considered to be twentieth century in Ó Súilleabháin's music. The complexity of Deirdre's musical identifications here reminds us that a belief based on incompatible constructions of musical categories does not necessarily translate into an antipathy towards music that is considered to be 'other'. It also suggests that while individual identifications may be interpreted with regard to collective identities, they are never wholly reducible to them.

For many people, though, it was not a case of either/or but more a question of degree. If traditional music was generally regarded as essentially Irish-sounding, then the Irishness of other music would be rated in relation to this essential belief. Steve, who was interviewed at the NCH in Dublin, gave such a response when I asked if he thought the contemporary pieces by Gerald Barry sounded Irish:

Steve
J: Is there anything about this music that you think is Irish?
Steve: I don't know. I thought at one stage I did, because I know another piece of
his, I did feel there was a hint of an Irish tune in there [*The Road*] ... but I mean
nothing very overt, nothing very evident or obvious ... . No, not really, maybe a
little hint of Irish traditional music, but besides that nothing really.

Steve also reported a similar response to aspects of Barry's Piano Quartet No. 1,
music made familiar to him through his work as a music teacher in a secondary
school. His use of the word 'hint' speaks more of Irish tunes as an aspect of
compositional material and/or technique rather than as a resource for repertoire.
Musicologist Gareth Cox (1998: 67) makes a similar general observation about the
same piece of music:

For Barry, this recourse to this national resource of traditional Irish music
for pitch material is not unusual, but as always, his source is obscured by the
selective and idiosyncratic treatment it receives ... .

From this analysis it could be speculated that the consciously chosen Irish elements
in Barry's work are not necessarily there to be heard. As it happened, Steve was
the only person among five interviewees who reported hearing anything Irish in
either of the Barry pieces premiered at the NCH in Dublin. Furthermore, it is
arguable that Steve's auditory perception on that occasion was in no small way
conditioned by his prior listening experiences and analytic knowledge of works
by this contemporary Irish composer.

At the UCH Limerick event, Betty found Mícheál Ó Súilleabháin's piece *Hup!*
to be Irish-sounding, but she qualified the sense in which she meant this:

Betty
J: Did you think the Ó Súilleabháin piece sounded Irish?
Betty: Yes I did. Not really, *idle-de-diddly*, you know – the real Irish – but it was
Irish, there were overtures there I thought. Here and there, the Irish came through.

Although Betty perceives this piece as hybrid rather than 'real Irish', her distinction
does not lead to the negation of Irishness in Ó Súilleabháin's work. Two types of
'Irish' meanings can be interpreted here. Firstly, we have intra-musical elements
that Betty associates with Irish traditional sounds – even if these 'overtures'
comprise just part of the overall musical fabric. Second, and more significantly
perhaps, Irishness is not just heard, but in more holistic terms is perceived to
'come through' parts of the listening experience.

Four interviewees at 'The Irish Ring' concert regarded a number of well-known
arias and ballads from the light operas of Balfe, Wallace and Benedict as forming a
distinct type of Irish musical tradition. Two of the arias identified in this way were

Illustration 5.1   Gerald Barry © Clive Barda

'I dreamt that I dwelt in marble halls'[1] from *The Bohemian Girl* and 'Scenes that are brightest' from *Maritana*. Yet even here, the identification of non-traditional repertoire as distinctly Irish did not usually translate into the perception of the same music as Irish-sounding. For example, the interviewees James and Joan did not find the selection of choruses and arias performed at 'The Irish Ring' event to have any generic Irish sound. However, Joan inferred that other sections of one ballad opera might be regarded in this way. The piece in question, 'The Cruisheen Lawn' could be described as a heavily stylized imitation of an Irish traditional song.[2]

---

[1]   This song has recently 'crossed over' into different genres of Irish music, with recordings of it made both by Enya and by the *a cappella* choral group Anúna (who were the original choir to perform in *Riverdance*).

[2]   The title of this drinking song comes from a phonetic adaptation of the Irish phrase *an cruiscín lán*, meaning 'the full jug'.

I did prompt a little here as I felt Joan was finding it hard to remember the title of something that she knew quite well:

> *Joan and James*
> J: Would you consider this music to be Irish?
> James: No, not in the strict sense.
> Joan: There's a gypsy sound of Rumanian, you know … .
> James: Yeah, I think it's Ruritanian music if you like, rather than Irish music – I wouldn't think so.
> J: Even, *The Lily of Killarney*?
> Joan: Oh no, *The Lily of Killarney* is more Irish.
> James: Yes, it's more Irish.
> Joan: There are parts of *The Lily of Killarney* which we didn't hear … [pause]
> J: 'The Cruisheen Lawn'?
> Joan: Yes, exactly. That's the one I'm thinking of. And there are other parts that sound Irish … .

Similar to the pattern noted among some interviewees' perceptions of pop-traditional genres, the use of recognizably Irish material by classical performers did not automatically result in the apprehension of an overall Irish sound. For example, some people regarded much of the material performed by The Irish Tenors and The Celtic Tenors to be Irish in origin, but they did not consider as Irish the overall sound produced by these artists. The following two statements are taken from different interview contexts. In each case I had asked respondents to rate The Irish Tenors in terms of 'Irish-sounding':

> *Eoin* ('Best Of Irish'):
> Well, they're singing like … [sniggers] … . No, not really. They're singing Irish things in a totally different, well, to me, in an un-Irish way.
> *Elaine* (Gerald Barry concert)
> The tenors, they are not singing the songs in a traditional Irish manner. They're singing in an opera style.

Both these statements suggest, once again, that in order for any music to qualify as Irish, it needs to be performed in traditional style or in the character of traditional music. Put another way, it could be said that, for these listeners, notions of stylistic authenticity came to dominate their overview of musical Irishness. However, this way of thinking was by no means unanimous, and was not shared by any of those interviewed at 'The Irish Ring' or Celtic Tenors concerts.

Interviewees at popular music events were the least forthcoming with articulations about Irishness and music. Just one person that I interviewed at the gig by Dara considered the song material of this act to have an overall Irish dimension. Indeed, the following statement by Liam represents the one instance in which the label of 'Irish rock' came up in the entire corpus of interview data, an absence that contrasts sharply with the term's currency in journalistic and marketing discourse:

Liam
J: Is there anything about the music heard tonight that sounds Irish?
Liam: Well, there's a whole ballad thing going on, I suppose. That's because Irish rock is more ballad like and that's what this music is ... .

As a listening subject at the same event, I would tend to agree with Liam's apprehension of ballad structure in much of Dara's material, though I did not hear this as specifically Irish in most cases.[3] A general adherence to ballad form could also be observed in the music of Pierce Turner. Although most of this might be categorized as international folk/popular, Turner occasionally parodied Irish traditional ballads or otherwise made musical reference to traditional repertoire in his original compositions. It came as some surprise that this appropriation of traditional material did not register as Irish-sounding (or at least not consciously so) with any of the people interviewed after this event. By contrast, the original material of Jimmy MacCarthy, that is to say, his song repertoire, was considered Irish by those interviewed at his performance. However, as with the ballad opera material, the sense in which MacCarthy's repertoire was considered Irish did not correspond with the apprehension of any distinct Irish sounds. Rather, interviewees spoke either about the fact that many traditional and popular artists had covered his songs or about the Irishness inherent to the song lyrics.

Overall, the above selection from the interview data confirms that the general category of Irish music is assumed to be synonymous with Irish traditional music. In many cases, traditional and classical are regarded as antithetical musical styles and yet, ironically, Irish classical music is only deemed to have an Irish sound when it refers to elements from traditional music. A similar process operates in relation to popular styles and genres. Evidence from the interviews therefore suggests that relationships between Irishness and non-traditional styles are perceived either as problematic, as was the case with classical music, or as virtually non-existent, as in the case of rock music. It could be said, then, that tendencies among musicological, commercial and other interests to demarcate such labels as 'Irish classical' or 'Irish rock' are not reflected in everyday beliefs pertaining to these styles of domestic-produced music. The analysis of interviews thus far suggests that, for many people, the social fact that a particular musical product or practice *is* Irish means little unless the same music actually *sounds* Irish. However, it would appear that the identification of Irishness in music involves more than the auditory

---

[3]   One exception to this was the song '100 Angry Voices', which had a clear four-line folk ballad structure in Mixolydian mode and which was embellished with melodic ornaments. I may have heard these elements as 'Irish' because of my academic background in folksong analysis, and/or because my social experience as an Irish person led me to hear similarities between this newly composed song and a number of Irish traditional ballads.

perception of (traditional) Irish sounds. As statements by a number of interviewees suggest, Irishness ('the real Irish') cannot be identified in such music unless it also *feels* Irish.

'Irish sound' and 'Irish soul'

'The heart of the matter'

Not surprisingly perhaps, a direct association between traditional music and national identity can be found among some proponents of traditional music. Speaking two decades ago, Labhrás Ó Murchú of *Comhaltas Ceoltóirí Éireann* presented a nationalist narrative of Irish music history when he berated the reluctance of policy makers and others to embrace traditional music's newly found popularity:

> One cannot apply statistical criteria to something which is an element of the spirit. There is an accompanying philosophy with our native music which takes cognizance of the source of origin, its people, its welfare and its aspirations. (1987: 5–6)
> There are, of course, some agencies in Ireland who, as yet, have not reached the age of cultural maturity and who are out of step with the aspirations of the vast majority of our people. This reluctance on their part to give to the Irish what is Irish is probably a throwback to our history when the invader tried relentlessly to anglicise our nation as a prerequisite to conquest. Most have overcome the resulting inferiority complex; others have yet to do so. (1987: 10).

In this explicitly nationalist view, Irish traditional music has an inherent Irishness that is the birthright of Irish people. This idea of Irishness is founded on the concepts of native people and musical origins that combine in both elemental and spiritual ways. In short, Ó Murchú expounds a nativist-essentialist view of Irishness and music, in spite of the fact that in the same essay he celebrates the traditional music interests of the Irish Diaspora along with the significant number of non-Irish peoples who are attracted to the same music (Ó Murchú, 1987: 1–3). The fact that Ó Murchú feels confident to assume what music the vast majority of Irish people want and need may seem incredible, particularly when he eschews any form of quantitative substantiation. However, this is in keeping with the rhetoric of a nationalist hegemony that has evolved since the nineteenth century and that continues to exert considerable influence.

In a later article, Moylan (2001: 9) takes a more pragmatic approach than Ó Murchú inasmuch as he questions the assumed popularity of traditional music. However, he adumbrates Ó Murchú's essentialist outlook in his suggestion that the majority of Irish people are alienated from 'their own' music:

... in Ireland, to most people, Irish music is unfamiliar. In parts of Clare and Kerry, for example, people use the word 'music', unadorned, to mean Irish music. In the rest of the country, one finds the term 'Irish music' is seemingly necessary. This is so commonplace that few find it bizarre. It is a relic of the inferiority complex that has bedevilled life in Ireland since it was a colony.

It is interesting to note that Moylan, who assumes 'traditional' and 'Irish' as synonymous, further regards the apposition of 'Irish' and 'music' to be problematic. His particular use of the word 'unadorned' is suggestive of both musical practices and beliefs that supposedly obtain in organic, undifferentiated societies. While Moylan's assertion might very well hold in the case of some rural traditional sound groups, his idealization takes no account of alternative, potential conceptions that arise from other musical and/or social contexts.

The views of these traditional music ideologues can clearly be linked to notions of ethnic national identity. Ideas of national essence and Irish ethnicity are also behind 'softer' interpretations of Irishness and music. A feature of this kind of writing is the homogenizing discourse reported by McLaughlin (1999) in which all 'imported' musical genres are subsumed within the traditions and spirit of an indigenous Irish musical culture. In her book *Bringing it all Back Home*, Nuala O'Connor discusses the influences of rock, country, pop, electric folk, blues and other genres in relation to Irish music 'at home' and amongst the Irish Diaspora in North America and Britain:[4]

> All of these Irish musical forms are offspring of the same traditional-music parent. They do not co-exist happily together: some are regarded by others as bastards; some are at loggerheads; some are ignorant of their illustrious parentage. But they do share common features, not necessarily of musical construction, but of spirit, which identify them as Irish. (O'Connor, 1991: 7)

This idea of spiritual Irishness is one that is also shared by Philip King, artistic producer of the TV series *Bringing it all Back Home* and of subsequent documentaries about musical culture in Ireland and elsewhere. While King appears to appreciate music as an intercultural field, and while he acknowledges the mutual influence of indigenous and international genres, we are still left with the ideal of an unblended type of Irish music when he states:

> ... I've been really privileged to go from dreaming about music as a small boy, to sitting in rooms with people like Jack Clement and the Everly Brothers, to making films with Emmylou Harris, to watching Daniel Lanois at work. But most particularly, to be around the heart of the matter in our own music, to sit with Martin Hayes and his father in their kitchen, or to be in Donegal with

---

[4]   *Bringing it all Back Home* was originally broadcast in 1991 as a series of TV documentaries, and was subsequently produced in print, video and DVD forms.

> Dermot Byrne and Con Cassidy before he died and to see a truly organic, living,
> mutating thing, almost like a language, the ongoing pulse of the country that is
> the music. (Philip King interviewed in Murphy, 1998: 33)

King not only privileges Irish traditional music in this statement; he also emphasizes
a particular sense of history and place. However, the very rootedness of this music
is conferred with a national significance when he describes it as 'our own' and as
the 'ongoing pulse of the country'. Indeed, King regards traditional music to be
one of Ireland's 'great resources' and urges for greater recognition of this at an
official, national level (ibid: 32). (The idea of Irish music as a 'national resource'
will be further explored in the next chapter.)

A spectrum of cultural-national identifications is also to be found among
contemporary practitioners in traditional music. In the TV documentary series *A
River of Sound* (1995), the fiddler Martin Hayes states:

> Our music is the inspired music of generations. And it's not the music of any
> one individual, it's the music of a people. And it took all the people to create the
> body of music that we have now and all the experience we have. So it's not just
> one person's inspiration, it's a collective inspiration. So, it's imbued with a lot of
> power, I feel. (Transcribed from the video recording *A River of Sound,* 1996)

In a similar vein, musician and scholar Caoimhín Mac Aoidh (2006: 140) writes:

> If traditional music is to be genuinely part of the Irish soul then, when that lone
> flute player begins a tune, it should impact on those listening as a statement of
> historical, current and future meaning, spoken in a thoughtful and considered
> local accent in an expression of passion, humour, pathos or celebration. That
> is a breathtaking challenge to us as a people of culture as well as to us as a
> community of musicians.

Like King, Hayes and Mac Aoidh identify a collective consciousness in music
that is passed from generation to generation. And central to their statements is
the idea of inspiration, that is, a belief in the spiritual potential or 'soul' of Irish
traditional music. While these statements edge more towards the cultural end of the
identification spectrum, other traditional musicians express their idea of Irishness
in more explicit, national terms. Shane Mitchell of the Sligo band, Dervish had
this to say following a performance by the band at the Rock in Rio festival in
Brazil, 2001:

> I've always said that Irish music can be presented the way it is … . We do
> everything from the heart, including playing our music, and I think that was
> reflected tonight in the gig we played … . Irish music is finally taking its place
> centre stage, and I'm very proud to be part of that … . It's one of the few
> natural resources we have in Ireland … the music speaks for itself. The music

we played tonight survived through hard times, it survived penal times, and its own strength carried it through. What we played tonight wasn't much different. (Shane Mitchell interviewed in Long, 2001: 59)

Once again, the idea of history and musical continuity features in this identification with Irish traditional music, but in place of the associations that both Hayes and Mac Aoidh make with 'a people', Mitchell's concept is rooted in the idea of nation. Like King, he opines that this music needs to be regarded as a national resource and, by comparison with other periods of Irish history he celebrates the contemporary status of Irish traditional music both at home and abroad. At the same time, Mitchell is clearly engaged with the music that Dervish play, with what he believes to be the spiritual qualities retained by the music itself and released as the performers 'play from the heart'. In this way his statement serves to show how the two sides of identification and meaning here – inherently musical and culturally Irish – are practically inseparable.

Alternative conceptions of 'Irish sound' and 'Irish soul'

Combined, the various citations above would suggest a fairly close homology between Irish traditional music and communities of Irish people although, as we have seen, what might be called the pan-traditional view is subject to a range of cultural and national articulations. Furthermore, this implied homology between traditional music and Irishness comes into question when different types of vernacular music and diverse social contexts are considered. However, the negation of simplistic essentialisms does not of itself discard the idea of Irishness in music, albeit if the notion is now applied in a more general sense. Although the assumed 'expressive fit' between traditional music and ideal-type rural communities is critiqued by John Waters (1994: 38–45), the same writer nonetheless goes on to make claims to a kind of Irish cultural identity that binds together the music of U2, The Smiths, The Cranberries and others. There are two aspects to Waters's argument that I will discuss here. One is the idea that Irish popular musicians become interested in their cultural and national identity through dealing with the alienation brought about by nativist versions of Irishness:

U2, like many of the recent generations of Irish people, came to be interested in their Irishness through trying to escape it. Having being force-fed the clichés, they threw them up. Suddenly they became hungry. (Waters, 1994: 133)

Related to this, Waters argues that since the late 1970s Irish popular musicians have come to re-articulate and recapture a 'soul' feeling of Irishness (see also McLoughlin and McLoone, 2000). Having dispensed with narrow Gaelic essentialisms, Waters identifies this as a reconnection with Ireland's cultural otherness – other to, and yet articulated within, the mainstream of Anglo-American cultural forms:

There are voices from deep in the tribal memory, an echo from the heart of the Indo-European consciousness. Through an incision made by The Smiths, The Cranberries have penetrated deeper into the bank of memory. Put on the soundtrack of *In the Name of the Father*,[5] wait for the opening duet between the *bodhrán* and the Lambeg,[6] and slide further in. Neither the Smiths nor the Cranberries, nor for that matter U2, would thank you for drawing similarities between them. Nor is this useful in enjoying the noises they make. The fan does not have a loyalty to a band on the basis of its roots or nationality, but in terms of a relationship suggested by the music. It is not a question of creating connections for the sake of it, nor of reclaiming the Smiths for Old Ireland.[7] It is a matter of acknowledging the possibility of relationships so as to reconstruct parts of the mirror which we lost in fragments to the world. (Waters, 1994: 193)

Here, Waters invites us to hear the same connections that he experiences when he listens to this music. He believes that there is a looser yet deeper sense of Irishness other than that suggested by the narrow relationship between Irish nationhood and traditional music sounds. However, as much as Waters considers the idea of Irishness in music to be widely dispersed and differentiated, he nonetheless articulates this within a grand narrative that somehow brings us to back to an imagined Irish essence. Arguably, Water's view of Irishness and popular music does not differ much from those of many traditional music commentators insofar as it includes the ideas of continuity, collective consciousness and inherent musical features – only now on a much grander (and vaguer) scale. Thus, as with Nuala O'Connor and Philip King, Waters engages with pluralistic notions of Irishness and music that are nonetheless governed by a homogenizing conception. Ironically, the combining threads of Irishness that Waters hears in this music (*bodhrán*, the vocal quality of The Cranberries' lead singer Dolores O'Riordan and so on) return us to what are perceived as traditional Irish sounds.

In many cases, Waters might well be right in saying that neither musicians nor fans are necessarily interested in nationality or roots. The evasive concept of music with 'Irish soul' (not unrelated to Ó Súilleabháin's 'Irish psyche') suggests a way of linking Irishness and music that does not sit comfortably in either category of *sounds*-Irish (normally confined to traditional music) or *is*-Irish (confined to domestic production). It can, however, be linked with the quality of *feels*-Irish, as suggested by the statements of some interviewees in the section above. This more general sense of Irishness presents an attractive idea for musicians and others who

---

[5]   The music for this modern political film, produced by Bono and Gavin Friday, included both traditional and hip-hop/rock sounds and featured, among others, the voice of Sinéad O'Connor.

[6]   Lambeg drums are associated with the marching traditions of the Orange Order (a Protestant sect) in Northern Ireland.

[7]   Waters refers here to the fact that The Smiths were a Manchester-based band with Irish family connections.

might wish to articulate both the 'foreignness' and 'nationalness' of their music and/or cultural identity. To take one of the most famous of Irish popular musicians, Bono presents a good example of ambivalent attitudes towards Irishness and music, starting with a negation of narrow essentialisms before moving on to a broader idea of what it is to be Irish musically:

> I rebelled against being Irish, I rebelled against speaking the Irish language, Irish culture … Batman, Robin, Superman – that was more part of my experience than Finn McCool and the legends and mythology of Ireland … .
> I think there's an Irishness to what U2 do; I'm not quite sure what it is. I think it's something to do with the romantic spirit of the words I write, but also of the melodies that Edge makes on the guitar. Now the rock 'n' roll element that comes through Larry would hardly be Irish, yet the abandonment in the way he plays the kit is intrinsically Irish … .
> I think … Irish music reminds us of the humanity that we're losing, of a past we all share. It's a common past and Irish music is a part of it. (Bono interviewed in O'Connor, 1991: 130)

These three separate statements by Bono suggest a number of broad ways in which Irish popular musicians might deal with their Irishness. To begin with, traditional and conservative concepts of Irishness are rejected, not only because they are largely irrelevant to the social experience of many musicians, but also because they represent an ideology that is incompatible with a rock aesthetic. The second statement presents an acceptable face of Irishness insofar as it eschews any narrow nationalism or musical essentialism. To a limited extent, Irishness in music can be identified with regard to specific elements, but it mainly refers to an ephemeral quality that is represented through individual behaviours and perspectives ('romantic', 'abandonment'). Third, Irish popular musicians are conscious of the continuities between traditional music practices and their own music making and, more generally, are conscious of their cultural 'roots'. While the above observations are based on specific views articulated by Bono in the early 1990s, similar views by artists regarding Irishness and music have consistently featured in interpretations of Irish popular music over the past two decades, notably, Clayton-Lea and Taylor (1992), Cogan (2006), Hegarty (2004), O'Connor (1991), Prendergast (1987), Skinner Sawyers (2000), Swan, (2003), Waters (1994) and in the *Hot Press*/RTÉ TV documentary series *Out of Ireland: From a Whisper to a Scream* (2000). At another level, this pattern might be more representative of the discourse of cultural commentators than that of the musicians themselves, since all of the above publications and projects to varying degrees assume the connectedness of different genres of Irish popular music through a general, albeit at times problematic, sense of Irishness.

As already noted in the opening chapter, McLaughlin (1999) provides a persuasive critique of such homogenizing tendencies, and sets out to interrupt this discourse by suggesting that some Irish popular musicians have negotiated their own sense of identity and place. In particular, he argues that the band U2 liberated themselves from the burden of national representation through experimenting and metamorphosing in successive albums and tours, from the 'traditional' Anglo- and Afro-American rock values reflected in their 1980s output to a more radical engagement with the 'avant-garde' of European rock/pop aesthetics in the early 1990s (McLaughlin, 1999: 168–87; 199–225).[8] However, this apparent transcendence of place by U2 is appraised somewhat differently by cultural critic Kieran Keohane, who picks up some of the thread of John Waters's interpretation cited above:

> Rootlessness, transcendental homelessness, to live in the stratosphere of stardom, or to be a Zuropean,[9] to have 'gotten over' one's (problem with) Irishness and Irish tradition, to be post-modern (that is, to have a post-national sense of identification), is still existentially unsatisfying. (Keohane, 1997: 292)

There are two aspects to these positions that I wish to comment on here. First of all, McLaughlin's interpretation might lead us to ascribe an inherent value to disengaging music production from local issues and/or regard 'international sounding' as somehow more 'progressive' and therefore more artistically valid than 'Irish sounding'. Keohane meanwhile appears to problematize the very idea of stardom in the context of Irish popular artists. By so doing he 'psychologizes' the cultural identity of the individual musicians concerned, and inadvertently promotes stereotypical ideas of authentic 'Irish' performance.

An overarching homogenizing discourse can also be observed in 'outsider' interpretations of Irish music and culture. For example, in a book entitled *Ireland and the Irish,* John Ardagh uses the following subheading: 'The music revival: from *Sean Nós* and The Chieftains to U2's world conquest' (Ardagh, 1995: 277). While most of his account of Irish music is given over to traditional music, Ardagh also seeks to accommodate artists such as Sinéad O'Connor and U2 in his interpretation of Irishness and music:

> As for today's biggest names, Sinéad O'Connor and U2, here the influences are not so clear … . She [O'Connor] claims to dislike modern Irish society, and most critics would say they find no Celtic influences in her singing. Others suggest that there is nonetheless something Irish about her directness, emotionalism and intensity … . Equally in the case of U2, the Irishness lies if anywhere in the expression. … . Irish musical experts … claim to find no traditional influences

---

[8]   In spite of this, McLaughlin points to domestic and international reception of U2, which firmly associates the band with the 'place' of Ireland and in particular with Dublin. The pervasive use of the Irish national flag by fans at U2 concerts, both in Ireland and abroad, would seem to support this interpretation.

[9]   Keohane's use of 'Zuropean' here alludes to U2's *Zoo TV* tour of 1992–93 and to the subsequent release of the album *Zooropa* in 1993.

in the music itself, which is pure modern rock; but they will accept that the directness of style, the feelings, the concern for storytelling, are in some ways Irish. (Ardagh, 1995: 285–6)

Similarly, in *The Complete Guide to Celtic Music* Ruth Skinner Sawyers accommodates the apparent 'un-Irishness' of U2's music in her commentary on *The Joshua Tree* album, released in 1987:

> The themes were hardly Irish – America as the Promised Land, life in the modern world, personal despair, spiritual yearning – nor were the musical influences – blues, gospel, and even country blues. Yet somehow the group's Irish spirit shone through. It sounded both Irish and American – but it also transcended nationality and musical boundaries. In a way, this was soul music. Irish soul music. (Skinner Sawyers, 2000: 240)

It goes without saying that the qualities described by both Ardagh and Skinner Sawyers – 'spirit', 'expression', 'soul', 'emotionalism', 'intensity' and so on – could apply to other types of music or other cultures. Perhaps the most obvious association in this regard would be the concept of Blackness as it has been applied to various Afro-American styles of music (Gilroy, 1993). Indeed, associations between Irishness and Blackness are made quite liberally in various forms of Irish popular music discourse. As examples, the connections made between Afro-American and Celtic 'soul' in Van Morrison's music (see McLoughlin and McLoone, 2000; Onkey, 2006), or in purely fictional terms, the description of the Irish as 'the blacks of Europe' in the 1991 film *The Commitments*.[10]

The widespread use and apparent acceptance of this homogenizing discourse was underlined (both metaphorically and literally) in the Ireland entry for the 1994 edition of *World Music: The Rough Guide*, entitled 'Irish Soul'.

> Irish Soul: Irish traditional music has fed into the mainstream for decades – and it's not lying down yet awhile.
> Alan Parker's engaging film 'The Commitments' centred on the activities of a young soul band. Soul bands in the James Brown mode are thin on the ground in Ireland, much less Dublin city, but soul musicians ... that's another story ... (O'Connor, 1994: 5)

The first observation to be made here is the insider/outsider dialectic of national identity that this article by Nuala O'Connor presents. (The same writer penned a revised version of the article for the second edition of the *Rough Guide* in 1999.) While it is arguable that any piece about Irish music in a volume on world music could be viewed in this way, the particular emphasis and implied association between the terms 'soul' and 'tradition' would appear to intensify that dialectic.

---

[10]   The screenplay was adapted from the eponymous novel by Roddy Doyle (1989).

'Soul' as a musical term connotes the more rooted aspects of Afro-American and, by extension, the 'mainstream' of global popular music. Yet, when 'soul' comes to be applied to Irish music, the introduction and body of this article seem to suggest that traditional music is the mainstream.

In a subsection from the same piece (and its revised version) entitled 'Shamrock and Roll', O'Connor (1994: 11, 1999: 179) suggests that the interface between Irish traditional and Anglo-American popular styles was mostly unidirectional 'as rock musicians raided the storehouse of Irishry to lend a Celtic air to their songs'. However, she goes on to claim that the traditional singing style of *sean nós* can be heard in the voices of Van Morrison and Shane McGowan amongst others: 'That voice, primitive and complex at the same time, is as much a part of the Irish tradition as an array of instruments ...' (O'Connor, 1994: 14). (See also p. 157). These statements by O'Connor not only serve to homogenize the diversity of vernacular musical practices in Ireland but at the same time authenticate certain types of musical expression over others; as well as capitulating to stereotypical conceptions of Irishness, the word 'shamrock' presents a pun that de-authenticates the fusion of 'indigenous' traditions with international genres. Arguably, this insider-for-outsider type of presentation exaggerates the extent to which a similar tendency may obtain in the domestic scene. However, the dualistic conception that Irish music is essentially Irish traditional music and yet has something to offer to the wider world of 'soul' music can very much be seen as a recurring theme in hagiographic accounts of Irishness and music. Such ideas can be linked to notions of authenticity within increasingly globalized contexts, and these are themes to which I shall return in Chapter 8.

The interviewees

Unlike the musicians, journalists and other cultural commentators cited above, the people I interviewed at various music events did not volunteer such all-encompassing labels as 'Irish soul' and 'Irish sound', at least not in any self-conscious way. However, more subtle articulations of 'soul' and 'feel' did feature in many people's appraisals of particular musicians and/or the sounds made by the same artists (see pp. 154–9). As already discussed, identifications of this sort can accommodate perceptions of Irishness in non-traditional popular genres. Yet, while there may well be strong links between the general labels of 'Irish soul music'/ 'Irish sound' and more specific readings of 'soul' and musical Irishness, the absence of any explicit reference to the former type among 67 interviewees suggests that homogenizing and celebratory expressions of Irish popular music are not necessarily shared by the general public.

Overt statements about Irish national identity and music were presented by a number of interviewees at traditional music events. Such beliefs typically arose in response to my question about the sounds of the music. That is to say, although I did not ask people about cultural and/or national identity, opinions related to these issues nonetheless came to the fore. Generally speaking, these interviewees confined statements to their own feelings of cultural-national identity, and, in contrast to some of the traditional music ideologues cited above, were not prescriptive about which music was or was not appropriate for other Irish people.

Tom (Hughes's pub) was particularly forthcoming on the matter of identity:

Tom
J: Do you think that there's something particularly Irish-sounding in the music here tonight?

Tom: Well, I think it's a very difficult thing to identify in words, but … you hear Irish music anywhere in the world, in any atmosphere, any circumstance, you hear it, you will immediately think that that's Irish music – that's part of me, that's me. I mean, I think that Irish music characterizes Irish people in a very, very strong way … .

Although my question here is primarily addressed to the sounds of the music heard, it would seem that hearing Irishness and thinking or feeling Irishness are inseparable processes for Tom. Furthermore, he believes that Irish (traditional) music articulates not only his nationality but also his very social experience. There are insider/outsider aspects to this expression of national identity in that the music not only characterizes what is Irish but also distinguishes it from what is not Irish.

Other interviewees at traditional events also identified with the music but expressed this more in cultural than explicitly national terms. Both Maurice and Jimmy, interviewed together at the traditional session in Noone's pub expressed ideas of continuity and heritage when speaking about the strains of traditional music heard in the background as we chatted:

Maurice and Jimmy
J: Well, about the music here tonight. Can you tell me things about the music right now that you like?

Jimmy: The sound. The fact that, the music you hear tonight, you could go back to hundreds of years ago … you'd still hear the same music like nothing has changed … .

Maurice: Well, you see, he stole my word … because what's going on in the background there now evokes traditional music as it was played in … less affluent days. The music hasn't changed. Now the pub here has reflected itself in a backward tradition in that the pub reflects the music that you hear now which is of – for want of a better description – the music of a hundred years ago. So, in a way, the music is a success because the modern world is retracting back to it, and the music doesn't have to … prove itself. It just doesn't have to prove itself.

Jimmy: … it's like a sound that has always been there, and that will go on for this generation and for the next generation. It'll be there for eternity, it'll go on forever … .

The contexts of identification here are those of tradition and continuity, and these appear to be important cultural values in the face of modernity and change. However, while Maurice and Jimmy were enjoying the music or 'sound' in the pub that night, their enjoyment seemed to be based mostly on the *idea* of Irish traditional music in a pub setting. Jimmy emphasized the idea of tradition in traditional music. His aspiration was not just that it would be there for him, but that it would be available to all Irish people, now and in the future. These strong associations between Irish identity and traditional music need to be interpreted in the light of the varied musical tastes registered by the interview cohort as a whole. Also worth bearing in mind is the range of social experiences reported by this group of people living in Ireland. For example, Maurice qualified his response to my question about musical tastes by stating that he was both 'a child of the sixties' and 'a city boy'. As such, Irish traditional music did not hold a particular interest for him as music and yet, he identified with it quite strongly:

Maurice

The music seems as it should be – to me anyhow, and it's ironic, more of a nuisance than a pleasure but I still want to hear it there. And I still want it to live. It's a peculiar irony but that's the way I feel. But I'm a city boy and I had plenty of other places to go to. But country people had only that to go to. You see, when you interview city boys, it complicates it but nonetheless, it's ... in our genes. My grandfather was from Laois so something transferred. If I never heard it, I have a love of it, a feeling for it, an understanding of it.

This statement suggests two levels in which Maurice might identify with music. First, there are his own personal tastes ('I'm more of a blues man'), which he links to his social experience as an inner city Dubliner or 'Dub' of a particular generation. Second, there is music with which he is not particularly engaged (traditional) but which for him may reflect broader parameters of identity (national, intergenerational, genetic).

Maurice's somewhat distanced position regarding traditional music was echoed in the views of other people who attended the session at Noone's pub. The following statement is taken from an interviewee named Mary:

Mary

J: How then, would you describe your tastes in music?

Mary: Mine would be wide and very varied. Many different types of music – I'd like jazz, I'd like blues, I like pop, I like rock, I like eh ... You know, I actually like Irish music, not mad into country music but I like difference or variety in music. You know, when I would think of music ... I start by what I would choose to listen to, but yet I am always going to associate Irish music as part of what I know.

Again, it would appear that while Irish (traditional) music is not at the top of Mary's list of preferences, she identifies with it in general cultural terms. To describe music as 'part of what I know' implies not only her own social experience but is also suggestive of something that is culturally embedded.

Cathal, another interviewee at Noone's, was more explicit regarding cultural and national identity:

Cathal

J: How would this session fit into your overall musical interests?

Cathal: From my point of view, in terms of like, my upbringing, like, I enjoy live events and the *seisiún* [session]. Like, this music is part and parcel of Irish life – that you can always walk into a bar and the fact that you can hear someone just striking up a chord. That's part of our life and I hope it never changes … .

J: Would you go to other live music events?

Cathal: Yeah, from time to time but I would never go to an Irish … to this form of music. I would never pay to go to something like this.

J: And … would this type of music feature in music you listen to on CD recordings or cassettes?

Cathal: No, never. I kind of don't like to listen to it purposely, but I know if I go to a certain pub then it's going to have live Irish music, and from time to time I would go to that pub … .

The first statement here by Cathal reveals an identification that combines the overall sound of traditional music with a general sense of Irishness. Here, traditional musical culture is characterized not only as a kind of heritage but is also seen to represent a distinct way of life that somehow encapsulates the essence of Irishness. However, in common with both Maurice and Mary, Cathal's cultural identification with Irish music does not necessarily correspond with his individual musical tastes and interests. Like Maurice, his pleasure in traditional music seems to be more focused on what the event signifies rather than on the music itself. When I asked Cathal what he thought might be Irish-sounding about the music he picked up on something that his friend Malcolm had said just before about the style of fiddle playing, but then seemed anxious to return to a more general interpretation of the music's Irishness:

Cathal

Yeah, the fiddle is predominant. Maybe, it's the fiddle that gets people tapping their toes … . I think it's a great deal more for maybe … my father, my parents' generation. They grew up with that. It may have been a part of the way of life and some of us in our generation embrace it … .

I would be traditionalist so I say: 'Keep these guys coming because they're part of our culture … .'

While Cathal's statement acknowledges that there may be specific qualities of Irishness in traditional music, it is the symbolic role of traditional music in Irish culture that assumes more significance in this instance. Looked at another way, it could be argued that, for Tom, Maurice, Jimmy, Mary and Cathal, the categories of 'music' and 'Irish traditional music' are valued in significantly different ways. This is not to suggest a crude distinction between musical and social meanings (see pp. 145–7). Rather, I would say that these opinions illustrate how extra-musical meanings can be more self-consciously expressed in cultural-national identifications than in the case of other types of socio-musical identifications. Of course, extra-musical meanings can also come to bear in the apprehension of different musical genres; we might speculate that this is indeed the case when Maurice's self-designation as a 'blues man' is linked to his own terms of 'sixties child' and 'city boy'. However, what is significant and common to the responses of this subgroup is the explicit way that Irish-musical identifications are articulated. With the possible exception of Tom who also expressed a particular interest in some stylistic aspects of traditional music, these cultural-national identifications were not based on any specific intra-musical aspects. It was not a case of the sounds not being heard or the music not being enjoyed (even if it was in the background and an occasional 'nuisance'). Rather, it was the sense in which the *idea* of the music as opposed to the music per se became central to these processes of identification. Nowhere did this come through as strongly as in Maurice's belief that: 'If I never heard it, I have a love of it, a feeling for it, an understanding of it.'

The pattern of identification outlined above broadly finds resonance with a central theme in Harry White's cultural critique on the production, reception and perception of Irish music. That is to say, not only is 'traditional' regarded as synonymous with 'Irish', but also, the emblematic status of Irish traditional music figures more in the imagination than does the music itself. However, as I will argue throughout the remainder of this book, this is by no means the only way in which Irish music and Irish national identity are associated. Furthermore, even within what might be called the cultural-national spectrum of musical identifications, there can be a variety of interpretations and articulations. For example, while Máire (Hughes's pub) echoed some of the themes of belonging and continuity expressed by the above interviewees, she did so in the context of her direct engagement with traditional music. In response to my question about the things in the music that she might like (I had not yet introduced the word 'Irish' at this point of the interview), Máire said:

Máire

… . If I'm actually listening to something I prefer to listen to slow airs and then I'd actually get up and dance for the fast airs … . And I think the other thing I'd identify with is probably more the sound, like the sound of the wooden flute or whatever … it's sort of memories of the fact that it is more … I don't know, something you identify with … . I can't give you anything technical.

Máire's identification with the traditional session is grounded in her attention to the music itself as much as it is to what it more broadly signifies. The phrase 'memories of the fact that it is more' suggests the notions of continuity and tradition, but these too are rooted in her own family background and childhood memories (mentioned elsewhere in the interview) and in her regular engagement with traditional music as an attentive listener and recreational dancer.

Cultural Irishness or 'Irishness by association'

The taken-for-granted reality of Irish music as synonymous with Irish traditional music has consistently been criticized by a number of commentators writing from the perspective of classical music interests (for example, Acton, 1978; Corcoran, 1982; Deane, 1995; Pine, 2005: 1–38, 213–60). In the introductory chapter, it was reported how several musicologists question this assumption by presenting an ideology-critique of Irish nationalism and the emblematic status that is has largely afforded to traditional music. And yet, along with other advocates for the development of classical music in Ireland, the same critics in many ways sustain the idea of a 'national' music, albeit with a more civic sense of nationhood and culture. Ironically, then, even though classical musicians and scholars tend to problematize relationships between Irishness and music, collectively they constitute a powerful national group when it comes to the negotiation of symbolic recognition and material resources. Thus, while many commentators consistently lament how classical music in Ireland has yet to realize the 'visibility', support and status enjoyed by the same cultural arena in comparable European nation states,[11] it could be said that national institutions service the area of classical music more than any other type. The NSO, The NCH, Opera Ireland and The National Chamber Choir are part of a long list of such institutions, and this has been intensified in recent years by calls for a national academy of music and other performing arts (Pine, 2002).

Issues of national identity also feature in the appraisal of individual composers and/or musical works. For example, four essays in a volume of the annual *Irish Musical Studies* (Cox and Klein, 2003) examine the Irishness of Irish classical music from a number of critical and analytical perspectives, some of which will be referred to in Chapter 7. Elsewhere, Bracefield (1996) problematizes a tendency among Northern Irish composers to eschew any direct engagement with contemporary political issues in their works. Thus, while the mainstream of Irish musicology has by-and-large adopted revisionist and anti-essentialist perspectives on Irish cultural history, its overarching critical stance has nevertheless sustained a focus on national issues and debates.

Although some classical music proponents, for example, the composers Frank Corcoran (1982) and Raymond Deane (1995, 1997), contribute to a generally negative, modernist appraisal of Irish music history, other composers and musicians see it differently insofar as they interpret the lack of substantial

---

[11] For example, see White (2005: 36–50). Smaczny (2007), meanwhile, presents a comparative, historical analysis of 'musical national traditions' in Ireland and the Czech lands.

classical music traditions in liberating terms. Both Ó Seaghda (1999) and White (2003) develop this point in relation to the opinions of contemporary composers Donnacha Dennehy and Gerald Barry. Dennehy, for example, states:

> Up to Ó Riada's time, there was a feeling that you had the burden of European tradition on your shoulders and, almost contradicting that, a feeling that we were on the periphery. Nowadays, it's as if it's being turned around. We're in the mainstream of European culture to an extent, but we can *play* on the fact that we're on the periphery to allow us to do what we want. I see a lot of parallels between what is going to happen in Irish new music and the way the Americans ploughed their own furrow in the 50s, with Cage or Feldman .... (Donncha Dennehy interviewed in Ó Seaghda, 1999: 29)

This suggests a way of imagining music that is Irish without the 'baggage' of traditionalism or, for that matter, modernism. Eve O'Kelly, director of the Contemporary Music Centre based in Dublin, also interprets this as a trend when writing here about the composers, Eric Sweeney, Eibhlís Farrell and Gerald Barry:

> These composers were the first to be able to dispense with the weight of their Irishness, as it were, feeling the need neither to demonstrate it nor rebel against it ... .
> He [Gerald Barry] feels Irish and regards it as an important part of his being, but writes music with an international voice ... . (O'Kelly, 1995: 96, 98)

These statements serve to illustrate how, in some quarters, a civic sense of Irish musical identity is deemed possible.[12] In other words, while the idea of a national musical essence is to be avoided, the potential uniqueness of Irish music need not compromise the music's universality and artistic intent. The above statements serve to underline the individual output of living Irish composers, and although there is a suggestion that the plurality of modern classical music in Ireland somehow amounts to 'we', this falls short of recognizing any collective compositional 'school' or style. Arguably, these beliefs and assumptions serve to authenticate de facto Irish classical music that is not traditionally derived (*is*-Irish), whereas traditional-inspired Irish classical genres (*sounds*-Irish) cannot aspire to the same artistic level. This adumbrates the distinction made by White (2003) between 'modern' and 'ethnic' articulations of Irish contemporary composition. As we have already seen, this kind of civic/ethnic distinction does not hold in the case of traditional music, the more obvious reason being that traditional music is generally regarded as Irish-sounding. Arguably though, the conceptual differences run deeper insofar as the ideas of ethnicity and culture (or collective consciousness

---

[12]   In many respects, this mirrors the way in which issues of national identity come to be negotiated by Irish writers (see, for example, Deane, 2003; Kearney, 1989).

in music) tend to be treated as inseparable concepts in the discourse of traditional musicians and their followers.

Notwithstanding the tendency to equate Irishness in music with traditional sounds, a number of interviewees approached the general category of Irish music in broader cultural terms. That is to say, Irishness in music could also be defined by association with extra-musical (Irish) phenomena, a category that could be described as 'Irish by association' and coming close to White's conception of cultural Irishness (2003: 16). However, even with these types of statements, it was difficult for interviewees to eschew essential concepts of Irishness insofar as some music defined as Irish was not deemed to be inherently Irish. I now report on cases where interviewees made 'Irish' references to musicians, composers, places and texts. In some cases, a definition of Irish music that was close to the definition used in this book – all music produced in Ireland – presented itself. The following dialogue comes from my interview with Sophie who had attended the Gerald Barry Retrospective concert:

> *Sophie*
> J: Did you think Barry's music tonight sounded Irish?
> Sophie: Well, I'd have to say, in general, yes, it did sound Irish. Everything by an Irish composer is Irish. So, it is Irish, no matter what it sounds like. Maybe it doesn't sound very Celtic or anything, but it's Irish, like.
> J: Well, what kind of way would it sound?
> Sophie: Traditional?
> J: No, what I mean is: Would it be easy to distinguish it from … music by an Estonian composer, say? If you were to think of the Irish piece and the Estonian piece would there be things in the Irish piece that would be distinctive?
> Sophie: I don't know. I might be able to distinguish it, but I couldn't say.

Here, it could be said that while Sophie has no hesitation in regarding Barry's music as Irish by definition, she has difficulty in reconciling this aspect of her statement with her description of the sounds heard in the same music. Sophie's inclusive definition of Irish music extended to forms and styles that she did not like. Here, in her assessment of the girl band B*witched, she once again distinguishes between what is and what sounds Irish:

> *Sophie*
> It's kitsch and it's embarrassing and, you know, it's teenybopper stuff. It doesn't appeal to me at all and I don't think that it sounds Irish. I mean, unfortunately, it is Irish [laughs]. You can't get away from that fact!

Combined, these observations by Sophie suggest a more sociological interpretation of the term 'cultural Irishness' insofar as, irrespective of her musical preferences, avant-garde classical and commercial pop are equally considered as aspects of Irish culture.

While many interviewees expressed a clear association between traditional music and their own sense of cultural and national identity, a smaller number of interviewees at classical events identified cultural Irishness in particular pieces of music. In many cases, however, these could be described as tenuous links, as this statement by Dick, who attended 'The Irish Ring' concert of ballad opera, illustrates:

> *Dick*
> … there is nothing particularly Irish about any of it really. I mean, one of the reasons why … two of them were written by Irish men but were set in other countries and the only one that was set in Ireland was written by a German so … [laughs]. But no, I'd say that they're Irish insofar as we have associations: one of them is set in Killarney and then Balfe and Wallace were Irish.

A stronger sense of cultural identity was expressed when repertoire was deemed Irish by virtue of literary connections. Two interviewees at two different events made reference to the links between Irish-produced classical music and prominent Irish literary figures such as Shaw and Joyce. One of these, James, who attended 'The Irish Ring' event at the National Concert Hall, Dublin considered these associations to be of cultural importance:

> *James*
> J: How would this [concert] tie into your musical interests in general?
> James: In the literary sense, it's a music that's very strongly associated with James Joyce and Dublin of this time, and his works are littered with extracts from this particular kind of music. If you read through them, you'd be surprised at what turns up in one form or another. I think that's something that should be remembered really.

In a way, James echoes a critical engagement by some Irish musicologists with the interweaving histories of music and literature in the late nineteenth and early twentieth centuries (see especially, White, 1995, 1998a: 94–124). A broader cultural interest in such musical-literary associations gives rise to the occasional staging of themed musical events.[13] Meanwhile, Smyth (2002, 2007: 207–10) describes how rich descriptions of Irish-produced music have permeated the works of many Irish novelists (including James Joyce[14] and, more recently, Bernard Mac Laverty and Roddy Doyle), and how these and other writers in different ways have sustained ideas of inherent Irish musicality across a range of musical genres.

Doreen was one of just two people I interviewed at the recital of piano and vocal music by E.J. Moeran at the John Field Room, NCH, Dublin. In this extract,

---

[13] One such example during the course of my fieldwork was a concert advertised as 'The Music of George Bernard Shaw', staged at the NCH, Dublin in October 2000.

[14] See also White (2005: 111–20).

she alludes to an Irish literary association when speaking about Moeran's musical settings of poems by James Joyce:

Doreen
J: Can you tell me some things that you may have liked about this music?
Doreen: The unusual harmonies in his music. Yes, it reminded me ... at one point I felt this was *Lied* only in Irish style, you know, with such an important part in the piano ... like German *Lieder* only in Irish style, written for the voice and piano, but it was very much that that struck me.
J: In what way did you think it had an Irish style?
Doreen: Well, not so much that it had an Irish style, but that it had an Irish composer, and of course it was the poems of James Joyce. And he composed melodies to go with them ... .
J: And do you think that the piano music and the songs were Irish-sounding?
Doreen: Not particularly, no.

Doreen regarded the music to be Irish by virtue of its association with the nationality of both composer and poet, and with the specific Irish settings of the texts. While she began by describing this as an Irish classical genre, she later qualified this by stating that the music did not particularly *sound* Irish to her.

The associations made between language and music were quite different when it came to the Irish language (Gaelic, *Gaeilge*). While the English language was referred to in respect of literary texts (culture equating high art), interviewees who mentioned the Irish language linked it more to national characteristics and essential qualities (culture as tradition/heritage). Liam was one of the people that I interviewed following the Dara gig at the Temple Bar Music Centre in Dublin. When asked if the music he had just heard sounded Irish he replied:

Liam
Well, it's very hard to define a race ... what defines a race? Language defines a race – to me. And this is not Gaelic ... but I don't know if the Irish are Gaelic anymore ... so, that's a complex question.

Indeed, this is a complex answer in that, on the one hand, Liam appears to take an essentialist position regarding Irish music and language and, on the other hand, questions the validity of any Gaelic-Irish cultural package in a contemporary context. The first part of Liam's statement is somewhat similar to a view expressed by Tom (Hughes's pub):

Tom
Instinctively, you know that probably, second to the Irish language it [traditional music] is the thing that characterizes and distinguishes Irish people more ... than anything else.

Unlike Liam, Tom is unambiguous in the way he regards traditional music and the Irish language as essential aspects of Irishness. However, he goes on to imply that Gaelic Ireland is more of a national ideal than it is a part of his own social reality:

Tom

J: So, do you speak Irish then?

Tom: I don't use it often enough. I mean, I feel about that, you know, that I should do it. I would have a reasonable understanding of Irish but my spoken Irish would be poor.

These statements by Liam and Tom are redolent of nationalist imaginings of Irishness that go as far back as the nineteenth century. However, in different ways, both are cognizant of the contradictions such ideological positions hold in the face of contemporary realities.

The same situation, vis-à-vis traditional music and the Irish language, was interpreted in a more positive light by the aforementioned James ('The Irish Ring'):

James

J: And other types of music, would you listen to traditional music or types of popular music?

James: I'm very fond of traditional music. There are some kinds of traditional music that I don't understand like *sean nós* but generally I think it has come into its own in the last fifty years. It went through a bad period when it could have become extinct, almost like the language in a sense. But obviously, with *Comhaltas Ceoltóirí Éireann* it has ... breathed life into it, and it'll be ... I suppose it'll be captured, encaptured now and it'll go from strength to strength.

Here, James implies that traditional music and the Irish language ('the language') are part and parcel of Irish national identity and therefore worthy or revival, and like his description of musical-literary associations, there is a narrative aspect to his sense of Irish nationhood here. Indeed, it could be interpreted that, in contrast to Tom above, James has no great difficulty in reconciling his fondness for Irish traditional music and language with the fact that he may be an 'outsider' to some aspects of 'national' culture. This brings us back to the distinction made earlier between a sense of national identity arising from the *idea* of Irish music as opposed to identifications of Irishness that are experienced in audition.

Two patterns can be inferred from the above statements linking non-traditional music with explicit statements of national identity. First, a specific sense of cultural Irishness is echoed in the way that some interviewees make associations between Irish classical music and literary texts. Second, other interviewees imply negative relationships between non-traditional musical styles and their Irishness on such grounds as inauthentic style or 'non-national' linguistic-cultural origins. Although this type of response is redolent of essentialist constructs of Irish culture, it does not follow that such ideas are received uncritically. For example, while Liam's statement echoes the ideology of Gaelic Irishness (he cites the 'trinity' of music, language and race), he regards as problematic the very notion of Gaelic Irishness in the context of contemporary Irish society.

Chapter 6

Irishness and music in a changing society

Irish society has undergone some dramatic changes since the emergence of its 'Celtic tiger' economy in the early 1990s. In this chapter, I explore how ethnic and cultural conceptions of Irishness are increasingly confronted by or are adapted to economic ideas of national identity. Hegemonic articulations of Irishness are further interrupted by an increasing heterogeneity amongst the Irish population which increased from 3.6 million persons in 1996 to 4.2 million over the decade that followed (Central Statistics Office, 2007a). Related to this has been a reversal of historical emigration patterns, with the trend over the past ten years being one of sustained immigration. Indeed, at the time of writing, 'non-Irish nationals'[1] make up 10 per cent of the resident population (Central Statistics Office, 2007b: 24). These changing demographics bring interesting challenges to stereotypical and essentialist notions of Irish cultural identity. As Loyal (2003: 89) interprets, an established, 'restricted hegemonic view of "Irishness" is now coming into conflict with the labour market imperatives of the increasingly globalised Tiger economy'. Arguably, the pace of economic growth and demographic change experienced in turn-of-the-century Ireland has impacted in some form or another on the day-to-day existence and cultural beliefs of most people living in the state. Accordingly, much of the discussion below explores opinions about Irish-produced music in the light of these new socio-cultural contexts. At the same time, the chapter also includes a brief consideration of the potential range of identities afforded by some of Ireland's 'less spectacular' music scenes.

Consumer culture and the search for new identities

In tandem with the rapid growth of Ireland's economy at the turn of the twentieth and twenty-first centuries have been a number of observable changes in the social conditions and general lifestyle patterns of the population. These socioeconomic developments in turn can be linked to new trends in cultural production and consumption. Rather than interpreting these relationships in terms of cause and effect, I would argue that economic, social and cultural factors – as much as these can be filtered out at the theoretical level – have all played a part in recent developments in Irish-produced music and in the perception of that music.

---

[1]   This official designation of 'non-Irish nationals' can be regarded as an improvement from earlier categorizations of the same groups of people as 'non-nationals' or worse, as 'aliens'.

Consumerism and national identity

Consumerism, in both its ideological and material aspects, was established relatively late in Ireland; prior to the first economic expansion of the 1960s the dominant political beliefs and lifestyle aspirations could be characterized as a form of 'ascetic developmentalism' (Tovey and Share, 2000: 436). As with other modern societies, patterns of consumption in contemporary Ireland go beyond the need for material goods, and are also involved with the consumption of symbols and meanings and with identity itself. Sociologist Eamonn Slater adopts Baudelaire's idea of the *flâneur*[2] to describe the present-day Irish consumer, arguing that, in bypassing any substantial industrial stage, Ireland has 'leapfrogged' into a modern consumer culture and society (Slater, 1998: 1, 3). Slater (1998: 3–6) goes on to identify a number of 'themes' characterizing Irish modernity that I adapt and summarize here:

1. Popular culture (including music) has undergone a process of *commodification*.
2. *Globalization*: the consumption of commodities from other destinations and, conversely, the production in Ireland of commodities for world markets. This two-way process includes the 'crisscross' of signs, images, information and sounds.
3. As in other modern societies, the *aestheticization* of everyday life resulting from the constant flow of signs, sounds and images (see also Featherstone and Lash, 1995). Related to this, commodity production, including that in the cultural arena, has increasingly become more *visualized*, primarily through the media of television, film and advertising.
4. *Signification*: as already stated, commodities not only satisfy material needs, but may also be markers of lifestyle and identity. The same can be said of activities, inasmuch as they can be transformed into markers of identity. Thus, in modern society, the area of culture is increasingly subject to processes of signification.
5. A growing tendency towards self-conscious engagement with activities among individuals, social groups and larger institutions is referred to as *reflexivity*.
6. The diversity and complexity of modern Irish society, along with the doubts raised through self-conscious activity, can result in the *fragmentation* of Irish identities.

The idea of the modern Irish *flâneur* reminds us of some of the subject positions described in the preceding chapter when several pub customers indicated that they identified with the *idea* of Irish traditional music more than with the music per se. Additionally, the combined, reported musical tastes of interviewees suggest a range

---

2 See also Middleton (1990: 93, 98).

of interests and potential identities that include domestic and international music in every conceivable style. This plurality of musical tastes appears to corroborate the ideas of commodification, globalization and, by extension, fragmentation. In general, Slater's set of themes serves to remind us of the complex nature, not only of Irish society, but also of the processes involved in interpreting the beliefs of people within that society. It needs to be stated that this set of analytical constructs could equally apply to other 'late modern' societies but, arguably, these processes are intensified in the context of a nation state that has only recently and rather spectacularly embraced consumerism. Certainly, data pertaining to the consumption of music products in Ireland over the past decade provides some evidence of this phenomenon (see pp. 57–61). While, on the one hand, economic Irishness and contemporary articulations of cultural Irishness would appear to eclipse the old essentialisms, a tendency towards signification and reflexivity might equally draw on or appropriate aspects of ethnic Irishness, as Graham (1999) suggests. Furthermore, it could be argued that Ireland's peripheral location, small (albeit growing) population and relatively recent independent status are all factors that ascribe particular significance – and with it, reflection and debate – on the meaning of national identity. This reflection and debate not only looks to general lifestyle issues ('traditional values' in the face of 'consumer culture'), but it is also involved with the field of domestic cultural production and, more generally, with the relation between production and consumption. It goes without saying, of course, that Ireland is much more than part of a global economy, and it is indeed arguable that national debates concerning civil and moral issues (family law, equality issues, church–state relationship, and so on) have had a far greater impact on people's lives insofar as they have resulted in considerable legislative as well as material change (Tovey and Share, 2000: 447–8).

It could also be said that the social experience of many Irish individuals and groups is unlikely to correspond with that of the imaginary cosmopolitan stroller who seeks meaning and identity in a world characterized by 'post modern' *bricolage*. For example, while some people may come to regard Irish traditional music as a commodity with exchange-value, other individuals might take the same 'commodity' and associated activities as a signifier of Irish identity. For others again (or the same people in different circumstances), traditional music might be valued for its immediate use, as played between friends or played back for dancing. This is not unrelated to the theoretical distinction drawn between participatory and performance music (pp. 65–6), and the possibility that both modes of cultural engagement might lead to recorded and/or broadcast products. On this point of individual agency, it has been noted that sociological studies of Irish culture, including those focusing on mass media, have generally ignored the perspective and agency of consumers and the centrality of cultural forms in their everyday lives (Kelly and O'Connor, 1997: 2; Tovey and Share, 2000: 365). Thus, while Slater's set of themes cited above can be useful in interpreting much of the contemporary debates surrounding Irishness and cultural production, this perspective needs to be balanced with an awareness that access to and participation in such 'new' national imaginings is very likely to be influenced by a range of social factors that include class, gender, ethnicity, geographical location and generation (Kelly and O'Connor, 1997: 1). Therefore, insofar as there may be a tendency to sideline real social issues in post-modern analyses of Irish identity, the very question mark surrounding contemporary notions of Irishness and the fragmentation of national identity that this implies might itself be representative of a new discursive hegemony. In other words, reflexive and critical approaches to national imaginings may still be susceptible to what Martin McLoone (1991) describes as 'the big We'.

New identities?

A critical examination of Irish identity has certainly featured in a number of documentaries broadcast on Irish television over the past decade, and, by generally adopting a self-reflexive mode of presentation, have called into question many of the received linear narratives of nationalist ideologies.[3] The very title of one such TV documentary, *Treo?* [trans. 'Direction?'] suggested an uncertain future for Irish identity and culture in the face of economic expansion and globalization. This bilingual presentation, which was broadcast during prime time on the mainly English-medium RTÉ Channel 1 in 1998, brought together the opinions of three leading academics, an Irish language poet, two arts ministers, a traditional musician, a film producer and a newspaper columnist. Interactive and observational modes were virtually absent as the viewer was presented with a stream of statements from each of the contributors without the benefit of hearing the interviewer's questions. Subliminally, the programme's nominal search for the future direction of Irish identity was further projected by the insertion of dichotomous pairings of sounds (traditional Irish/contemporary techno) and images (urban, cosmopolitan/desolate rural landscapes).

Hardly surprising given the theme of this documentary, all contributors spoke of Ireland in terms of 'we' and 'us', and each of the statements contained aspects that could be categorized in terms of insider/outsider perceptions of national identity. Overall, the programme's narrative could be interpreted as one advocating the strategic accommodation of Irish cultural traditions within the context of late modernity. One contributor was the junior arts minister Eamon Ó Cúiv who stated:

> I think that there is great international pressure on our identity. It's strange that we have come to value and respect ourselves because of this international pressure. International communications have been crucial to this process. Look at the status of traditional music now, compared to the 50s. Look at the status of Irish dance. Look at *Riverdance,* compared to how dance was regarded ten years ago. Look at the value placed on Irish [language] even by those who do not speak it. International cultural pressure has brought about these changes. I don't

---

[3]   See O'Brien (2004).

believe such pressure is ever wholly positive or wholly negative. We must try to embrace the positive and reject the negative. (Transcribed from a recording of the original broadcast, 1998)

This statement by a government minister with partial responsibility for state cultural policy is significant in a number of respects. First, Irishness is not necessarily deemed to be under threat from technological change and international communications. Second, the conventional 'package' of Gaelic culture is reappraised inasmuch as it is no longer considered feasible as a whole way of life. However, its separate components may continue to act as signifiers of Irish cultural identity. Most noteworthy perhaps is the way in which the minister, while appearing to embrace modernity, nonetheless perpetuates a narrow view as to what constitutes Irishness in the case of music, dance and other cultural activities.

In the same programme, poet Nuala Ní Dhomhnaill assessed the impact of globalization on Irish culture in more problematic terms:

We need to figure out our values, what we want, the meaning of culture. Is culture simply language or are there other aspects to it? Should we encourage modern developments of the culture? Or is that pretence? Giving an Irish façade to a culture that is not ours? Do we still have lessons to learn from the old culture? Have we reflected fully on some aspects of our culture? (Transcribed from a recording of the original broadcast, 1998)

Here, Ní Dhomhnaill's emphasis on artistic intent and values appears to rebuke any facile celebrations of contemporary Irish identity. At the same time, the dichotomy she establishes between 'the culture'/'a culture that is not ours' implies a unitary, authentic Irish culture and, in this sense, her statement lends itself to the overall homogenizing discourse of *Treo?*. Such assumptions about the essence of Irishness, along with a conflation between culture as art and culture as a way of life, also featured in a statement by independent film producer Philip King (see also pp. 101–2). However, King adds a third dimension to the meaning of culture in his statement, namely, the idea of heritage. Moreover, he associates heritage with economic conceptions of Irishness when he comes to regard it as a cultural resource:

What is our greatest natural resource? ... We have no coal, no oil, no atomic energy, thank God. But we have something else that comes from within. We have the grey matter, an amazing imagination. Many wonders emerge from that imagination ... . From that imagination a film is born, or a song is born. A record comes into being ... . That is our national resource. If the opencast mining done on it is not too severe ... this wonder will always be ours. (Transcribed from a recording of the original broadcast, 1998)

In a sense, King's statement lends itself to contradictory readings when he presents, respectively, images of individual creation and the economic utilization of 'our national resource'. While he proposes a more optimistic future regarding the interface of Irish and international cultural forms, King, similar to Ní Dhomhnaill, assumes some form of cultural Irish *Urtext*.

Another significant event exploring the apparent tensions between Irishness and modernity took place at the 2006 gathering of the McGill Summer School in Donegal, which took as its theme 'The Soul of Ireland: Issues of Society, Culture and Identity'.[4] Here, the debate not only focused on matters of cultural identity but also touched on the 'dark side' of 'Celtic tiger biography' (Coulter, 2003: 18) by examining social issues such as affluence/poverty, immigration, and sectarian tension (Mulholland, 2006: v–viii). However, such a sociological approach was not replicated in parts of the debate pertaining to cultural expression: thus, although one of the conference strands would explore 'the soul of Ireland in traditional music', there was no similar thematic engagement with other styles or contexts of domestic-produced music. Caoimhín Mac Aoidh and Tomás Ó Canainn, both of whom contributed papers on traditional music, differed in the ways that they responded to the conference's 'soul of Ireland' quest. While Mac Aoidh (2006: 134) broadly regarded traditional music as 'a reflection of who we are' (see also p. 102), Ó Canainn (2006) spoke about the 'magic' of the same music, not from a national-cultural viewpoint, but rather from the perspective of an insider within a particular sound group. Another type of Irish music was referred to in the summer school's opening address given by finance minister Brian Cowan. In this, the minister confidently asserted that the soul of Celtic Tiger Ireland was in 'good shape' (Cowan, 2006: 1–2), and part of his justification for this assessment was based on a progressive and inclusive appraisal of Irish culture and Irish music:

> It is possible to take a snapshot in time, idealise it and call it a national culture. I reject this approach because it misses the essentially dynamic nature of a strong culture .... . National identity and culture should evolve, not stay rooted in the past .... .
> Pointing to growing similarities with other cultures is not the same as showing that we are losing our distinctiveness. For example, many of our foremost music groups do not play traditional music, but it would be a foolish person who tried to deny them their essential Irishness. They are not overt representatives, but they have undoubtedly been influenced by their country, and, more importantly, they speak to the experience of Irish people.
> In music, just like in sport and so many other areas, we are showing our ecumenical side and it is a very positive thing. (Cowan: 2006: 6)

Arguably, these statements by a high-ranking government minister present a welcome counterbalance to the homogenizing rhetoric of other politicians such as Eamon Ó Cúiv cited above. At the same time, Cowan sends out mixed messages when he refers to high-profile musicians who, while not denying their 'essential

---

[4]   This annual, multidisciplinary colloquium celebrates the life and work of the Donegal writer, Patrick McGill (1889–63).

Irishness', somehow fall short of representing that very same quality. Under this way of thinking, Irish popular music production is regarded as a global economic success, while local consumption of the same music is acknowledged as socially significant. And yet, the same music does not *really* qualify as part of national culture, whether as part of 'our' heritage and way of life (traditional music) or as an exemplar of high art (classical music). As I shall now report, the resilience of this ideology continues to impact on 'official' representations of Irishness and music.

Representations of Irish music

Certain types of Irish music have not only featured in general explorations of Irishness, but have also been exposed and 'showcased' through a series of grand narrative texts and exhibitions.[5] Two major music documentaries of the 1990s were *Bringing it all Back Home* (1991) and *A River of Sound* (1995). Both of these productions, directed by Philip King, focused on the history of traditional music and its derivatives. Also throughout the 1990s and well into the first decade of the twenty-first century, Ireland's most popular TV chat show, *The Late Late Show* actively promoted Irish traditional music on several occasions, the first and perhaps most navel-gazing programme of which was *The Late Late Irish Music Special*, broadcast in December 1993. Along with a succession of other tributes to well-known musicians such as The Dubliners, The Chieftains and Sharon Shannon, this live broadcast was subsequently released in video format. While these productions functioned as much for entertainment as they did for any narrative purpose, they were similar to the music documentaries in the way that they centred on traditional genres while at the same time incorporating other styles of Irish music (U2, Sinéad O'Connor and The Corrs appeared on several of these tribute shows). I should add that musical performances in an eclectic range of domestic and international genres regularly feature in the weekly broadcasts of *The Late Late Show*. However, the representative imbalance of the tribute shows is suggestive once again of an essentialist view of Irish music. In this respect, the first broadcast documentary series outlining a history of popular music in Ireland, *Out of Ireland: From a Whisper to a Scream* (jointly produced by *Hot Press* magazine and RTÉ in 2000), signalled a significant departure from dominant narratives of Irish music.

Irish-produced music took a prominent role in two major international festivals in 1996, namely '*L'Imaginaire Irlandais*' in France, a celebration of Irish cultural forms that lasted six months and the Frankfurt Book Festival, which in that year adopted the theme 'Ireland and the Diaspora'. Again, the music components of

---

[5] As O'Brien (2004: 250) notes, throughout the 1990s there was a plethora of 'one-off documentaries on bands and musicians, most of them assuming an unproblematic link between the artist and the culture'. However, a few of these productions 'successfully drew the threads of socio-cultural commentary through the unique personalities of their subjects' (ibid.) Amongst their number were *Christy* (1994) and *Luke* (1999) which celebrated, respectively, the careers of Christy Moore and Luke Kelly, onetime singer with The Dubliners.

these festivals appeared to focus on traditional and traditional-derived music while other types of Irish music, particularly avant-garde classical music, tended to be marginalized in the representation of Irish culture (Deane, 1997: 27–8). Shortly afterwards, in 1997, the CMC devised a touring audio-visual exhibition entitled 'Finding our Voice: Music in Ireland Today'. The exhibition, which traced 'the development of music in Ireland in the twentieth century' (Contemporary Music Centre, 1998: 5) continued to tour locations in Ireland and the UK up to the year 2005. Of note here is how the phrase 'music in Ireland' was used to in preference to the more problematic term 'Irish music'. Seemingly more pluralistic in outlook, CMC's history of music in Ireland was effectively confined to the 'development' of Irish classical composition. However, as with the popular music documentary *From a Whisper to a Scream*, it could be argued that 'Finding our Voice' did open up ideas about Irishness and music insofar as it presented an alternative history and also because it re-appraised the discourse through which Irish music is defined.

The late 1990s also saw the establishment of 'interpretive centres' for both Irish traditional and Irish popular music. *Ceol* (the Irish word for music) was the name given to a traditional music museum in the trendy, regenerated quarter of Smithfield in Dublin. Close by in the city centre, the *Hot Press* Irish Music Hall of Fame offered its visitors an audio-visual experience of the history of Irish popular music.[6] As already mentioned in Chapter 3, the statutory agency Culture Ireland has actively promoted the showcasing of Irish dance, theatre and music at international events since its establishment in 2005. It would be fair to say that the music programming of Culture Ireland has to date been more inclusive than the international festivals of the 1990s insofar as contemporary classical and jazz productions are included alongside traditional performances. At the same time, Culture Ireland appears to mirror the unwritten policy of other national agencies (for example, the statutory organization Music Network and *The Journal of Music in Ireland*) in which less spectacular and/or commercial domestic genres are excluded from celebrations or other representations of Irish musical life.

What all of the above-mentioned nationally themed productions, festivals, exhibitions and centres illustrate is, that from the early 1990s onwards, various forces in Irish society and beyond would contribute to a growing self-awareness and narrative structuring of Irish musical culture. While the majority of these appear to have been informed by essentialist and/or homogenizing narratives of Irishness, we can also see how alternative histories and conceptions of Irish music have recently begun to emerge. Common to the various constructions of an Irish musical heritage are a set of implied associations between music, time, space and place (Bennett, 2004; Connell and Gibson, 2003: 236–7). These mediated representations of Irishness are not only proffered to those 'inside' the culture, but also, insofar as conceptions of national identity can be linked to commercial interests, are equally addressed to tourist and other 'outsider' groups. Quinn

---

6   Both of these centres closed in 2001 although the 'Irish Music Hall of Fame' operated as a touring exhibition until 2005.

(2003) highlights this insider/outsider dialectic in her research investigating the 'interconnections' operating at regional cultural events such as Wexford Festival Opera and the Galway Arts Festival, and interprets a general pattern whereby 'Increasingly, the places being reproduced are carefully packaged, highly mythologised, commodified places where image and marketability assume greatest significance' (Quinn, 2003: 78).

Economic national identity and music

If the nation-building phase of Irish history can be characterized as a struggle between the seemingly oppositional ideologies of ethnic and civic Irishness, it could be said that, in recent decades, Irishness has come to be defined more by a conflation of economic and ethnic conceptions. Mac Laughlin (1997b: 2) has this to say on the subject:

> The modernisation of Ireland and of Irish society in the Sixties and Seventies has now been followed by a process of postmodernisation since the Eighties, and not just at the level of Irish music, dance, cinema, identity politics and literature; the very country itself is being restructured and recreated.

Mac Laughlin is critical here of what he considers to be a new, unofficial dispensation of Irish identity. While Ó Giolláin (1997: 40) also remarks on the same phenomenon, he acknowledges the fact that such changes are reflected in social practice, as much as they are in official and or economic celebrations of Irishness. At one level, a recent increase in the activities of traditional music, speaking the Irish language and Irish dance may be regarded as native and traditional, but the potential meanings implied by these cultural phenomena may be quite different in the contexts of a differentiated modern society: 'What has been revived is also, in a way, new, because it is now situated in a changed environment' (Ó Giolláin, 1997: 40). I would argue therefore, that there is a dialectical relationship between the more recent symbolic reinventions of Irishness (Irish music labelled as a type of world music, *Riverdance* and so on) and with what happens on the ground. For example, while it has been observed that the international success of *Riverdance* led to increased amateur participation along with new forms of Irish dancing at the domestic level (O'Connor, 1998, 2003), it has also been argued that a gradual process of innovation in Irish dance competitions was one of the conditions leading to this success (Ó Cinnéide, 2002: 46–57). To take the same cultural product, Bill Whelan's original score for *Riverdance* has continuities with a production and reception base of Irish music going back to the 1970s (see p. 35); at the same time, it is conceivable that this product is heard as new to many people among Irish and international audiences alike. This dialectic can operate in more subtle ways also. For example, the prominence given to the low tin whistle in the 1997 film *Titanic* led to the subsequent adaptation of the low whistle in the instrumentation of many Irish traditional groups.

At the beginning of the twenty-first century, Ireland is undoubtedly a country of diverse musical interests and activities, to say nothing of its differentiated and increasingly plural social structure. Given its ideological and material transformation from an era of nation building towards a seemingly more open, materially wealthy and technologically advanced society, why then do traditional markers of Irish culture appear to have acquired greater significance than ever before? If Irish (and other) consumers are free to assemble their own *bricolage* or sets of identities in some great post-modern bazaar, why do essentialist conceptions of Irish music appear to have such resilience? Thus far in the book, I have suggested that this state of affairs is partially explained by the relatively unique status of traditional music in Ireland, and by the residual influences of cultural nationalism. However, if we return to the third ideal type of national identity, the economic, then we may uncover other factors that contribute towards the perpetuation of 'ethnic specific' Irish musical associations.

By itself, the term economic could be used to define Irish music on the basis of its saleable products. As discussed in Chapter 3, this way of approaching the category of Irish music is generally adopted by industry interests. The short-lived MBI (2001–04) was jointly funded by national government and music industry agencies. The initial remit of MBI was to embrace 'all types of music', and it was established to provide 'a forum for the industry and actively promote strategic policies for the development of the music industry and the maximisation of its contribution to the national economy' (O'Connell, 2001). What was not clear, however, was how MBI could achieve its plural embrace when it blatantly privileged the economic factor over artistic and broader socio-cultural considerations. At best, it could be argued that defining Irish music in terms of its contribution to the national economy is to reflect an indifference to the more contentious aspects of national identity and music in Ireland. However, as I argue below, some dominant conceptions of Irishness and music are retained and to an extent exploited in this era of late modernity and 'globality' (Nederveen Pieterse, 1995: 49).

An example of how industry perspectives can be brought to bear in the discussion of arts and education policy presents itself in the following statement by Niall Doyle, the one time chief executive of Music Network and subsequent director of music for the national broadcaster RTÉ:

> When Irish chic is passé, and international *Riverdance* mania has slowed to a trickle, the Irish music industry will be relying solely on the quality of its creative products. It will be relying on the strength of its creative foundations – diversity and education, and it needs to look now to ensuring that development. (Doyle, 1997: 25)

Doyle (ibid.) goes on to characterize this new alignment of public and private interests as 'the Art and Industry sides of the policy debate', with the 'higher organisational strata of the industry' driving the agenda. The economic imperative also appears to inform the editorial line adopted by Niall Stokes for *Hot Press* magazine when interpreting a lull period for Irish rock against the international success of Irish commercial pop:

> ... the fact that we're achieving this level of success in pop, as against rock music does raise questions ... . The only effective response is to ensure that we also continue to nurture serious artistic talent in rock music, traditional music and dance – or whatever form the new cutting edge takes. (Stokes, 2000: 5)

Stokes is speaking here from a national perspective ('we') and like Doyle above he interprets the meteoric rise and success of Irish-produced acts as a double-edged sword. Both commentators put forward a similar strategy of 'investment' in musical creativity and talent as a means to ensuring the economic viability of Irish music. As sections of the analysis in Chapter 3 would suggest, there is much scope for the development of musical infrastructures and music education in Ireland. However, the critical issue in this discussion revolves around the perceived purposes of any such investment. Leaving aside the utilitarian role that is implied for education and/or the 'nurturing' of talent, it is noteworthy that Doyle and Stokes assess the problem in terms of exportable Irish music products, and neither writer addresses the problem in terms of domestic industries and/or scenes. However, in a later editorial article, Stokes shifts his focus to national production and consumption, and while he is at this stage optimistic about the extent and diversity of local production, he problematizes the dominance of international products in domestic markets (Stokes, 2003).

Yet, a purely positivistic interpretation of the relationship between music and national economies does not take into account the potential that non-commodity cultural forms may hold in this equation. In Chapter 5 it was shown how a theoretical distinction between the emblematic status of Irish music and the material reality of Irish musical practices is reflected among the opinions of interviewees (identifications with the idea of Irish traditional music as opposed to identifications arising from the actual sounds and practices of that music.) By extension, it seems plausible to suggest that economic conceptions of Irishness and music can arise from, on the one hand, a consideration of globally successful Irish-produced commodities in various genres and, on the other hand, market-led appropriations of the very *idea* of Irish music, which generally comes to be associated with traditional music and/or the homogenizing labels of 'Irish sound' and 'Irish soul'. This suggests a process of market branding, not only of Irish music, but also of Ireland itself. Mac Laughlin (1997b: 6) is particularly scathing of what he considers to be this economic appropriation of Irish culture:

> ... Ireland has become a country where people are more attached to symbols and brand names than to any real places or any organic traditions. New power elites

here are constantly inventing and re-inventing symbols for the country so as to literally market Ireland and Irishness around the world.

While Mac Laughlin may be exaggerating a tendency among some people to buy into these most recent enterprises in the commodification of Irish culture, the implication that we have arrived at a new form of national hegemony merits some consideration. Without doubt, the past decade or so in Ireland has witnessed what might be described as the emergence of cultural-economic entrepreneurs, sharing some lineage with the 'moral-cultural' entrepreneurs of earlier folk revivals. We have already seen how the film producer Philip King employs the discourse of cultural-economic entrepreneurship or 'artrepreneurship' (Kuhling et al., 2006) when he uses terms such as 'our greatest natural resource' and 'open-cast mining' in reference to Irish culture.

Perhaps the most explicit and unapologetic expression of a cultural-entrepreneurial view comes from the business academic, Barra Ó Cinnéide (1999, 2002):

> The broader social and cultural context driving entrepreneurship is underestimated … . Ireland's prosperity depends critically on understanding, appreciating and exploiting, if you will, our unique characteristics and traditions. (Ó Cinnéide, 1999: 154–5)
>
> [Speaking about *Riverdance*] … the promoters have made it a unique product by branding it as a quintessentially Irish product like Guinness. (Ó Cinnéide, 2002: 169)
>
> As the so-called 'Celtic Tiger' became established in the mid 1990s, a small number of commentators came to identify that non-economic factors were at work in the growth of the economy. (Ó Cinnéide, 2002: 183)

In this view, national culture and national prosperity are inextricably linked. Indeed, Ó Cinnéide not only suggests that Irish cultural traditions are behind the recent economic boom, but also that these cultural traditions are based on unique or essential Irish characteristics. Although Ó Cinnéide speaks in one breath about 'the marketability of Irish ethnicity and the nation's favourable international image', he also identifies the need for shows such as *Riverdance* to incorporate modern and global cultural forms (2002: 195–6).

Arguably, this apparent fusion of tradition and modernity, and of culture and economy is not based on symmetrical relations. While Ó Cinnéide's work does suggest a close link between cultural change and economic growth, as well as a changing dialectical relationship between national identity and international image, it nonetheless shows how the most recent global projections of Irishness have largely come to be dominated by economic interests. Furthermore, as much as these enterprises situate Irish traditions and artefacts in (post-)modern contexts, thereby effecting the simultaneous images of ethnic and cosmopolitan Irishness, the branding or 'unique selling point' of Irish culture is encapsulated by an essential and static sense of Irishness. This has implications, not only for the perception of a 'sell out' or de-authentication of traditional music (O'Connor, 1998: 52), but also for the perception of all music categories in Ireland.

In much popular music, where quintessential Irishness appears to be lacking, the rather nebulous idea of 'unique Irish characteristics' can be invoked to bring such music under the seemingly advantageous label of 'Irish'. For classical music products and events, there is an observable tendency towards market branding when, increasingly, the words 'Irish' and/or 'Celtic' are used in the nomenclature of performing groups, recordings and international shows. From a purely economic point of view, all of these strategies make sense given the limited size of the domestic market for most types of Irish music products (Clancy and Twomey, 1997: 52). If the Irish music sector is to grow, the argument might go, then it must fill a niche in international export markets. And, rather than considering that musicians' careers have been constricted by or, worse still, determined by economic conceptions of Irish music, it could well be that many such individuals not only adapt to, but themselves also exploit the possibilities offered by this dominant trend. For example, Quinn (1996) describes tourists' perceptions and experiences of traditional music in Ireland and how these can impact on the cultural and economic activities of local communities. Similarly, McCann (2001) and Kneafsey (2003) observe how traditional musicians can equally negotiate both 'commercial' and 'traditional' aspects of their musical worlds. These examples suggest that there may be more subtle processes in the negotiation of 'Irish cultural capital' other than the blatant exploitation of 'Irishry' and/or the mass production of indigenous cultural forms.

However, these trends cannot be interpreted as socio-economic 'facts' alone. We have already seen some possible effects that this recent conflation of essentialist and economic conceptions can bring to bear on domestic production and consumption (in both commodity and non-commodity forms), on statutory arts and education policies, and on the very idea of Irish music. From an artistic perspective, it could be argued that these dominant economic conceptions act to undermine ideas of diversity and originality in Irish music, not only on the basis of their commercial imperative, but also because what is 'unique' for the purpose of market branding translates as 'same' within its own production base. Thankfully, however, we have not reached a stage when Ó Cinnéide's analogy between Guinness and Irish culture has come to be realized in every possible respect (although the use of recorded traditional music in Irish theme pubs throughout the world presents one disturbing example of the 'same-unique' formula). A focus on the interface between economic national identity and music does not mean that the 'older' conceptions of national identity, the ethnic and the civic, have necessarily been displaced. It could be said, though, that the map of Irish identity can no longer be characterized by the opposing conceptions of traditional culture and modernity as, increasingly, Ireland is imagined as part of a global economy.

Cultural-entrepreneurial discourse presents a multifaceted view of Irish culture that adapts embedded ideas (tradition/heritage, way of life, high art) to its mainly economic perspective. I now propose a number of ways in which economic conceptions of musical identities and national identities in Ireland may become interrelated, and here I draw on aspects of Adorno's social theory of music (Adorno, 1976):

- *Music production and national success*: From a purely positivist view, Irish music is the sum of its saleable products. Given the disproportionate share of world markets that Irish-produced music is believed to hold, the international success of Irish music is assumed as a cause for national pride.
- *Circumstances of production*: Irish culture (traditional and traditional-derived forms), Irish ethnicity and the whole way of life in Ireland can all be considered as national resources. These qualities hold potential benefits not only for the field of cultural production, but are valuable for the economy as a whole.
- *Forces of production*: The Irish are assumed to be inherently musical and their musical products are unique, are of high quality and have universal appeal.
- *Global market branding*: Irish music finds a niche in global markets through its identification as a distinct quality brand. This is linked not only to the actual musical products, but also to Ireland's 'image' and reputation. Thus, the label 'Irish music' not only relates to a range of material products (from the output of diverse artists to a generic 'traditional sound') but also to the music's potential to signify desirable aspects of an 'Irish lifestyle'.

All forms of social identification involve an insider–outsider dialectic, and, as has been charted in previous chapters, this has been a recurring theme in past configurations of national identity and music in Ireland. It seems fair to speculate, though, that the rapid success of an Irish export music industry in the Celtic Tiger era has heightened Irish people's sensitivity to outsider perspectives on the Irish and their music. I use the word 'sensitivity' here as it is not assumed that all people in Ireland will buy into 'hagiographies of the Celtic Tiger' (Coulter, 2003: 10), or that they will necessarily echo the celebratory discourse of 'artrepreneurs' and other media commentators. Furthermore, even where individuals and groups appear to adopt an entrepreneurial outlook, there may be varying levels of cultural and economic interests involved, though never to the exclusion of one or the other. Thus, the term cultural-economic entrepreneurship might be used to embrace activities as far removed as producing a 'stable' of Irish pop groups to the promotion of international centres for traditional music.

A number of interview statements cited in the previous chapter find resonance with aspects of the cultural-economic entrepreneurial discourse interpreted above. However, the areas that these held in common were based on essentialist beliefs about Irish people and Irish music and on a general consciousness of insider–outsider perspectives; nowhere in the interview data was any explicit association made between cultural-national identity and the recent economic successes of Irish-produced music. Indeed, it was more likely that interviewees expressed their distaste for the current fashion in all things Irish. We saw how Eileen, a traditional music aficionado, reported her dislike for media celebrations 'about the Irishness of Irish music', feeling that the whole area had become 'over schmalzified'. Other interviewees were conscious of transformations in Irish society and Irish music, but this did not seem to be a cause of celebration for them. For example, Betty, who attended a classical concert in Limerick offered this opinion during a group discussion about the Irishness of internationally successful acts:

> *Betty*
> J: What do you think about *Riverdance*, The Corrs … in terms of how Irish they sound?
> Betty: Well, I suppose it depends on the Irish you're talking about. I think it corresponds very well with present day Ireland – middle America really … .

Betty's critical perspective here questions any simplistic reading of Irishness and music; at the same time, she implies a tendency towards homogenous cultural production in an increasingly open society. These statements by Eileen and Betty can be linked to the notion of musical authenticity (see Chapter 8). While both interviewees are aware of the increasingly globalized and 'mediaized' contexts in which Irish music may be consumed, this appears to be a cause for concern rather than for celebration.

A plurality of Irish musical identities

One of the more spectacular developments in Irish society over the past decade has been the increasing heterogeneity of its population, a trend that arguably has given further cause to interrogate received notions of Irish identity and culture. In December 2001 the music magazine *Hot Press* highlighted Ireland's cultural diversity by running a special anti-racist feature entitled 'One nation under a groove'. Attached to this issue was a CD compilation entitled *Go Move Shift* [7] that included tracks by well-known domestic artists in addition to musical contributions from some recently arrived immigrants. *Hot Press* editor Niall Stokes introduced the feature thus:

> There was a time, not so long ago, when Ireland was an almost completely mono-cultural place. Not any longer … . You can see it, you can feel it in the streets of Ireland's cities and towns … . Suddenly, we are surrounded by a huge variety of different accents and voices … . There is a new and different buzz about the place, a sense of excitement and colour that is a joy to experience. There is a great cultural shift involved, and how we respond to it is a matter of

---

[7]   The album took its title from the protest song written and originally recorded by British folk singer Ewan MacColl. 'Go Move Shift' was subsequently recorded by Christy Moore, and in this version has come to be regarded as a standard of Irish folksong repertoire.

vital importance. It is absolutely essential, that, as a society, we should avoid the kind of divisiveness that has plagued other countries in relation to issues of race and ethnic origin. It is essential that we avoid the blight of racism ... . It is my belief that music and musicians can play a vital part in inspiring a more enlightened and liberated climate here. Irish traditional music draws heavily on the traveller lodestone. Rock' n' roll wouldn't exist without the blues, a music that was forged by the black population, living as an underclass in the racist southern states of the US. For most musicians, the leap of faith has already been made. Music transcends cultural differences and barriers. Its seeds intermingle. It changes, evolves and grows, taking on new shades and influences. This is something that musicians instinctively know. We are one. We are all the same. (Stokes, 2001: 49).

While *Hot Press* has always been at the vanguard of left-oriented, socially critical reporting (notwithstanding the magazine's close associations with 'the music industry') this feature stands out in the way that music is involved in the expression of a particular vision of an intercultural Ireland. It would be difficult not to agree with Stokes's demand for a non-racist society, even if his view that music somehow erases cultural difference might be considered utopian. His arguments for an intercultural approach appear to be based on loose comparative homologies (Irish traditional and blues both being the music of oppressed peoples) and on an overarching rock ideology. At the same time, the 'we' offered by Stokes differs from that used in conventional national imaginings insofar as it marks out distinct social groups and subgroups that include the marginalized of Irish society. Furthermore, by Stokes's words and by the wide range of genres represented in the CD, this national imagining of Irish musical culture is as much based on reality as it is on political aspiration insofar as it reflects at least some stylistic diversity in its contemplation of Irishness.

Such a reappraisal as to what constitutes 'our culture' was also expressed by a number of interviewees at events. First, I will refer to some remarks made about the group Afro-Celt Sound System (ACSS), the very name of which describes the mixture of cultures, languages and genres that are involved in this Irish-based production.[8] (The ACSS are one of the acts included on the *Go Move Shift* CD.) Jimmy, one of the interviewees at the session in Noone's pub characterized the ACSS sound as 'a hybrid kind of music – but still Irish music that would appeal to a contemporary audience'. While Jimmy recognized what might be called the 'contemporary Irishness' of the ACSS, he reported that his own identifications of Irishness in music were more likely to occur when listening to 'pure' traditional music. Another interviewee, Cian (Pierce Turner gig) appeared to regard ACSS as a stronger marker of his Irish identity:

---

[8] Vallely (2003: 206) takes a critical view of the Afro-Celt Sound System's musical authenticity, interpreting the group's sound as neither African nor Celtic, but rather as a type of electronic music produced and managed by multinational interests.

Cian

J: In terms of Irish-sounding, how would you rate the Afro-Celt Sound System?
Cian: I would like to think that they are Irish. I would hope so, yes, very Irish,
I think. I heard it mixed in a pub in San Diego recently and that's what I felt. I
think … ok, although it's like, African-Celtic music, but I still think it's … yeah,
it's as Irish as it comes.

Many of the 67 people that I interviewed identified the ACSS in terms of *is*-Irish
and/or *sounds*-Irish; Cian, however, was the only person among this group whose
apprehension of ACSS's music involved a *feeling* of Irishness, not just in the
music but also in his own response to it. Like a number of other interviewees, Cian
seemed to be able to focus more on the national aspects of his own identity when
removed from the day-to-day immediacy of living in Ireland. It is also interesting
that Cian hinted at a similar aspiration towards the kind of Irish society envisioned
by Niall Stokes when he used such terms as 'I would like to think' and 'I would
hope so' with regard to the ACSS's Irishness.

By coincidence, a second group to feature on the *Go Move Shift* CD also
elicited a response pertaining to a contemporary sense of Irishness amongst some
interviewees. While I had specifically asked interviewees for their assessment
of ACSS in terms of 'Irish-sounding', Eoin, whom I interviewed with his friend
Mick at the 'Best of Irish' traditional concert, included the traditional group Kila
in his response. Kila, in the words of band member Rossa Ó Snodaigh (2001),
regard their brand of traditional music to be in the category of '*nua*-traditional'
or 'new traditional' Irish music.[9] This refers not only to the assimilation of new
instruments and other 'world music' to their sound, but also to the atmosphere of
Kila gigs in which the highly energetic performances of the musicians quite often
lead to improvised dancing among audience members:

Eoin and Mick

J: The Afro-Celt Sound System. How would rate them in terms of Irish-
sounding?
Eoin: It is fairly Irish.
Mick: I suppose it's half and half, kind of. Maybe a little bit more than half Irish …
Eoin: Bands like them, Irish-Afro-Celt or whatever … and Kila, I consider them
very Irish. Well, Afro-Celt half Afro because they're playing African instruments,
but Kila would to me be pure Irish, taking in different twists of – like, they can
have an Eastern European thing going – but … totally Irish as in, not following
right on tradition but contemporary Irish and very much so.

---

[9]   Ó Snodaigh's conception was articulated in a brief position piece that appeared in
The Journal of Music in Ireland. This provoked a critical response from Terry Moylan
(2001) in the next issue of the same publication.

Like Cian, Eoin and Mick were among the youngest of the people that I interviewed. Eoin and Mick were themselves traditional musicians albeit with an eclectic range of music interests. Eoin's response in particular shows how the ideas of tradition and innovation can come to be accommodated in contemporary ideas of Irishness. He appears to be conscious of the inherent contradiction of his own response – Kila are both 'pure Irish' and 'not following right on tradition' – but it is this very tension that for him articulates a sense of contemporary Irishness in the music.

Other responses from the interviewees suggested that some types of Irish-produced music were inappropriate in the changing contexts of contemporary Ireland. Stephen and Meadbh who had both attended the Pierce Turner gig in the company of Cian, were not impressed by the performer's repartee with the audience or with some of the song lyrics, particularly those aspects pertaining to insider/outsider views of Irishness. As noted earlier in Chapter 4, Pierce Turner is a singer/songwriter who has been based in Manhattan for over two decades but who carries out extensive tours in Ireland on a regular basis. Stephen and Meadbh had not heard his music before and were attending the gig on the recommendation of a friend who was an avid Turner fan. The following responses occurred at a stage in the interview when I asked them if the live music that they had heard that night sounded Irish:

Stephen and Meadbh
Meadbh: He seemed to always go, talk about Ireland, not like in the past tense, but like of quite a while ago. Like, every reference was to either a girlfriend of a long time ago, newspapers, little things like that.
Stephen: That's right, yeah.
Meadbh: So, you couldn't really say he's influenced by Ireland as such, he's influenced by his memories of his idea of what Ireland is.
Stephen: It's a good point … . It's a bit clichéd in some respects … I mean, just in terms of Irish culture and what's happening at the moment, it didn't … . I mean those kind of aphorisms don't have much to do with us right now … I mean, I would say we need a different kind of mirror. That's kind of old hat … it's pointing in the wrong direction. You know?
Meadbh: His whole thing about Spanish students [Turner had made reference to his experience of the large number of English-language students that traditionally swell the population of Irish cities during the summer]. It's just so outdated, like very outdated when I think of the book I've been reading about changes in Ireland with refugees and so on.

Although Stephen and Meadbh are speaking mainly about song introductions and less about song lyrics, their negative reception of Turner's music appears to be strongly influenced by what they consider to be anachronistic representations of Irishness in a contemporary context. That said, it should be stated that both registered some enjoyment of the music as sound; indeed, following some probing, both reported the apprehension of Irish-sounding musical elements. However, in

Stephen's own terms, the overwhelming sense in which Irishness was perceived was in the lyric and narrative aspects of Turner's performance, and this was deemed to be inappropriate in the context of an increasingly heterogeneous Irish society.

There were some similarities between Pierce Turner's gig and the concert performed by singer/songwriter Jimmy MacCarthy insofar as aspects of MacCarthy's life history and perspectives on Irish culture were offered both during and between song performances. Brigid and Pat were among a group of people with whom I spoke after this event in Dublin:

Brigid and Pat
J: Do you think Jimmy MacCarthy's music sounds Irish?
Pat: Well, sure! It doesn't sound any other way. Yes, sure, sure.
Brigid: I think it's bordering very much though on ... emigration. It's kind of lingering on, and maybe it's only now he's getting recognition, maybe that's the way we look on it. Five, six, ten years ago, it would have been reflecting what was really happening ... .
J: Apart from the lyrics, does he, did he make what you would consider to be an Irish sound here tonight?
Pat: Sure, sure, and it's a pity a lot more Irish people didn't go to hear it.

As might be gathered, the fact that I virtually repeated the same question might indicate that I was particularly interested in specific things that people heard in the music. Pat's response here typifies that of a significant number of interviewees who, while affirming the Irish sound of a certain music or musician, do not go on to describe the qualities on which their affirmations are based (see p. 147). Brigid, however, identifies something in the song lyrics that relates to her memory of the socio-economic conditions that obtained in the 1980s (notably, high rates of emigration and unemployment); the fact that this is part of the artist's own experience and indeed common to the social experience of many Irish people appears to articulate a particular sense of Irishness in this case. Brigid's positive response to what might be termed a lyric-narrative genre of Irish popular song is quite different from that of Stephen and Meadbh above. While these interview statements do not indicate any substantial reason why this is so, my own impression during those separate interviews suggested that differences in age and social experience had at least something to do with it (Brigid would have been a young adult in the 1980s).

Issues of age and/or generation were mentioned in many interviews, and such differentiation was applied in equal measure to performers and audiences, and by both younger and older interviewees. Usually, this arose when I asked people about particular musicians and whether they sounded Irish or not. May was a sprightly woman in her 70s who attended the 'Irish Ring' operatic concert with her husband Dick.

May and Dick
J: In terms of Irish-sounding, what do you think of The Corrs?
Dick: Yes, they're good.
May: Yeah, they're good, but … they're not for our generation. You know I can appreciate their music … .
J: And those popular groups like B*witched, does any of the music sound Irish?
Dick: No.
J: Even when you can hear the fiddle?
May: No, I know exactly what you mean and that doesn't appeal to me at all. It's not for our generation.

May makes two distinctions here. First of all, she does not identify with (Irish) music that is not of her generation. However, while both The Corrs and B*witched are excluded on these grounds, she values the former more than the latter. Whether this arises from her perception of inherent musical patterns, authentic Irishness or combinations of these is not clear. Elsewhere, several respondents of mixed age had de-authenticated both the musical quality and Irishness of girl band B*witched by describing their music in such terms as 'teenybopper' and 'kids stuff'.

Many interviewees at both the 'The Irish Ring' and Celtic Tenors concerts offered insights into their own musical lives. What identified these as belonging to the same musical-social group were their love of choral and operatic music, and their self-awareness in terms of age, generation and memory. This extract from an interview with James (in his 70s), Rachel and Gráinne (both in their mid-40s) offers one poignant case:

James, Rachel and Gráinne ('The Irish Ring')
J: What things did you like about the music tonight?
James: I think what attracts me is the nostalgia. The older people will remember … older people when they were very young who were very interested in this kind of music. You notice tonight that the place [NCH, Dublin] wasn't full. That's the first time I've heard any of this type of music where seats weren't absolutely sold out. So there must be a lot of people who are very interested in it over the years … disappearing.
Gráinne: Well, I'd say the younger generation, my children's generation would not have heard that type of music. But I remember 'I dreamt I dwelt in marble halls' with Joan Sutherland singing from my father's records. We used to hear those songs over and over again. That's the one that came back to me.
Rachel: That's one of my favourite pieces also because, again, my grandmother used to sing it.

Nostalgia is an idea that comes through in many of the interviews, and it is a theme that will be revisited in Chapter 8. What I wish to comment on here is the sense of a particular musical tradition that is expressed by these three interviewees here. This tradition is based on what has come to be understood as Irish repertoire, and on semi-professional performances of the same music, sustained by the agency of local amateur choral societies; in fact, both James and Rachel had sung in the chorus that night (suggesting 'dual membership' of a particular sound group and a more general musical-social group). Meanwhile, although Gráinne had not sung in this particular choral concert, she indicated that she had participated in a *Messiah* performance some weeks earlier.[10]

Likewise, May and Dick had not participated in the chorus that night but they too were members of another Dublin choral society.

> *May and Dick*
> J: What things do you like about the music tonight?
> Dick: Well, it's beautiful.
> J: In terms of things likes tunes and harmonies?
> May: Yes, there are some lovely tunes.
> Dick: They'd nearly bring you to tears.
> J: Really?
> May: I would associate it with things that Mother sang, you know – choruses that my mother would have talked about. And also that I would have been familiar with … .
> Dick: Well, let me put it like this. I'm 75 years old and there have been three generations involved with it.
> May: Yes, very much like that.
> Dick: I mean, I heard that music first when I was a toddler … .
> May: It's very old music, certainly … very warm sounding.
> Dick: And it's holding remarkably well.

Again, we can see that the appreciation of this music has much to do with the ideas of age, generation and tradition. Indeed, without knowing the context of this interview excerpt, it would be easy to imagine that Dick and May were talking about some type of folk music. What did emerge with some consistency throughout the interviews at choral/operatic events was that many people shared the same musical preferences and concert-going habits (constituting a fairly distinct musical-social group) and that many of these were also members of choral performing societies (belonging to a particular type of sound group). One of the interviewees, James, explained the extent to which such networks might operate:

> *James*
> The other aspect – I don't know whether it would concern your [question] – is the importance of choral work. You get to know a lot of people, you learn a lot

---

[10]   The history of 'Handel reception' in Ireland goes back to 1742 when *The Messiah* premiered in Dublin. The oratorio continues to be produced by several choral societies each year. Additionally, the 'Hallelujah chorus' and other excerpts are sung in cathedrals and some churches during religious services at Christmas.

about music and you enjoy being a member. You get to know hundreds of people, people from other choirs, husbands, wives, boyfriends, girlfriends, children.

I include this statement because, although it does not directly concern my inquiry, it suggests that much more needs to be known about unspectacular music scenes in Ireland today, particularly those aspects pertaining to people's everyday lives. I use the word unspectacular here because many musical-social practices are excluded from histories and contemporary accounts of Irish music. One such example already noted in Chapter 2 is the substantial fan base of Daniel O'Donnell whose music could be described in such terms as 'country and Irish'/ 'easy listening'/ 'middle of the road'. The resilience of O'Donnell's fan base appears to fly in the face of fashionable imaginings of contemporary Irishness and music. Mac Laughlin (1997a: 142) interprets this as a moral and cultural conservatism that is 'deeply entrenched in the landscape of a modern "hidden Ireland"'. He goes on to propose that:

> He clearly belongs to a popular quasi-Irish culture that refuses to disappear in postmodern Ireland. Widely reviled by 'intelligent' Ireland as its favourite figure of ridicule, O'Donnell's popularity appears to defy explanation. (Mac Laughlin, 1997a: 142)

The term 'quasi-Irish culture' is somewhat problematic here, given that Mac Laughlin critiques official versions of Irishness while at the same time claiming that the reception of O'Donnell and, more generally, 'country and Irish' music refers to a widespread social practice in Ireland. However, his adaptation of the term 'hidden Ireland'[11] is useful in the ways it suggests how mythical constructions of Irish music and place can be challenged by a closer examination of local musical practices.

One person's self-reflexive response to my question about the potential Irish sound of The Irish Tenors (and similar groups) suggested an openness to the idea of multiple music traditions in Ireland and, linked to this, a recognition of different social experiences for different groups of Irish people. The 'principal speaker' here is Fionnuala who was interviewed along with Deirdre, Máire and Betty at UCH, Limerick:

Fionnuala, Deirdre, Máire and Betty
J: When groups such as The Irish Tenors or The Celtic Tenors sing Irish ballads, does that sound Irish to you?
Betty: I suppose it does really.
Fionnuala: To me, it's a sound that maybe, that I haven't been exposed to in live terms, let's say. It talks to me about a class situation in Ireland where people sang melodies and sang songs in the parlour around the piano. I didn't grow up in a family like that.

---

[11]   This term was first coined by the historian Daniel Corkery (1925).

Deirdre: Mm.
Máire: Is that really more English than Irish?
Deirdre: Oh, very much so.
Fionnuala: Well, yes. But it is Irish, it did happen certainly, and the type of songs they sing, there would be an element in Irish society and that was their type of music.

Fionnuala's theory here seems to reject any simplistic polarization of Irish music versus un-Irish (or English) music. At the same time, her use of the past tense and the implied homology between social class and classically oriented Irish music suggests a sensitivity to nationalist-colonial tensions. As it happens, Fionnuala identified herself as coming from a *Gaeltacht* [Irish-speaking region], and in other parts of the same interview she gave me interesting accounts of *sean nós* dancing from that part of Ireland. One thing that struck me when comparing this interview transcript with others was how Fionnuala's views appeared to be based on her perception of social realities. This was in sharp contrast to opinions that seemed to be based more in mythological ideas of Irishness and music, such as the idea of 'The West' representing all that is essential in Irishness (see p. 187). There was a certain irony to Fionnuala's eschewal of this, given that aspects of her own social background (Irish language, Western seaboard, traditional music and dance) matched such an idealized, collective imagining of Irish culture.

The examples cited in this section, while not in any way presenting a comprehensive picture, suggest a plurality of musical identities in Ireland. The brief discussion around one musical-social group and its associated sound groups illustrates how ideas of collective consciousness can also be applied in the context of non-traditional genres of Irish music. That is to say, while choral and operatic music produced in Ireland is not generally associated with any specific form of inherent Irishness, the various activities associated with this musical repertoire nonetheless constitute a fairly distinct musical identity within Ireland. We have also seen how the interaction of changing social contexts, musical genres and individual experience can lead to alternative articulations of Irishness and music. In particular, the identification of Irishness in some contemporary genres would appear to depend not only on the apprehension of actual sounds, but also on whether or not the same 'Irish' values and/or social experience were shared by producers and consumers.

Chapter 7
The music

This chapter sets out to uncover specific ways in which Irishness might be heard in Irish music. It begins by outlining a general approach for the interpretation of musical meanings. Subsequent sections are then organized around observed patterns and issues that emerge from the interviews, and these I categorize as: general expressive qualities; style, sound and soul; instruments; structural features and sensory elements; and lyrics. The overall discussion is further broadened to include the opinions of musicians, musicologists and other commentators.

Musical analysis and musical meaning

What kind of analytical approach can be applied to the general area of Irish music, given the apparent differences between its musical styles and the likelihood of differing perspectives on the significance of texts and/or contexts in interpretations of musical meaning and value? In the opening chapter I argued for the consideration of Irish music as constituting part of a unitary, musical-historical field. The breadth of this perspective enables us to examine a number of structural relationships that might obtain between various musical genres (Middleton, 1990: 119). For example, the use of particular modalities in traditional, popular and classical forms of Irish music could be compared and contrasted. However, we would need to regard continuities of this kind as something that were in the first instance confined to the level of musical materials and conventions, since the meaning and use to which such musical elements are put might reveal quite different patterns. A sensitive application of musicological language is another important principle in considering a range of musical styles. Exclusive use of an 'external metalanguage' (that is, from analytical musicology) is inappropriate for the study of non-classical music; so too is the confinement of discourse to 'internal metalanguages' that serve only to confirm the constructed ideologies of particular genres (Middleton, 1990: 123), for example, Irish traditional music interpreted only by reference to the discourse of its practitioners. One possible solution for the researcher of any cross-cultural musical field is 'a method which is both self-reflexive and explicit about the values implicit in its own terms' (Middleton, 1990: 119). Musical analysis has already played a supportive role in this book insofar as it has been implicit in the interpretation of what people hear and think about Irish music. Here, I acknowledge my own particular way of listening to and thinking about music, which to some degree has been conditioned by an analytic perspective, and

I recognize that this may well be different from many people's approach to and apprehension of the same music events and/or products.

Notwithstanding the importance for this study of some 'intra-musical analysis', it needs to be reiterated that musical meaning does not reside in musical sounds and structures alone; rather, the *significance* of particular musical experiences arise from the *codes* involved, the *competence* of participants and the *pertinence* of musical-social contexts (Middleton, 1990: 172–3).[1] In a sense, the 'grand text' of this book is made up of the primary and secondary significations[2] of Irish-produced music that constitute people's musical experiences. Primary significations arise from the temporal and sonic properties of music, while secondary significations relate to the contexts in which music is heard. The importance of musical code is already implied by the very categorization of traditional, classical and popular music in Ireland. We can also see how these codes may differ at the level of sub-style. The idea of pertinence, meanwhile, can help us interpret the different types of discourse that may be applied to the same musical genres. Related to this is the whole area of competence in particular codes: for example, how might traditional music be interpreted differently by its own sound groups as opposed to groups who have only peripheral contact with its stylistic conventions? It should be noted that the idea of competence here is not necessarily an exclusive or 'expert' term, but rather one that encompasses both propositional/discursive and non-propositional aspects of musical experience (Walser, 1993: 39–40).

I now set out my strategy for the employment of musical analysis in this chapter, which I adapt from Middleton (1990: 172–246). First, my purpose is to interrogate theories and beliefs about various sound patterns and structures of Irish-produced music, rather than to propose some form of objective meaning in the music itself. Second, I do not privilege musical structure over expressive ideas and/or 'para-musical details'. What emerges from the interviews are a number of analytical categories, some of which correspond with broad musicological terms, others of which relate more to everyday discourse about music. Third, while recognizing the literal meanings offered by the sung word, for reasons of scale I do not engage with analyses of song texts in this chapter (though reference is made to the words of one song cited by an interviewee). However, I do focus on the musical effects of language and how the paralanguage of song performance can affect meaning.

My overall approach to musical meaning thus far in the book has been premised on a conventional theoretical distinction between intra- and extra-musical meanings (Martin, 1995: 64). While the very notion of 'extra-musical' suggests some form of social construction, intra-musical meanings, that is, meanings pertaining to patterns of sound, are also established and maintained through social processes (Green, 1988: 32; Martin, 1995: 71). Thus, the two sides of musical meaning cannot be easily reduced to notions of primary versus secondary significations, or interpreted as a simplistic dualism of denotation and connotation. As Green

---

[1]   Middleton adapts these terms from Gino Stefani's theory of music semiotics.

[2]   Middleton (1990: 220, 2000: 104).

(1997: 7) argues, contexts of production and consumption affect our experience of music and should not be considered as 'extra-musical appendages' inasmuch as they can 'form a part of the music's meaning during the listening experience'. On the other hand, aspects of meaning that relate to intra-musical elements are neither autonomous nor essential since they are contingent on the competence and subject-position of listeners and on the pertinence of musical-social contexts (Green, 1997; Middleton, 1990; Walser, 1993).

Talking about music

In spite of the fact that I asked all interviewees a number of direct questions pertaining to music and sounds, specific statements about intra-musical elements were not forthcoming from many of the respondents; this was a marked tendency among the group of interviewees at popular type events. I should qualify this by saying that much data was eventually gathered, though this often required additional questioning and probing. Furthermore, many of the responses to my questions about music and sound were generally short phrases or just one or two words. This apparent reluctance to elaborate on intra-musical elements contrasted with the more extensive (and often more forthright) opinions that were offered at other stages of the interviews. It could be speculated here that listener competence did not always match the musical codes of the genres performed. For example, it might have taken a certain type of musicologist to discuss at length the works of Gerald Barry, or an accomplished traditional fiddler to describe with confidence the stylistic and individual nuances of Martin Hayes's playing. While there did seem to be different levels of experience and confidence in regard to speaking explicitly about intra-musical elements, I also had the impression that there was a general 'cultural' reluctance to engage in any kind of musical analysis. In other words, people's hesitation in making explicit musical statements should not necessarily be interpreted in terms of their lacking musical understanding.

General expressive qualities

The interview data revealed two distinct patterns among descriptions of the expressive character of various Irish-produced music, wherever these arose. The first of these was the idea of 'lively', and this term or variants of it were more often than not applied to the instrumental music heard at traditional events, as well as to the recorded products of some traditional artists (in particular, those of Altan and The Chieftains). Thomas, who had attended the Jimmy MacCarthy gig, made a distinction between, on the one hand, artists who sounded Irish but who in his opinion lacked the character of Irishness (The Corrs, The Irish Tenors) and, on the other hand, musical acts such as Altan whose Irishness he characterized as 'more lively'. He went on to state:

Thomas

I think real Irish music I would sort of define as being very rooted, and sort of got a bit of ... gimp[3] about it. I don't know exactly how to, how you would explain that but I know it when I hear it.

At the same time, other listeners did regard groups such as The Irish Tenors and The Celtic Tenors to sound both Irish and lively, although these would have been in the minority. The perceived absence of liveliness, particularly during instrumental dance tunes was often a basis for critical comment. For example, at the traditional music concert in Ashbourne, Angela and Jim, while celebrating the playing of Martin Hayes, found the other performers lacking in some respects:

Angela and Jim

J: How about the other performers, what did you like about their playing and singing?

Angela: I got a bit tired of that box [concertina] playing. It was a bit pedantic ... .

Jim: Well, it's not easy to be beside Martin Hayes, you will always be in the shade ... but apart from that, a certain amount of life and colour was missing from the others tonight.

There may be no great surprise in the fact that the feature of liveliness receives so much mention, particularly if we consider the assumed links between Irishness and traditional music, which arguably, has in turn come to be almost exclusively associated with dance forms. Even when traditional dance music is regarded as just part of a pub atmosphere, to quote Cathal (Noone's pub), 'it gets people tapping their toes'. For Máire (Hughes's pub), the experience of music and dance appeared to be inseparable:

Máire

J: What sort of things in this music do you like?

Máire: I suppose the things that I ... any music like that, if it's not singing, it's just fast. I just want to dance to it, so ... I don't know if I find it frustrating here just listening to it ... . I find it hard to just sit down and actually listen to that kind of music for a long time ... and actually not dance.

As noted earlier, Máire was one of a number of interviewees who reported a keen interest in set dancing.

The music–dance association also emerged in interviews conducted at the concert featuring contemporary Irish classical music in Limerick. The first people that I interviewed at this event were a young couple, Brendan and Anne. In the following extract they were speaking, firstly about Bill Whelan's piece,

---

3   Colloquial expression meaning 'spirit' or 'liveliness'.

Inishlacken, and later about Mícheál Ó Súilleabháin's *Hup!*, which had included the performance of a traditional dancer:

Brendan and Anne

J: What things about this music did you like?

Brendan: I thought it was typical Bill Whelan, like kind of the uplifting Riverdancy tune to it.

Anne: Mm. I thought you could hear the *Riverdance* side to it but then it moved away from the *Riverdance* thing.

J: In what ways did you think it was different from *Riverdance*?

Brendan: I was waiting for dancers to come on. I haven't gone to *Riverdance* but I thought it'd be great to put this to dance.

J: In the case of these two pieces, did you think they sounded Irish?

Brendan: Yes I did.

Anne: Yeah … maybe it was in the shoes or something, you know the tap of the hard shoes.

This suggests that, for some people, traditional-derived contemporary compositions may lead to a pattern of music-dance connections not unlike that expressed by Máire in respect of traditional music and set dancing. The general feeling of movement and steps along with the image of dancers appear to be important markers of Irishness for Brendan and Anne. This expectation of dancers coming onto stage is interesting because it suggests a visual presentation of the music, an association that can perhaps be linked to the plethora of such productions and broadcasts from the mid-1990s onwards. Arguably, this case suggests how for many Irish people and for younger people in particular, productions such as *Riverdance* have exercised a formative influence in collective imaginings of Irishness and music.

Another general type of expressive response to Irish music, albeit with less frequency, related both to the melodic character of songs and instrumental pieces (slow airs) and/or the perceived vocal qualities of particular singers. The terms used to describe such general apprehensions of Irishness could not have been more different from the perceived quality of liveliness, and I have categorized this set of responses with the term 'haunting'. The following set of remarks are collated from different interviews:

Carmel ('Best of Irish')

J: You mention that the music here tonight sounds Irish. What makes it so?

Carmel: The airiness and the loneliness. It seems to capture a time and place. And then there is the use of minor keys.

Marie (The Celtic Tenors)

J: In terms of Irish-sounding, how would you rate Enya?

Marie: Well, I think she has a haunting kind of sound, and to me a lot of Irish music has that haunting kind of sound … and that's why, it's not the particular

songs but I think she just has an Irish quality rather than anything else, you
know.

Cathal (Noone's pub)

J: Is there anything about the music here tonight that sounds Irish?

Cathal: Well, I don't know if this is relevant or not, but some of my foreign friends
think that *Riverdance* and Irish music generally is haunting and passionate, and
I can see what they mean.

For both Marie and Cathal, the relationship between musical sounds and the notion
of 'haunting' is not made clear, though Marie does seem to identify a haunting
'Irish' quality in Enya's vocal timbre. Carmel's statement suggests two sides to her
identification with the music, both of which can be seen as related. The idea of place
and time are expressions of extra-musical meanings whereas the reference to the
music's 'minor keys' is an aspect of meaning derived from an intra-musical quality
(see pp. 166–7). 'Airiness and loneliness' can be said to straddle both sides since
these terms could equally refer to extra-musical or intra-musical ideas. Significantly,
the singer Helen Hayes had introduced her repertoire at the same concert by referring
to the 'sad and reflective nature' of traditional ballads, a comment that came to be
echoed in Carmel's description of the entire performance.

The expressive characterization of Irish music as either 'lively' or 'haunting' is
reflected in many representations of Irishness, notably, in TV and film. Here, I refer
not only to Irish-produced film scores but also to major Hollywood and British
productions that involve Irish themes and/or Irish(y) music, some examples being
the films *Far and Away* (1992) and *Titanic* (1997)[4] and the BBC drama series
Ballykissangel (1996). Typically, music written in Irish reel or jig style is used to
depict some brawl, chase or other 'humorous' event, while a solo female voice
is often used to evoke feelings of passion, loneliness and suffering. Although the
cliché of Irish music as *diddley-eye* might now be interpreted as 'stage Irish', kitsch
or even camp, the association between Irishness and dance tunes is nonetheless a
resilient and adaptable one.

Going against a tendency towards the 'Ballykissangelization'[5] of pseudo-
traditional music, some recent cultural products have re-presented the sound-
image of Irish dance tunes in more 'authentic' formats. An example here would be
the appearance/performance of traditional group Gaelic Storm in the film *Titanic*
(as opposed to a studio orchestra performing 'Irishy' tunes). It could also be said
that under the broader and more vague category of Celtic music, beliefs in the
haunting character of Irish music not only come to be perpetuated, but are in fact
magnified. Arguably, this associative property has been exploited by a number of

---

[4]   See O'Shea (2006–07: 126–9) for an analysis of the musical stereotypes used in
the score to this film, which broadly correspond with the categories of 'lively' and
'haunting'.

[5]   I adapt this term as coined by Ruth Barton (2000) in relation to 'Irishy' imagery in
TV and film.

Irish musicians. For example, Enya's high-profile involvement in the soundtrack to *The Lord of the Rings* in 2001 was shortly followed by a TV advertisement promoting the release of the revised CD album, *A Day without Rain*. The advertisement ran with the slogan: 'Enya – the voice of Ireland is now the voice of the world'. It would appear then that, far from disappearing in a national context, these quintessential ideas about Irish music may well persist in contemporary global settings, an awareness of which constitutes part of the social experience of people living in Ireland today. This returns us to the sounds of *Riverdance*, which can be equally regarded as lively (by Brendan and Anne) or as haunting (Cathal and his 'foreign friends'). On listening to the contrasting sections of this music it is not difficult to see how such perceptions and responses might arise.

The identification of Irish music as 'lively' and/or 'haunting' is also to be found in the discourse of some Irish musicians and musicologists. An example from the first category is presented in this statement made by the traditional harpist Máire Ní Chathasaigh. This was part of an interview in a programme entitled *Sounds Irish* which was simultaneously broadcast on Lyric FM and WYNC, Minnesota on 17 March (St Patrick's Day) 2003:

> I've always thought that something which is characteristic of Irish melodies is a surface prettiness and beauty with a sort of melancholy undertow. I think that's what makes it – Irish melodies – so special, that balance between the happy and the melancholy. (Transcribed from a recording of the original broadcast, 2003)

In the musicological field, Graydon (2003) adumbrates this dual representation of Irishness in his essay on three twentieth-century Irish composers. Having de-authenticated an earlier folklorist tendency in Irish compositional style as 'nationalist idiom', Graydon argues that the works of Frederick May, Brian Boydell and Aloys Fleischmann represented a move towards European modernism that still retained 'unconscious elements' of the composers' cultural Irishness. Rather like the 'haunting'/'lively' dichotomy reported above, in Graydon's essay an overall sense of Irishness in music tends to be viewed as either: (a) 'plaintive', 'contemplative', 'lament', 'melismatic', or; (b) 'brighter', 'upbeat', and generally rhythmic (ibid: 60–61). We can get an idea of both types in his interpretation of May's String Quartet in C Minor (1937):

> Notwithstanding its internationalism, its innate 'Irishness' shines through in the 'brighter' sections of the piece … . The same can also be said of a later, equally tranquil section, which in intonation rather than construction leaves one with a subtle scent of its composer's nationality. (Graydon, 2003: 60)

A tendency to read Irishness in the works of modern Irish composers cannot be attributed to musicologists alone, as many composers themselves have expressed similar beliefs (for a discussion, see Cox, 1998: 67–8; Graydon, 2003; Klein, 2003). In general, though, a distinction could be made between, on the one hand, general musicological conceptions of Irishness in music, and, on the other hand, statements by individual composers about the conscious or unconscious use of musical materials and/or ideas that are believed to be inherently Irish. The composer and cultural commentator Raymond Deane (2002: 13) is critical of composers and others who adapt such phrases as 'melodic country' and 'rhythmic obsessiveness' to their characterizations of Ireland and its music. As Deane quite bluntly points out, melody and rhythm could be said to feature in any number of music styles and traditions.

So from where did the idea of Irish music as either quintessentially lively or haunting arise? Gerry Smyth interprets this dualistic conception as one that is inextricably linked with colonial, and later, nationalist imaginings of an inherently musical and inherently repressed people: [6]

> ... music became a compensation for being born into a politically vanquished race – comfort when they wished to remember and a distraction when they wished to forget. Thus was born the remarkably long-lived Janus-faced stereotype which pits elegiac Paddy Sad (think misty mountains, low whistles, and slow airs) against festive Paddy Mad (think smoky pubs and diddley-eye jigs and reels) in a constant battle for the 'meaning' of Irishness. (Smyth, 2004a: 4–5).

In a similar vein, Kieran Keohane suggests that some Irish artists perpetuate aspects of the Paddy Mad/Paddy Sad split persona, although whether this is done consciously or unconsciously is more difficult to determine. Thus, the group of Galway 'lads' who make up The Saw Doctors come to be read as 'mad' while the various female artists contributing to the album series *A Woman's Heart* convey a general feeling of melancholy and loss (Keohane, 1997: 277, 281). Considered together, these two examples strongly suggest that the Janus-faced stereotype of Irish musical expression is at least partly influenced by received ideas of gender differentiation.[7]

Style, sound and soul

Instrumental playing

Style was a term that came up with some frequency in the interviews, and was applied both positively and negatively. These positive and negative statements

---

[6]   O'Shea (2006–07: 128–9) develops a similar argument.

[7]   Here, I would point to the lack of any substantial engagement with issues of gender in the literature on Irish music (see, however, Davis, 2005; O'Shea, 2006–07; Schiller, 1999). Space does not permit me to address that lacuna in this book, although I have previously explored representations of gender and race in the production and marketing of 'Irish-Celtic music' (O'Flynn, 2006b).

were used either to define styles of music or to evaluate the musical authenticity of particular musicians and genres. Most people that I interviewed at traditional music events listed instrumental style as an Irish-sounding feature; of these, only a minority went on to explain how this was heard. A small number did describe style in some detail, with the use of ornaments and other melodic patterns (e.g. 'lyrical' or 'flowing') chief among the patterns identified. Another type of response was to compare Irish traditional style with similar instrumental traditions, for example, from Scotland or Cape Breton. The following examples are taken from different interviews conducted at the traditional session in Noone's pub:

Muireann
The style of fiddle playing is very particular and the sound ... which is distinctively Irish. I think you'd actually recognize that, as opposed to Cape Breton or whatever.

Malcolm
I think that the quick alternation on the fiddle is quite Irish whereas Scottish music would be ... the Irish, they have the rhythms that go quite fast. With that, they have the same kind of genres so I'm thinking back to my Scottish youth when I played traditional. But I think the chords you have and the quick repetitions, that's a very Irish thing.

Although Muireann had earlier identified melodic ornaments as something uniquely Irish, she did not elaborate on what she meant by differences in Irish and Cape Breton styles of playing. Malcolm, however, was more explicit in making a comparison between Scottish and Irish traditional playing.

Other interviewees – notably, those who themselves were traditional players – appeared to be conscious of regional differences in instrumental style. Marian and Carmel, two interviewees at the 'Best of Irish' concert in Co. Meath both indicated that they originally hailed from the northern county of Antrim. As they had also identified themselves, respectively, as a fiddler and button accordionist, I decided to adapt the general line of questioning somewhat:

Marian and Carmel
J: Would you have an interest in Mary MacNamara's box [concertina] playing tonight?
Carmel: Oh yes, I have a CD with her playing.
J. Would the East Clare style differ from that in County Antrim?
Marian: Oh, it would. It's different.
Carmel: Very different, yes – different rhythms.
Marian: Well, the Northern would be more staccato style. This would be much more laid back.
Carmel: ... and more lyrical.

These two women, along with Eoin and Mick who attended the same gig, and Malcolm at the Noone's session, were the only respondents who went beyond the general label of style by elaborating on specific instrumental techniques. The binary distinctions of these responses (quicker/slower, staccato/lyrical, unadorned/ornamented) were consistent with observations made earlier by Keegan (1997) on verbal categorizations of regional style. In the case of other interviewees, it was less than clear what precise elements constituted the 'generic' Irish style that they reported hearing.

Singing

Singing style was also identified as a potential marker of Irishness in music, though not with the same frequency as with instruments. There was just one featured singer, Helen Hayes ('Best of Irish' concert) over the course of the live traditional events. The songs that Hayes performed were all in the English language, and her singing style could be described as 'natural' insofar as the breathing was unforced and the timbre quite mellow. Her melodic line blended an overall clarity of pitch with subtle, microtonal inflections at various points of each song. Mick, who attended this concert, regarded the singing of Helen Hayes to be 'totally Irish. The whole tone, it's completely one hundred per cent Irish'. Speaking at the same concert, another interviewee, Jim, remarked: 'Very traditional Irish style. It's nice to hear an Irish inflection on songs that are over a hundred years old.'

Singing style was also a reason why practically everybody that I interviewed had no hesitation in considering the music of Dolores Keane to be Irish-sounding. This emerged in response to a subsection of my final interview question, in which I asked interviewees to compare the voices of Dolores Keane and Mary Black (both well-known interpreters of ballads and newly composed songs) in terms of their respective 'Irish' sound. In the 'Ireland' entry for the 1999 edition of *World Music: The Rough Guide*, Nuala O'Connor describes Mary Black as 'Ireland's most popular singer' whereas Dolores Keane is attributed as being 'The possessor of perhaps the purest voice in Irish music' (1999: 181, 182). The qualitative distinctions implied by these adjacent descriptions of the two singers were echoed in many statements made by interviewees. What follows is an extract from an interview conducted at UCH Limerick with Fionnuala, Deirdre, Máire and Betty:

Fionnuala, Deirdre, Máire and Betty
J: If you were comparing Mary Black with Dolores Keane, who sounds more Irish and why?
All: Dolores Keane.
Fionnuala: You can't take her accent away … .
Betty: You can't take it from her.
Deirdre: She can be up and singing the liveliest jazz and she has the 'nyaa' all the way.
Máire: But even her talking voice … .

Deirdre: Ah, she has it all the way.

Máire: Mary Black? Mary is from Dublin, isn't she?

Betty: Her accent comes through to me, and I suppose that is Irish as well.

Deirdre: Well, there's no doubt that Mary Black is ... [pauses] ... very good, but I would, if I was to rate them, I'd say Dolores is more Irish. It's just her ... you cannot describe it ... it's just her distinctive style.

Three key words used here are style, accent and what Deirdre refers to as 'nyaa', an expression commonly used in reference to aspects of *sean nós* singing style. Depending on the context, 'nyaa' might be understood as microtonal inflection, glottal stops, nasal timbre or combinations of these elements. Broadly speaking, it tends to be regarded as a particular and unique kind of (Irish) 'vocal grain' (Barthes, 1977: 179–89). Similar to the opinions expressed among some other interview groups, in the above extract both Dolores Keane and Mary Black are regarded as Irish. However, Dolores Keane is afforded a greater degree of Irishness, and I would argue that this arises from a differentiation made between Irish sounds that are heard as unique and Irish sounds that are heard as continuous with other musical cultures and/or styles. (Máire's question regarding the geographical origin of Mary Black raises an issue that will be explored more fully in the next chapter, namely, the importance of region and place in imaginings of Irishness in music.)

Accent was a term that was used with some frequency when I inquired whether certain artists sounded Irish or not. This was a very positive marker of Irishness for singers such as Christy Moore and Dolores Keane, both of whom could be described as having strong 'country' accents (a term generally used to describe all rural accents). Sometimes, accent was referred to as the only identifiably Irish aspect in a musical act. For example, Mick ('Best of Irish') described The Cranberries as 'rock 'n' roll with an Irish accent'. The following extract reports part of an interview held following The Celtic Tenors concert when I asked whether or not there was any Irish sound to a range of domestic pop and rock acts:

Clare, Marie and Ita

J: What about the various Irish boy bands and girl bands?

Clare: Boyzone – they could be from anywhere, the same as Take That, for instance.

Marie: ... unless you were tuned into the accent.

Clare: Well, that's where I think B*witched have it – in the Dublin accent.

Ita: And Westlife have it too.

Marie: But you still wouldn't pick it up as being Irish.

J: How about U2?

Ita: No, nothing.

Marie: Their accents are Irish but their songs? ... No, I don't think so.

In these responses, accent is recognized as Irish but this of itself does not render the music Irish. Like many other interviewees, Clare, Marie and Ita were unequivocal about the Irish sound of Dolores Keane, identifying her Galway accent as a clear marker of Irishness. This suggests a distinction between a literal meaning of accent, which would refer to regional variations in speech production, and a broader conception of accent that would also include vocal timbre as well as the personality or 'soul' of the artist. As already stated, the two Irish performers that were most associated with this quality were Dolores Keane and Christy Moore.

This is how Bren and Thomas, who attended the Jimmy MacCarthy concert together, compared the voices of Mary Black and Dolores Keane:

> *Bren and Thomas*
> Bren: Well, I think that Mary Black sounds ... well, sounds very polished.
> Thomas: She could be from anywhere whereas Dolores Keane has a strong accent and comes across ... and has more of a personality or something. I don't know. I wouldn't listen to her music very often, but just from what I've heard.

If Thomas did not listen very often to Dolores Keane, I doubt if he would be acquainted with the 'personality' of the singer in the way that the word is usually understood. However, 'personality' here is more likely to refer to an expressive character that is interpreted from the vocal sound, and it is interesting to note how this quality is measured in opposition to a vocal character that is described as 'polished'.

Something similar happened when I put the same question comparing Mary Black and Dolores Keane to Doreen, who attended the recital of music by E.J. Moeran. Doreen had identified herself as a classical piano teacher who also played tin whistle at a local traditional club in South Dublin:

> *Doreen*
> J: If you were to describe one as being more Irish-sounding than the other, how would you rate Mary Black in relation to Dolores Keane?
> Doreen: I think Dolores Keane is more Irish.
> J: Why is that?
> Doreen: I just said that instinctively without ... I think her music is quite a bit more Irish, there's more of a basic Irish melody to it.
> J: And if they sang the same melody?
> Doreen: Yeah, I still think Dolores Keane, because Mary Black has more of a trained voice, whereas Irish traditional melodies and singers, you can just ... they have music in them, you know, they just sing from the heart.

Of note here is that a person who had sought out (and apparently enjoyed) the performance of an art music song cycle should regard musical training and musical soul as almost mutually exclusive concepts, at least where Irish music was concerned. However, not everyone that I interviewed responded to my (admittedly provocative) question in such black and white terms. For example, Marie, who attended The Celtic Tenors concert felt that this was too difficult a comparison to make; while Dolores Keane had a definite 'nyaa' in her voice, Mary Black also had a unique vocal quality that was Irish, but less obviously so. That said, an overwhelming number of interviewees were unequivocal in the distinctions they made between the two singers.

While it could be speculated that most listeners perceived a difference in the tessitura of the two singers (Keane as a deep alto, Black as a light soprano), this distinction was not articulated during any of the interviews. Overall, it is not difficult to see how the particular qualities of Keane's voice (low range, nasal timbre) might be perceived as more unique and therefore more Irish than the sounds produced by popular or classically trained singers. However, this type of belief needs to be examined in the wider practice of *sean nós* and traditional singing in Ireland, encompassing as it does a wide variety of vocal qualities and techniques, as the following entry in *The Companion to Irish Traditional Music* suggests:

1. Tone quality, or 'timbre', may vary from extreme nasality, to a hard or constricted tone, to a relaxed, 'open' one.
2. Registration may exclusively use chest voice, or have a preference for the highest register, or head voice. (Henigan, 1999: 338)

Although this eclectic conception of traditional singing would appear to accommodate equally the potential Irishness of both Dolores Keane's and Mary Black's voices, we have already seen how the majority of interviewees apply a more constricted view of 'vocal Irishness' in their appraisals of these singers. For some singers, it seemed that no matter what they produced, it would come to be perceived as Irish, a phenomenon that could be described in terms of an Irish 'vocal authority' (Potter, 1998). To quote Deirdre's remark about the varied repertoire of Dolores Keane once more: 'She can be up and singing the liveliest jazz and she has the 'nyaa' all the way'. Here, Deirdre suggests that no matter what is sung by this performer, it will be heard as Irish, and in so stating appears to be less critical than Nuala O'Connor (1999: 182) who writes: 'In recent years her [Dolores Keane's] choice of material has drifted close to MOR [middle of the road] and light country, which many feel unsuited to such a fine interpreter of traditional songs.'

Another Irish singer who would not usually be labelled as traditional, but was yet regarded as Irish-sounding was Sinéad O'Connor. One interviewee at the Celtic Tenors event described this singer in the following way:

Marie
I think she does sound Irish ... I don't know why but I think she does. I know she sings all sorts of things but I still think she sounds Irish. There's something about her.

Again, we have the idea that irrespective of repertoire, a certain performer may create an inherently Irish sound. With Marie's statement, it could be speculated that the instinctively felt 'something about her' is a reference to O'Connor's voice, personality or both of these. Mick, who had attended the 'Best of Irish' concert offered this view on the Irishness of O'Connor's voice:

> *Mick*
> J: How about Sinéad O'Connor, would she sound Irish to your ear?
> Mick: Yeah, she'd be very close to the Irish sound ... . It's just, I don't know, it's the flavour in Sinéad O'Connor's voice, I mean, like in Dolores Keane's. There's a ... you can tell there's a whole Irish buzz but with Bono you can't get that at all, like.

Two interrelated levels of musical meaning can be inferred from this. First, there is the general expressive plane that is described by Mick as 'a whole Irish buzz'. He also identifies one inherent musical element that partially explains the music's general feel, namely, that of vocal grain. It is noteworthy that Sinéad O'Connor was the only rock performer who was consistently deemed to be Irish-sounding, not in any specific way, but more in the general sense of 'Irish soul'. The fact that no other (internationally successful) popular artist was identified in the same way is significant, particularly in the light of claims made in the various narratives of Irish popular music that were discussed in Chapter 5.

Illustration 7.1   Sinéad O'Connor on *The Late Late Show*, 1990 © RTÉ

Vocal grain was mentioned most often in relation to Dolores Keane, but such remarks were never far from statements about the singer's musical character, personality and even ethnicity. These themes emerged with some force during my interview with Maurice and Jimmy at Noone's Pub:

Maurice and Jimmy
J: Comparing Mary Black and Dolores Keane: how would you rate them in terms of an Irish sound, if any?
Maurice: I like Dolores Keane. Mary Black is ... a nice singer but it's commercially driven.
J: What is it you like more about Dolores Keane?
Maurice: She sounds like a fuckin' knacker.[8] Now, that's not ... [laughs] ... now that's an insult to both knackers and Dolores Keane. It's just she fuckin' sounds as if she's one of them ... no, not a knacker. She sounds as if she lives on an island.
Jimmy: The Galway accent.
Maurice: Maybe it is, yeah.

The link that Maurice makes between this singer's vocal character and a marginalized Irish ethnic group is remarkably similar to the findings made by Van De Port (1999) in a paper entitled 'The articulation of soul: Gypsy musicians and the Serbian Other'. In this case, however, Maurice – with the help of Jimmy – shifts from the notion of the traveller to an idealized version of 'native' Irish ethnicity that comes to be represented by 'The West' (more of this in the next chapter).

Instruments

The symbolic power of musical instruments can be observed at various stages of Irish cultural history, from the earliest Celtic mythologies to the antiquarian movements of the eighteenth century, and subsequent nationalist iconographies from the nineteenth century onwards (Boydell, 2007; Buckley, 1990; McCarthy, 1999: 30–33; White, 1998a: 15–21). Ideological and cultural associations between Irishness and musical instruments continue to the present day (O'Shea, 2006–07; Schiller, 1999), the most obvious example being the endurance of the harp as an official emblem of Irish nationhood (see Boydell, 1996; Lanier, 1999). Although most of the instruments used in contemporary Ireland can be found elsewhere, it would appear that, in both symbolic and material terms, particular musical instruments are regarded as signifiers of Irishness.

Two of the more distinctive instruments among those commonly used in traditional music performance are the *bodhrán* and the *uileann* pipes. It was

---

[8] A pejorative term that is sometimes applied to the distinct ethnic group of Irish travellers.

therefore not altogether surprising that a number of interviewees identified these as constituting a unique Irish sound. However, there were even more references to Irish adaptations of more 'universal' instruments, primarily the fiddle and the flute. The following statements regarding the Irishness of traditional instruments are collated from different events, with all responses but the last made in the contexts of informal pub sessions:

Karl (Hughes's pub)
To me, this is inherently Irish. Every country's got its own little thing, you know, and you've Irish bagpipes, the Turkish have bagpipes of their own and instruments, you know, they subtly vary from country to country. Bit like cooking, really. But yeah, this seems Irish to me.

Cameron (Hughes's pub)
Well, to me it's the type of wooden flute. I mean, you don't really hear the wooden flute in anything else.

Jonathan (Noone's pub)
What I like about this is ... it's very traditional really. The only thing that really goes away from the Irish sound – it's really just the guitar playing a chordal accompaniment

Malcolm (Noone's pub)
The fiddle. It sounds traditional, Celtic and Irish. Yeah, the fiddle, and the drum thing, whatever you call it. There's plenty of that.

Thomas (Jimmy MacCarthy gig)
In real Irish music you would get traditional instruments other than guitar – I mean the *bodhrán* and the *uileann* pipes, the fiddle. They would make it distinctly Irish.

Perhaps the first and most obvious observation that could be made here is the relative ease with which many people spoke about instruments, including the way that these material objects were unproblematically associated with a distinct sense of Irishness. Statements byThomas, Cameron and Karl were most explicit in this regard, underlying the involvement of negative conceptions in the formation of national identity ('different instruments than in other countries', 'not found in anything else', 'distinctly Irish'). Both Jonathan and Thomas implied a relative valorization of the Irishness of instruments in their specific remarks about the use of the guitar. However, as has already been observed in much of this analysis, such comments also need to be interpreted in the light of subjects' overall position vis-à-vis the musical style in question. For example, from an overall profile of the interview that included Jonathan, I would surmise that his implied designation of the guitar as a non-Irish instrument was not based on an essentialist historical view of traditional music and its instruments. Rather, I had the impression that the guitar had little value in his aesthetic of traditional music on the basis that its accompaniment function (in this context) interrupted the mainly heterophonic base of traditional music performance (see p. 165–6).

In all of the interview quotes above, it would be difficult to separate out the sonic and symbolic ways in which various instruments came to be heard as Irish. One exception to this was an opinion put forward by Muireann, who attended the session at Noone's pub. Although Muireann also suggests the idea of timbre in this quotation, a sense of national identity with an Irish musical instrument is very much to the fore:

Muireann
J: In what way would this music be different from other traditional music?
Muireann: Well, see him there? [points to group of core musicians] He's playing *uileann* pipes there which are the Irish adaptation really of the bagpipes in the nineteenth century. So there's something there we really made our own, we personalized for ourselves. So that's a very Irish sound, I think.

Also coming through in this statement is a narrative, not only of Irish identity, but one that reflects a particular historical understanding of traditional music in Ireland. Arguably, such a way of thinking about traditional music would not be unique, given the emphasis placed on traditional music history in the culture at large, from its place in secondary school music syllabuses to the frequent narratives and documentaries that are broadcast on radio and TV.

An ambiguous attitude towards The Corrs has already been reported in earlier chapters. It needs to be emphasized that this arose in the context of my specific question about the potential Irishness of the sound produced by this group. However, for some respondents, the perception of Irish instrumental sounds in music by The Corrs related negatively with their appraisal of this musical act as a whole. The following is part of an interview conducted after the Gerald Barry concert in Dublin:

Sophie and Fiona
J: In terms of Irish-sounding, how would you rate The Corrs?
Sophie: I hate The Corrs.
Fiona: I hate The Corrs, and they, I think they play on the whole Irish *hi-diddle-di-dye* sort of historic sound that's kind of, like, awful. I think that they're the kind of sad side of traditional music … . I think they're terrible, but they do sound Irish, unfortunately.
Sophie: I really don't like The Corrs, just for the same reasons – that whole sort of, you know, commercial Irish chic. We see the fiddle or violin in the background to make it less rubbish so the Americans will buy it.
Fiona: I mean, even on their CD, and I've heard it, they have these little takeouts of about three minutes of like, Irish dancing music. You know, they have their hit songs and then you get maybe, you get a two minute break with … [Sophie then lilts an improvised *diddle-di diddle-di* melody in jig time, both laugh]. … You know, there's the *bodhrán* and the violin there, and it's just wicked, awful. But they're probably very good musicians and, you know, they are appreciated … .

Before commenting on this, I should state that, earlier in the same interview, both Sophie and Fiona, had registered a high level of appreciation for the traditional group Altan, and both were unequivocal in regard to that group's Irish sound. Thus, when Fiona suggests that it is unfortunate that The Corrs sound Irish, it is not because she fails to appreciate traditional music or 'traditional' instruments per se; rather, her displeasure arises from its particular meaning, as she reads it, in the overall context of The Corrs. The complexity of these responses, in which the use of traditional instruments may be regarded concomitantly as Irish-sounding *and* in-authentically Irish, echoes the equally complex set of opinions relating to the Irishness of repertoire and/or musical materials that were described in Chapter 5. In each case, subject positions may be governed by particular ideas of style and authenticity.

Not surprisingly perhaps, the identification of instruments as Irish-sounding occurred at none of the classical events that I attended. There were however some references to the Irishness of certain instrumental sounds at two of the featured popular gigs, though these did not in any way match the force and clarity with which instruments were identified as Irish by those at traditional events. Stephen, who had attended the Pierce Turner gig, had this to say in response to my question about whether or not the music sounded Irish:

> *Stephen*
> ... I think there was a recognizable element of Irishness but ... they were very, kind of peripheral ... .
> Well, in the narrative ... but more in the background music, you know, with the accompaniment of fiddles ...

Another two interviewees at the Dara rock gig associated a similar use of strings with an overall Irish sound. In the interview extract that follows, Darina speaks in general terms about aspects of the music that she had enjoyed that night:

> *Darina*
> J: If you were to describe this music in terms of style, how would you describe it?
> Darina: Celtic pop
> J: What makes you say that?
> Darina: Em, just a very, you know, Irish kind of sound ... with the string section.
> I just thought it was very Irish sounding. I mean, though there was definitely a rock element to it as well.

Similar ideas emerged during another interview at the Dara gig, when I was making general inquiries about things that people may have liked about the music that night:

Ann and Tanya
J: Okay, what kind of things did you like about tonight's gig?
Ann: The whole thing ... .
Tanya: It was upbeat.
Ann: It's not rock, it's not pop, it's just all those things
Tanya: Yeah, and a bit of classical too with all the strings ... well, they sound traditional Irish too.

Darina, Ann and Tanya refer here to an eclectic mix of styles, which, in contrast to Fiona and Sophie's reception of The Corrs, is not alienating to their musical tastes. It is interesting to note Darina's description of an overall style of 'Celtic pop' compared to that of 'Irish rock' used by Liam, another punter at the same event. Arguably, these constitute 'soft' and 'hard' definitions of more or less the same stylistic phenomenon in some types of contemporary Irish-produced music. For now, though, I wish to comment on the identification of classical strings as Irish-sounding. This association might appear somewhat fantastic, but interviewees' comments need to be considered in the specific contexts of the music heard that night. As a listening subject at the same gig featuring Dara, I recorded the following observations on casette while driving home in my car:

> For a band this size, and the possibility of texture and so on, there was a definite feeling of sections within the texture. At first, I just felt that we were getting synchronized tonic or dominant pedals, that is, drones on the strings. Related to that some gapped chords, basically, an open string sound. In one of the earlier pieces, there was a simpler use of strings that sounded 'Country-ish'. And then there were parts when the drum and guitar sections would withdraw, and we'd just have the singer Dara with strings alone. Once they plucked. And they did get to do what might be called a few riffs, almost a little like a Corrs-like Irish rhythm, but nothing as obvious as The Corrs ... .

I have quoted from this 'stream of consciousness' here to illustrate how the particular orchestrations and performance practices might lead an Irish listening subject to regard a classical string quartet formation within an Irish rock/pop act as somehow Irish- and traditional-sounding. As Cian (Pierce Turner gig) put it:

Cian
... this quartet kind of theme is coming through in many kinds of Irish music now at the moment. Now that we're talking about it, yeah, a lot of people are bringing in the quartet now – even Irish music. Yeah, I was interested, I had heard but had never seen a quartet at a live gig before.

It is arguable, though, that most if not all of the musical patterns referred to above could lead to similar conclusions of Scottishness or Englishness. At the same time, it needs to be remembered that the identification of strings as Irish-sounding not only arises from what is heard, but also from the wider contexts of domestic music production and consumption in which the use of strings has conventionally come to be associated with a traditional sound. These associations may further stem from what appears to be a preference for acoustic resources among many high-profile Irish popular acts such as The Hothouse Flowers and The Frames (see p. 33).

Structural features and sensory elements

I now report on comments that suggested the apprehension of specific musical patterns and sonic qualities. (Passing reference has already been made to the sensory elements of pitch, timbre, texture, pulse, rhythm and tempo as well as some larger musical structures, notably, instrumental dance tunes, slow airs, ballads and other song forms.) The idea of repetition came up with some frequency in interviews that were recorded at classical music events and at traditional music events. Significantly, ten interviewees at the informal pub sessions made reference to the repetitive structures of traditional dance music. Mostly, this involved positive terms such as 'musical continuity', 'alternations and repetitions' 'the repeated structures, and 'the way the dances go round and back to each other'. However, although many people celebrated this inherent musical pattern, it proved to be alienating for a minority. As Michael (Noone's pub) expressed it: 'they seem to have the same two or three bars and they just repeat and repeat and repeat'. Sophie registered a different kind of response to an altogether different type of repetitive musical structure that she had apprehended in Gerald Barry's piece *The Road*:

> *Sophie*
> I *loved* this piece. I just thought it was so complex, and so driven, and in a very, very strange way I could nearly relate it to dance music because it just had this constant thud of action going, going, going, going the whole time. I just loved it!

The dance music Sophie refers to here is that of contemporary dance or rave. It might be tempting to pursue links between this type of reception and the allusions made by some contemporary Irish composers (including Barry) to an 'obsessive character' that is supposedly common to traditional dance music and to much new Irish music. However, as reported earlier in Chapter 5, when I did ask Sophie if Barry's music sounded in any way Irish, the answer given was a definite no.

One of the two people that I interviewed at the Moeran recital in Dublin suggested a link between repetition and Irishness when he commented on the piano pieces performed that day:

> *Seán*
> J: Was there anything about the music today that sounded Irish?
> Seán: Well, I was thinking throughout some of the pieces with just the piano, especially 'The Lake Island' and the one about the market ... .

J: 'The Horse Fair'?

Seán: Yeah, I don't mean the tunes themselves but just the way the music was built on short little dancy patterns ... coming out of those tunes.

Interestingly, Seán's apprehension of 'dancy patterns coming out' bears a close resemblance to Geoffrey Self's description of Moeran's Rhapsody No. 2 as sounding like 'Irish jigs in embryo' (Self, 1986: 59). It is perhaps not so surprising that Moeran's music should elicit this kind of response if we take into account the considerable interest that Irish traditional music held for him, not least through his activity as a collector of songs and dance tunes in South Kerry (Self, 1986: 47).

The idea of rhythm was the musical element that was listed with the greatest frequency by interviewees. In fact, rhythm was the only technical musical term that was applied with any consistency.[9] When people used this word, it was either in relation to the technical aspects of duration, pulse and metre, or was generally linked to ideas of 'groove', 'feel' or 'gimp'. Rhythm was often cited as something that people liked about traditional music, and in many cases this coincided with the identification of Irishness in that music:

Karl (Hughes's Pub)
J: What sort of things in this music would you like?
Karl: There's a distinctive rhythmic structure in that Irish ... rolling sort of music.
Jim ('Best of Irish')
J: What things about the music tonight make it sound Irish?
Jim: The rhythm. It's the rhythm really that makes it Irish.

Most of the references to rhythm were included in short unambiguous statements such as these, and this indicated to me that the association between 'rhythmic' and 'Irish' was largely taken as axiomatic. As might be expected, those who identified rhythm-related features as Irish-sounding were in most cases the same people who regarded 'liveliness' as an essential quality of musical Irishness.

Just one other distinct category of sensory apprehension emerged from the interviews, and this I have termed as heterophony-modality since both of these musical concepts can be regarded as interrelated features of traditional music practice. Heterophony is something that is quite audible and visible insofar as it involves a number of instruments playing the same melodic line. Linked to the largely heterophonic texture of Irish traditional music, at least in 'pure' articulations of the style, is a tendency for harmonic and/or polyphonic layers to be understated or completely absent from the music. This relates to the tonal system

---

[9]   It should be remembered, however, that the apprehension of other sensory details emerged from interviewees' statements, though in less explicit ways. For example, the perception of timbre was certainly implied by the high number of references to vocal quality and to instrumental sound.

of Irish traditional music which is based in modality, rather than on the functional harmonic system. Most of the citations falling into this category came from people who performed and/or had studied Irish traditional music at some stage; in semiotic terms, this could be interpreted as listener competence matching stylistic code (Stefani, 1987). However, the fact that other audience members failed to list these musical qualities does not of itself mean that they did not apprehend them, though this might have been the case in some instances.

In a sense, the identification of heterophony as inherently Irish was already implicit in the high significance attributed to instrumental timbre and to the very repertoire of airs and dance tunes. I have already quoted the opinion of Jonathan at Noone's pub, who put a value on the predominant (single) melodic line of traditional music: 'it's very traditional really. The only instrument that really goes away from the Irish sound – it's really just a guitar playing a chordal accompaniment'. And yet, the inclusion of guitars in the musical texture at this traditional session serves to show how, while heterophony continues as a distinct feature in traditional music, accompaniment also has some presence. Indeed, various types of 'infill' layers have featured in many genres of traditional music for several decades now, from the piano vamping used in *céilí* bands to the guitar-based accompaniment style introduced by folk-trad groups from the 1960s onwards. The issue of including or excluding accompaniment, or of valorizing heterophony over other textures may have much to do with concepts of authenticity. Certainly, there are material and aesthetic reasons why traditional music might be regarded as an essentially melodic-based style. Arguably though, there are similar reasons to suggest that newer genres of traditional music have led to 'local' articulations of musical accompaniment that could also be regarded as Irish-sounding. Examples here would be Ó Riada's introduction of the harpsichord in the 1960s, the 'bouzouki-mandolin interplay' developed by Planxty in the 1970s and, in contemporary contexts, the minimal textures/harmonies produced by Denis Cahill (guitar) and Patrick Marsh (bouzouki) when performing with the fiddler Martin Hayes. Indeed, terms such as 'Irish bouzouki' and 'Celtic guitar' have come to be assumed in the discourse of many musicians and fans.

Angela and Carmel, who had both attended the 'Best of Irish' concert, though not together, made reference to the minor modality of much of the music heard that night:

> *Angela* ('Best of Irish')
> J: What things about this music might sound Irish?
> Angela: Gosh, that's a hard question. Mm, I actually think it's more, you know, trills and all that sort of thing. And definitely, you know, the minor notes or chords – whatever. That kind of sound makes it Irish.

As reported earlier in the chapter, Carmel suggested that the use of minor keys was important to the overall expressive character of the music heard that night. This identification of minor modality is noteworthy because, although the modes of many traditional airs could be categorized as either Dorian or Aeolian ('minor'), a higher proportion of tunes in the traditional repertory are based on Ionian or Mixolydian modes ('major') (Breathnach, 1977: 8–15; see also Ní Chathasaigh, 1999).

Two people who had attended classical music events referred to a relationship between conventional harmony and the idea of an Irish sound. The first of these, Seán apprehended something Irish in Moeran's use of pentatony throughout his piano piece, 'The Lake Island':

> *Seán* (Moeran recital)
> J: Was there anything about the music today that sounded Irish?
> Seán: … I suppose in 'The Lake Island', the way it wasn't in a normal major scale … if that makes any sense.

I had a distinct impression from Seán's overall interview that the employment of such 'folk elements' into classical music was something that he enjoyed. This was in contrast to Deirdre (UCH Limerick) who, as it was earlier reported in Chapter 5, had mixed feelings about the juxtaposition of two (apparently) different tonal systems in pieces by both Bill Whelan and Mícheál Ó Súilleabháin. On one side, Deirdre employed the terms 'past', 'purely Irish' and 'modal scales', whereas on the other (un-Irish) side, 'modern', 'harmonies' and 'dissonances' were the terms used.

Overall, it can be observed how some people are inclined to regard as Irish those elements that are considered to be more special and unique than elements common to 'Western' styles of music. Thus, we have the binary oppositions of major/minor, heterophony/accompaniment, modal/harmonic, trained voice/natural voice, and so on. Of course, these distinctions may apply to intra-musical elements as much as they do to people's beliefs about the same sounds and patterns. To adapt the dialectic proposed by Green (1988), what we hear conditions what we believe and, conversely, what we believe affects what we hear. Hearing minor modes can be interpreted as the apprehension of inherent sounds and patterns that are based in material experience. Hearing minor modes as essentially Irish involves a selective process whereby some of the sounds and patterns assume cultural significance whereas other, equally audible musical elements are not imagined in the same way.

Lyrics

As already reported in Chapter 5, several interviewees at classical concerts mentioned the association between some musical works and Irish literary themes. By contrast, most of the comments made about lyric content were in reference to contemporary popular song. Jimmy MacCarthy was highly rated as a songwriter by those who attended the performance of his music:

> *Des*
> He's a great songwriter, probably the best songwriter in Ireland …

Pat

... his songs are so spectacular ... as far as I'd be concerned, they're the best of Irish songs, and I mean, there's a lot of meaning to all the songs, and it means a lot to him, you know.

I have already mentioned the significant number of nationally successful musicians who have recorded songs by Jimmy MacCarthy. The overall impression that I got after interviewing nine people at this event was that the singer/songwriter was recognized as something of a national institution, particularly in regard to the number of contemporary 'classics' that he had penned. However, although MacCarthy's music appeared to be very much appreciated, most of those interviewed did not consider his music to have an Irish sound per se. On the other hand, the combined narrative of songs lyrics and general repartee did suggest a kind of Irishness to some audience members:

Thomas and Bren
J: Do you think this music sounds Irish?
Bren: Sounds Irish?
J: Yep.
Bren: I think it's a distinctive sound, alright. I don't know if it's particularly Irish in a way. His lyrics would be Irish by reference. But the music that you hear – it's very folksy.
Thomas: Yeah. No, I wouldn't rate it as Irish-sounding at all. No, no. Maybe his experiences that he relates to his songs could be Irish ... but not the sound.

Embedded in these statements is the assumption that an Irish sound requires recognizable elements from Irish traditional music. Given the national popularity of MacCarthy's material along with its overarching narrative, lyrics, originality and melodic style (which to my ear, suggests elements of the traditional ballad genre as well as international folk), it seems incredible that his music is not more generally heard as Irish. Here, I would go as far as to speculate that, MacCarthy's music would probably be recognized as an Irish sound were it not for the predominantly essentialist way of regarding Irishness in music.

This is not to berate interviewees such as Thomas and Bren who very kindly agreed to participate in the study. As will by now be clear, assumptions about the inherent Irishness of traditional music are common to the culture at large; indeed, in my own everyday discourse, I sometimes use the term 'Irish music' when what I mean is Irish traditional music. Furthermore, the fact that Irishness may not be apprehended in the sounds of some Irish-produced music does not deny the possibility for individual identifications with the same music to produce feelings of national belonging. Although we can assume that Bren heard no Irish sound *in* the songs performed that night, a highly individual instance of national

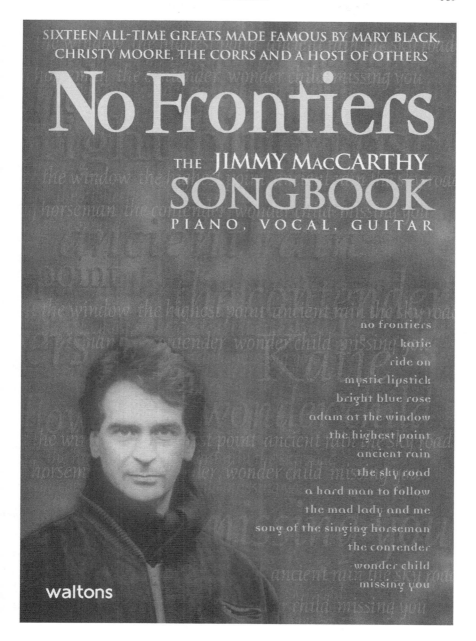

Illustration 7.2   Cover artwork for *No Frontiers: The Jimmy MacCarthy Songbook* © Waltons Publishing

identity was revealed when she spoke about the song 'Mystic Lipstick',[10] the lyrics
of which could be described as an allegory of an Ireland in transition:

> She wears mystic Lipstick, she wears stones and bones,
> She tells myth and legend, she sings rock and roll,
> She wears chains of bondage, she wears wings of hope,
> She wears the gown of plenty, and still it's hard to cope.
> *Chroí ó mo chroí,*[11] your heart is breaking ... . (MacCarthy, 2001)

Bren's reflections about this song immediately followed the interview excerpt
quoted above:

> *Thomas and Bren*
> Bren: I was just thinking of one song tonight – I heard it loads of times before
> but just seeing it performed live was very good – 'Mystic Lipstick'. It's got a
> very strong feeling for me, it just hit me there. I think it should be a national
> anthem. You know, it's a very strong song. I really like it.
> J: An Irish national anthem? [Thomas laughs at this question]
> Bren: Yes, an Irish national anthem.

Without going into an analysis of the song text, it is not difficult to see why Bren
might regard this as appropriate material to symbolize modern Ireland. Arguably,
this example gives us a window into another important site for associations
between national identity and domestic-produced music, namely, the strong
narrative element to many genres of songs and ballads.

It is of note that statements linking lyrics and/or narratives to Irish national
identity were mostly concentrated at the Jimmy MacCarthy and Pierce Turner gigs.
The reason why song words appear to assume a much higher significance in the
contemporary ballad genre than they do in traditional and/or classical performances
of sung material might be accounted for by different degrees of pertinence within
each stylistic code. Such different patterns in pertinence and significance across
the major style categories might also explain why, in comparison to those attending
classical and traditional events, the general group of interviewees at popular type
events were not forthcoming in their comments about inherent musical features.

There are two interrelated ways that style acts as an articulatory principle in
perceptions of Irishness and Irish music. At one level, we have the apprehension
of particular intra-musical elements that are usually associated with traditional
music. At a broader level, extra-musical ideas associated with traditional style
often govern the way that these 'Irish-sounding' elements (which sometimes cross
over into classical and popular genres) are appraised in terms of their potential

---

[10]   The song was first published in 1989.
[11]   Trans: 'Heart, oh my heart'.

Irishness. For many interviewees, the presence of traditional repertoire and/or the use of traditional instruments did not of themselves constitute an Irish sound. In other words, the whole of the music was considered to be more important than the sum of the parts. This was very clearly the case with the appraisal of singers. It seemed not to matter what singers sang; rather, their relative Irishness would be measured in terms of vocal technique, timbre and accent.

Equally important in these appraisals were perceptions about the personalities of individual singers. This conflation of ideas about the singer's persona and their unique vocal sounds suggests some currency to the notions of 'Irish sound' and 'Irish soul'. In most cases, sound and soul emerged as interconnected beliefs, and this may be one of the few ways in which Irishness is perceived among musicians performing in rock and pop styles. However, while articulations of this kind are applied to a limited number of performers, a belief in the wider categories of 'Irish soul music' and 'Irish sound', as expounded by some cultural commentators, is not reflected in the interview data. This emphasizes the role of individual agency in the construction of discourse about Irish-produced music. The collective opinions of people interviewed for this book suggest that although essential beliefs in the Irishness of Irish traditional music are often shared, the perception of Irishness involves much more than the apprehension of particular sounds and patterns: even when elements from this style are recognized as being in the music, this does not guarantee that the music itself comes to be regarded as in the style. This can be linked to an issue that emerged with considerable consistency in the fieldwork, namely, the notion of musical authenticity.

Chapter 8
Authenticity and Irish music

In this chapter, I shall argue that the idea of authenticity is central to a number of dialectical relationships that obtain in constructions of Irishness and music. Among these are the binary oppositions of commercial/real, traditional/innovative, urban/rural, and Irish/'Irishy'. The terms by which these dualisms are negotiated are often concerned with issues of musical style, but other themes to emerge are those of nostalgia and alterity.

Theorizing authenticity[1]

In what might be termed as its predominant form of expression, authenticity is negatively linked to the commodification of music products, and is constructed by the mythologization and fetishization of 'ethnic' and 'folk' musics. This conception of authenticity appears to be prevalent in an Irish context insofar as the Irishness of Irish music is typically defined in terms of 'ethnic specific' materials and practices. Yet, as both Frith (2000) and Taylor (1997) argue, similar constructions of authenticity are utilized in the marketing of various 'world musics' for global audiences. Earlier chapters in this book have already demonstrated how some cultural-economic entrepreneurs appropriate collective imaginings of essential Irishness in music to promote the idea of a (national) market brand. A significant number of music producers can be said to follow suit, as evidenced by the growing number of 'ethnic specific' musical hybrids, and the concomitant adoption of nomenclature, imagery and other paraphernalia that are suggestive of an overarching Irish or Celtic cultural identity. Conversely, modernist perspectives on contemporary classical music articulate a different type of 'cultural Irishness' by authenticating the 'subtle' and 'unconscious' integration of apparently Irish musical elements and/or Irish ideas within a 'European' mainstream of art music. Against this, Irish classical music that makes conscious use of the 'ethnic repertory' tends to be de-authenticated on the grounds of its inherent nationalism, mass appeal and lack of artistic intent. There has been no equivalent dichotomy in the commentary on Irish popular music although the general paradigm of originality versus mass appeal has regularly featured from the 1980s onwards, as various narratives have tended to privilege Irish rock at the expense of showband and pop genres and, more recently, dance and hip-hop (McLaughlin, 1999, 2004; McLaughlin and McLoone, 2000). Thus, while authenticity can be said to occur

---

[1] Some of the ideas explored in this section appear in an earlier essay (O'Flynn, 2007).

wherever there is discourse about music, it is 'an area that is marked by radical differences depending on the style of the music, the ethnicity and nationality of the musicians and other factors' (Green, 2001: 103). Inasmuch as this book examines more than one style of music, there is a need then to consider a plurality of potential authenticities and the interrelated contexts in which these may operate.

The material evidence presented in the preceding three chapters corroborates a widely held theory that 'Irish music' and 'traditional music' are regarded as synonymous terms by the culture at large. While this by itself is not wholly unexpected, what does come somewhat as a surprise is the clarity and extent to which authenticity emerges as a key articulatory principle in that process. This phenomenon particularly comes to the fore in Chapters 5 and 7 where it is shown that, above anything else, affirmations or negations of Irishness in music are mediated through varying conceptions of style. If we concur with the view that notions of authenticity are closely linked to those of identity (Stokes, 1994: 6), the frequency of such responses merits a closer examination.

Already, the book has revealed a range of subject positions in regard to traditional and non-traditional forms of Irish-produced music. Most respondents readily identified with Irish traditional music in broad cultural-national terms. Yet, while many of the people in this category appeared to celebrate traditional music, there was also a significant number who indicated a preference for more 'international' musical genres. In fact, the summary findings of preferences among the entire interview group suggested a wide range of musical interests, the emblematic status of traditional music notwithstanding. However, given my line of questioning, most of the statements pertaining to authenticity were made in reference to Irish-produced music, and a number of contradictory patterns emerged in this context. First, when applied to particular genres, the use of traditional materials and/or performance practices was deemed to be authentic by some and inauthentic by others. Second, issues of authenticity could arise equally from a consideration of texts (repertoire, musical elements, style/'soul'), contexts (venue, interaction, atmosphere) or combinations of these ('tradition'). These are reflective of a similar range of discursive parameters obtaining in academic folklore and in anthropology (Johnson, 2000: 283), and, more recently, in the jargon of world music (Frith, 2000).

What exactly is authenticity then? While accepting Martin Stokes's description of authenticity as 'a discursive trope of great persuasive power' (1994: 7), it is difficult to agree with his assertion that authenticity 'is definitely not a property of music, musicians and their relations to an audience' (ibid: 6–7). I am not suggesting that authenticity resides *in* actual music, but if the authentic is significant in discourse about music then it follows that it is involved in relations between and among producers and consumers of music. As Taylor (1997: 22) describes, for musicians and listeners alike, authenticity is real insomuch as it is believed in, talked about, and can actually influence musical behaviours. Moore (2002: 221) echoes this dynamic application of the term when he argues that a theoretical consideration of authenticity needs to focus on the activities of perceivers rather than on the intention of various originators.

For any listening subject, authenticity in music may be constructed with reference to (a) a particular sound experience or a set of similar experiences, and (b) the totality of an individual's sound experiences as they relate to overall social experience. In practice, these are processes that interrelate, although the ways in which people construct musical authenticity can vary greatly, with some constructions very much based in the apprehension of sonic details while others could be considered as more arbitrary (Moore, 2002: 209). Examples of both these tendencies have already been illustrated in this book insofar as some people identify more with the idea and emblematic status of Irish (traditional) music, while others register their identification in terms of actual practices and sounds. I do not suggest that these are mutually exclusive conceptions; rather they can be considered as dialectically related. Thus, on one hand, we have people who largely identify with Irish traditional music as an idea, and although they do not attend to the detail of that music, they nonetheless enjoy it as ambient sound; on the other hand, those who identify more with the sounds and conventions of traditional music (that is, members of a distinct sound group) can also have strong opinions as to what Irish music and, in particular, Irish traditional music should be.

A general pattern noted in Chapter 7 was the significance that the personalities of individual performers could hold in the recognition or non-recognition of Irishness in music. Moore (2002: 209) proposes three possible performance modes that can be linked to such constructions of authenticity:

First person authenticity: Artists speak the truth of their own situation.
Second person authenticity: Artists speak the truth of the situation of (absent) others.
Third person authenticity: Artists speak the truth of their own culture, thereby representing (present) others.

On the surface, it might be assumed that first and third person authenticities are the only modes applicable to a study that comprises musicians and listening subjects based in Ireland. However, as I argue below, notions of alterity may also be involved in authentications of Irish music. (The prevalence of third person authenticity has already been established in earlier chapters where patterns of national and cultural identifications with music were exposed.)

Authentic and inauthentic Irishness

Identification and authentication

There was a clear resemblance between the terms of authenticity used by the interview respondents and those found in domestic music journalism. In the latter case, it did not prove difficult to uncover examples of such discourse, and I offer just one example here to illustrate the kind of terms by which a professional traditional act might be celebrated:

> You couldn't accuse them of the quick buck ethos ... honesty and integrity are at the heart of Dervish ... . Being grounded to a real home place ... (Laffey, 2001: 14)

Here, journalist Seán Laffey authenticates a group of traditional musicians in terms of rootedness, truth and – in spite of the Dervish's professional status – their non-commercial ethos. Similarly, there was a high frequency in the interview data of words and phrases along the lines of 'real', 'honest' and 'organic'. Brendan, who had attended a concert of classical music in Limerick, referred to the singer Dolores Keane in these terms:

> *Brendan*
> It's more natural and more *nadúrthach, mar a dearfá* [trans. 'natural as one would say']. It's like, there's no kind of hidden agenda, you get what Dolores is, and that's it.

Brendan's authentication of this performer's Irishness is doubly expressed through the repetition and symbolic translation of the word 'natural' into the Irish language [*nadúrthach*]. Mikey, who was interviewed at the Jimmy MacCarthy gig with three other friends, had this to say concerning my question about whether the traditional group Altan had an Irish sound:

> *Mikey*
> Irish? Oh, God, aye. I know their music well. It just, well it just runs very deep. You know, they don't have to talk about it, they just do it, and the music is there, it's honest, and it runs deep.

Like Brendan, Mikey mainly alludes to a first person authenticity here, and, as noted in Chapter 4, understatement of performance has come to be regarded as an authentic quality in the practice and reception of Irish traditional music.

Most statements pertaining to ideas of authentic Irishness also referred to what it was not. The following examples are collated from different interview contexts:

> *Maurice* (Noone's pub)
> It is Irish and it is what we are. It's more authentic than what's recorded and what is produced by the record companies. It is obviously more natural because it seems that anything that's old and natural has, eh, very little monetary interest from the record companies ... . Yeah it's purist. That won't sell. It's the real thing and I want to hear that.

Brendan (UCH Limerick, speaking about a number of traditional-popular genres)
I totally dislike it … I think it's completely using … I mean, when you listen to real Irish music you can feel, I think you can feel what they're putting across. And they are just using it, you feel, you just hear it in your ear, like. You hear it in your ear, but you can't feel it inside you … .
Thomas (Jimmy MacCarthy gig, comparing The Corrs and Altan)
They [Altan] are much more, eh, I suppose, rooted. You've got a feeling that these people live a life, that they, you know, they play the music because they love … I mean, I'm sure The Corrs love music as well but I think they've just gone down the more commercial, mainstream way which is fine for them but … I mean, there's other people who buy their albums. But I'd say if you're looking for more authentic kind of Irish pieces then you need to go to the likes of Altan.

Maurice's statement, which implies a third person authenticity, is predicated on the opposition of, on the one hand, music that is immediate, natural and Irish, and, on the other hand, music that is mediated by commercial, technological (and arguably, multinational) concerns. Thomas's statement represents a 'softer' version of the authentic versus commercial paradigm, and differs somewhat from Maurice's in that it alludes to first person authenticity.

In the previous chapter it was shown how perceptions of vocal timbre and personality often became enmeshed in people's ideas of an Irish sound, and how articulations pertaining to the idea of 'Irish soul' were not necessarily genre-specific. In his statement quoted above Brendan attempts to unpack the various processes that might make some music sound more authentically Irish than others. The distinction he makes between what is perceived aurally and what is felt overall underlines the active agency of the listener in co-producing musical authenticity. While in musical-analytical terms the general idea of authenticity might be regarded as an intangible quality, it could be argued that, in many cases, the seemingly vague and arbitrary notion of 'feel' is very much grounded in real experience and is therefore central to the construction of musical meaning. This sense in which Irish musical identities can become embodied in perceptions of musicians' performance bears some similarity to the findings made by Román-Velázquez (1999) in a study of salsa musicians and their audiences in London.

Commerce and authenticity

Without exception, music described as commercial was also deemed to be less authentic and less Irish. Indeed, for some people, the condition of being 'non-commercial' was part of the very authenticity of Irish traditional music. Cathal, an interviewee at Noone's pub, underlined this type of position when he stated, 'I would never pay to go to something like this'. Cathal was among a group of interviewees who, while appearing to like traditional music only in a rather general sense (the *idea* of Irish music), identified more with what he considered to be part of a national collective music tradition (third person authenticity). The idea that tradition and commerce were incompatible terms also served to de-authenticate Irish pop acts that incorporated traditional sounds and/or performance practices into their music:

> *Bren* (Jimmy MacCarthy gig, speaking about The Corrs)
> Ah, I think they're a bit like packaged shamrock. I mean, they're very listenable but not much depth as far as I'm concerned.
> *Liam* (Dara gig, speaking about B*witched)
> … that's just commercialism. No, that's just manufactured sounds. Not Irish at all, no. It's really just … it's *Coronation Street* music. No thought required to make this music and no thought required to listen to it.
> *Stella* (Noone's pub, speaking about B*witched)
> No, they are not Irish sounding. They are just four or five girls making a commercial success with pop music and sticking in bits of Irish music here and there. Fair play to them, but it doesn't sound Irish to me.
> *Elaine* (Gerald Barry concert, speaking about B*witched)
> You've got a record company exploiting that resource and people will take that as being Irish. Traditional music with a pop formula because of the marketability of traditional Irish music at the moment … . The thing is where have they gone? They've gone because they've passed over all the *diddle de iddle-de* stuff. Well, that was their only sound really … .

All of these statements are based on the binary opposition of authenticity and commercialism. Of note here is how negative judgements of authenticity can override the Irishness that may be perceived in the use of traditional musical materials by these popular artists. Bren and Elaine not only regard the artists' music as inauthentic and un-Irish, but are also critical of tendencies to market and package such musical genres. The sense in which Liam opposes authentic/Irish to commercial/manufactured is articulated by reference to a popular soap opera, and this oblique reference to Britishness may also inform his views on authentic Irishness.

De-authenticating positions regarding Irish pop can also be found in domestic rock journalism. Although the general aesthetic of rock discourse may differ from that of folk/traditional, these two style categories bear many similarities in terms of the authenticating principles that prevail in their respective discourses (Moore, 2002). In the case of Ireland, McLaughlin (1999) illustrates how a particular conflation of the discourses of traditional music and rock music contributed to a situation where pop and Irishness came to be viewed as mutually exclusive ideas. Pop may also be subject to the de-authenticating discourse of the rock press in England, but given the embedded cultural status of pop that goes back to The Beatles and more recently featured a 'renaissance' of Britpop in the 1990s, it is arguable that Englishness and pop are more compatible ideas (see pp. 31–2). From the brief account of Irish musical genres presented in Chapter 2, it can be seen that Irish-produced pop has its own history. Moreover, findings from Chapter 3 indicate that Irish people purchase a proportionally high level of popular music products, much of which comprises 'commercial pop'. However, this aspect of the national-musical field has either been excluded from cultural theories of Irish music or negated by rock journalists and others. The recent national and international visibility of Irish-produced pop acts (as well as other successful Irish acts) has simultaneously been characterized as economically successful and culturally inauthentic, as the following selections illustrate:

> ... The likes of The Corrs and B*witched are, of course, highlighting the commercial face of intrinsically Irish pop music ... . And yet, while their music is readily identifiable, the culture – via words and ideas expressed – is not. While the likes of Irish music artists like Gavin Friday and Pierce Turner weave various strands of Irish culture through, generally speaking, un-commercial soundtrack and song – in the process creating genuine post-modern Irish expression, nuance, and flavour – the Celtic hip-hop people extol a somewhat more cut-price, mundane aesthetic. Welcome to the sell-out of the century. (Clayton-Lea, 1999: 16)
>
> Their [Westlife's] new album *Coast to Coast* ... may consist largely of bland ballads and slick layers of over-produced harmonies but it is music of a kind. Disposable and unremarkable, it's the generic sound of today, a soundtrack for the Celtic Cub Ireland where style triumphs over substance and the ring tone on your mobile phone sets you apart from the pack. (Carroll, 2000: 4)
>
> It's getting bland, and Ireland was never bland ... . It's just an industry to many people, some of its star performers are just painted tarts ... . (Jimmy Crowley interviewed in McGrail, 2002: 27)

Three broad types of Irish-produced popular music are critiqued in the above examples. In Clayton-Lea's article on traditional-sounding pop, two types of authenticating distinctions are suggested. First, we have the notion of commercial pop versus authentic rock, and it is interesting to note how the desired quality of 'un-commercial' can be heard in the music of some professional acts but not in others. Second, he adopts a distinction between what is valid cultural expression and what is not. In this, the writer rates words and ideas as bearing more cultural significance than what he believes are intrinsically Irish pop sounds. Westlife could be regarded as a more international-sounding pop act, and Carroll's critique above is addressed to a perceived identity-less audience of Irish consumers as much as it is to the 'blandness' of the group's overall sound. Singer/songwriter Jimmy Crowley uses the same term of blandness to de-authenticate traditional and folk performers who have entered a more mainstream, popular arena. Not only does he imply that Irish music loses its unique aura by such 'commercialization', but he also regards these performers' (first person) authenticity to be lacking.

Tradition and innovation

The assumed authenticity of traditional music can come into question when modes of production appear to conflict with idealizations of value and style. Two issues are discussed at this juncture. First, I interpret a number of negative appraisals on the activities of professional traditional musicians, a theme that is closely related to the commercial/authentic dialectic discussed above. Second, I examine some dualistic conceptions that revolve around the idea of a tradition/innovation split within the sphere of Irish traditional music.

For Maurice, the professionalization of traditional music somehow de-authenticated it:

> *Maurice* (Noone's pub)
> The Chieftains are The Chieftains. If they want to fuckin' be The Chieftains, they play Irish music, right? Ah, they're good, but you could put me here [points to the session musicians] and the fellas would be playing just as good, but they wouldn't be getting the fuckin' money. Dublin is where all the money is now, and you will hear people that played every night for the last 20 years, that the only thing they don't have is a fuckin' contract. But they don't want a contract, and there's their accomplishment.

This position is somewhat redolent of what Taylor (1997: 23) refers to as 'the discourse of selloutism'. By his own admission, Maurice identified more with the idea of traditional music than with the actual experience of it, and this may explain his apparent indifference to the particular sounds produced by different musicians. Here, it would appear that the authenticating principle of a non-monetary cultural transaction has a strong bearing on the identification of the music as Irish. This echoes Cathal's association between non-commodity forms and Irishness, cited above.

Marian and Carmel were two amateur traditional musicians that I interviewed at the 'Best of Irish' concert. At might be expected, these participants expressed a keener interest in traditional music than either Maurice or Cathal. Carmel was practically the only person among the entire interview group who equivocated about the Irishness of the traditional group Altan: 'They sound Irish ... yes. But they're very commercialized. I'm not saying that it's a bad thing but they're the music for the stand up stage.' This implies a distinction along the lines of participatory and performance music, with the former valorized at the expense of the latter. In the same interview, Angela went on to dismiss another professional traditional musician, Donal Lunny: 'I don't know about Irish, but he's certainly done very well for himself!' This can be interpreted as a double criticism insofar as, in addition to enjoying a successful career, Lunny arranges and performs music that clearly veers towards the innovative side of traditional music production. However, other amateur traditional musicians were less critical of their professional peers. When chatting with the musicians at Noone's pub, I asked for their opinions on an increasing tendency towards the professionalization and commodification of Irish traditional music. Contrary to what might have been expected there was no sense of disparagement in what was said, with a general attitude of 'fair play to them' or 'what they do, they do well'. It was already noted that a few musicians among this group were sometimes paid to perform at 'stand up' gigs. This gives one insight into the relative fluidity between and among traditional sound groups, insofar as the lines between amateur and professional activities are not always distinct, and musicians may equally engage in participatory and performance modes of production.

Given the growing professionalization and institutional recognition of traditional music in the country as a whole, it is arguable that authenticating practices for this musical style are constantly subject to contestation and debate. This is nowhere more apparent than in conceptions of a conservative-progressive split within the world of traditional music. While debates between 'purists' and 'innovators' can be traced back to the 1950s, the stakes appeared to intensify from the mid-1990s onwards. Much of this was sparked by the RTÉ/BBC TV series *A River of Sound* (1995) which, broadly speaking, linked a wide range of traditional genres and derivative hybrids in its overall 'progressive' narrative of Irish traditional music. One of the interviewees at the UCH Limerick event, Anne, adumbrated this 'development theory' of Irish (traditional) music when appraising pieces by Mícheál Ó Súilleabháin and Bill Whelan: 'Does it sound Irish? Yeah. Maybe it was in the movement, you know, in the Irish music ... . You can see it developing from the past to now'.

This is not to suggest that 'progressive' views of Irish (traditional) music are uncritically received. Indeed, *A River of Sound* promoted much controversy, and the coincidence of its broadcasts with the unprecedented commercial success of *Riverdance* only served to highlight what might have been perceived as its radical agenda. This is how journalist Tom McGurk interpreted it at the time:

> The dangers of popularity are real, as indeed too, are the dangers of the exclusivities of the traditionalists ... . I suspect that the debate this series will open up will not be just a matter of traditionalists versus modernists. Rather it may be about the competing claims of authenticity against homogenisation. The question in one way is profoundly simple: Is this series celebrating the continuum of traditional Irish music or is it actually about the onset of a new traditional Irish 'musac'? What a useful question too in the week that *Riverdance II* opened. (McGurk, 1995: 25)

Ostensibly 'neutral', the dualistic discourse of this extract privileges the notions of tradition, continuity and authenticity against those of popularity, mass mediation and homogeneity.

A River of Sound was shortly followed by the 'Crossroads Conference' in 1996, the very title of which suggested that, for some people at any rate, embedded notions of traditional music were problematic in a time of change for musicians and their audiences (see Reiss, 2003: 152–8). Mícheál Ó Súilleabháin (see pp. 42–3), who was centrally involved in the *River of Sound* TV series, was also a key player in this dialogue. He approached the conservative/progressive dispute in the spirit of rapprochement with a paper entitled 'Crossroads or twin track? Innovation and Change in Irish traditional music' (Ó Súilleabháin, 1999). Along with Hamilton (1999b), Ó Súilleabháin argued that there were historical precedents for both individual and collective innovations within the world of traditional music.[2] However, another presenter at the same conference, Séamus Tansey (1999: 213) saw it quite differently:

> There needs to be a split. Go your separate ways. Form your own Celtic twilight sub-culture as an appendage to the Irish traditional music that we know and love and that has come down to us for generations and from the very environment of this country … . Tradition versus Change. If that is change i.e. the mongrelisation, the bastardisation, the cross-pollination, the copulation of our ancient traditional music, with other cultures, then I say we want none of it … .

In Tansey's view, popular and classically oriented innovations have no place in traditional music (ibid: 212), and his use of the term 'Celtic twilight' is not only suggestive of inauthentic musical practices, but also devalues those aspects of Irishness that are not essentially Gaelic.[3] This is perhaps as strong a purist position that can be found, but I put it here to show both the passion and resilience of Gaelic-Irish essentialism in the face of rapid cultural change. But for many practitioners and scholars in the field, resistance to stylistic change has as much to do with artistic sensibilities as it does with expressions of cultural nationalism. Fintan Vallely, for example, puts forward the following reasons for viewing 'tradition' and 'innovation' as incompatible terms:

> Like language, and like any other music genre, traditional music in Ireland has its own internally regulated accent that is its sound. Any deviation is seen by those within it as different – maybe trying, often pleasant, sometimes hostile. Hanging on to a definite sound is a major hazard for any traditional music. (Vallely, 2003: 208)

---

[2]   See also Quinn (2008) for an analysis that reappraises 'the tradition' in the light of Martin Hayes's unique style.

[3]   The distinction between 'Gaelic' and 'Celtic' has a history in the rhetoric of Irish cultural nationalism. In contemporary contexts, 'Gaelic' suggests an adherence to traditional Irish values and may also signal an essentialist conception of Irish culture. 'Celtic', on the other hand, tends to refer to more general ideas of cultural expression and identity, and has increasingly come to be used in the marketing of hybrid music genres. Yet, this term may also lead to essentialist imaginings of Irishness insofar as its homogenizing assumptions serve to negate social and cultural diversity.

All in all, this suggests two ways of negotiating stylistic norms in Irish traditional music. There are first those musicians, scholars and others who have an interest in traditional music and who together negotiate, define and maintain a set of established conventions. This comes close to Howard Becker's conception of a relatively closed 'art world' (1982). Against this, there are musicians, scholars, entrepreneurs and other social actors who also feel that they belong to or are associated with this musical world but who at the same time wish to renegotiate the terms of their own membership, particularly in relation to the articulation of stylistic conventions.

Statements relating to tradition and change were frequently given during the course of interviews; collectively these mirrored the spectrum of opinions reported in the paragraphs above. Tom, who regularly attended the traditional sessions at Hughes's pub offered this view:

Tom

J: What kind of things in this music do you like?

Tom: … if I was listening to an individual musician, I'd be very interested in the way they shape tunes and construct tunes … and I would think that I would probably … I mean I would look for a certain identity in the way that they play. I like very innovative musicians but I don't like musicians who change for the sake of innovation, and I think that's a very careful balance in Irish music. Because Irish music, like you know, is constructed on the basis of people playing music and … the same tunes are played all the time with very little exception. So therefore, it is kind of … it's a very careful layering of the way they change, of the way the tunes are changed. Ah, I think that's probably the thing I would look for, like, in a musician, you know, how they play tunes, how well they play them.

J: Do you play yourself?

Tom: No I don't, no. I would be very, very critical of people who play tunes you know, who are messing about … .

This question was asked at a stage of the interview before I had introduced the word 'Irish'. Yet Tom responded to a question about musical enjoyment in terms of identity, which in turn was measured by reference to performers' first person authenticity. Overall, Tom's statement painted a picture of a relatively closed musical world in which style was framed by conventions and stratifications and by the articulating mechanism of authenticity (Martin, 1995: 172–87). This was all the more striking considering that Tom was not himself a traditional player, and it underlines the sense in which a 'consumer' can be regarded as an active member of a particular sound group.

I think it is reasonable to assume that Tom was aware of his own conservative position vis-à-vis traditional performance. Generally speaking, though, conservative or 'purist' perspectives were less common in this particular aspect or axis of authenticating discourse. One interviewee, Fionnuala, consciously

articulated a pro-innovative ideological position when her friend Deirdre implied
that the mixture of classical and traditional sounds in Mícheál Ó Súilleabháin's
music was less than authentic:

> *Fionnuala and Deirdre* (UCH Limerick)
> Deirdre: Oh, it was all so choreographed, it just didn't flow like the real
> traditional … .
> Fionnuala: Yeah, and I think that is a good thing. I think that's a healthy thing to
> bring one style and marry it with something else and see what comes out of it,
> because I think if any tradition stays static, that there's going to be no growth,
> it's just going to remain there, fossilized.

Fionnuala's theory of authenticity in this instance requires a consideration of
tradition *and* change. Muireann, who attended the session at Noone's pub was
representative of a number of interviewees who appeared to appreciate equally
both 'directions' of traditional music:

> *Muireann*
> I suppose I'm very interested in the whole way that traditional music is going
> and changing all the time, and I'm particularly interested in the music of Donal
> Lunny, and the kinds of things that he does – the way he's kind of pushing the
> boat out, and mixing other idioms into traditional music … . And still, the very
> traditional groups like Beginnish, which is like four or five very high quality,
> mm, traditional, *purely* traditional soloists, I love that as well.

Later on in the same interview, Muireann was critical of Donal Lunny's album
Coolfin on the basis that it was not innovative:

> … it's not going in any particular direction and it's not progressing from what
> he's done already, it's just repetition, and he's more or less stopped … it's as
> though he has stopped developing.

These seemingly contradictory statements suggest that the same listening subject can
employ different sets of authenticating principles, depending on the musical genre
in question (indeed, Muireann seems to adopt a modernist critical perspective in her
appraisal of Lunny's music). Furthermore, I would argue that individual statements
of authentication are articulated through a unique configuration of dichotomous
conceptions that are deemed pertinent in each case by the listener concerned.

'Irishy music'

It has already been established in this book and elsewhere how non-traditional
styles of Irish-produced music tend to be excluded from identifications of Irishness.
Non-traditional styles that incorporate 'ethnic specific' elements may come to be

heard as Irish but, ironically, the very use of such materials in non-traditional contexts serves to de-authenticate the music in question. One discursive category to emerge from the interviews was that of 'Irishy', that is to say, the perception of stereotypical Irishness in music without concomitant identifications of Irishness arising from the same music. Generally speaking, this involved a rejection of kitsch, 'twee', 'stage-Irish' or tourist-oriented performance. Florence, who I interviewed at the Jimmy MacCarthy gig, presented one such example:

> *Florence*
> J: Do you think Jimmy MacCarthy produces an Irish sound?
> Florence: Yeah, but not Irish in the 'Oirish'[4] sense.
> J: What things about him make you say that?
> Florence: The warmth of his personality. He encompasses more than Irish – inverted commas – which I'm not into. Irish twee, you know, comeallye[5] and tweed and all that kind of thing.

The Irish concert ballad came in for this type of criticism more than any other genre. The following interview extract offers some insights into why such a perception may arise:

> *Maurice and Jimmy* (Noone's pub)
> J: If you listen to performers like the Irish Tenors singing ballads, does that sound Irish to you?
> Maurice: Well, they're enjoyable enough but they're playing to the gallery ... nothing wrong with that. Irish, yeah but it's not ... It's too much too late. Not 'too little too late'. It's too much too late!
> Jimmy: My opinion is that they're something that's based back in the thirties, and their music is ... well it portrays the Irish as people who produced all these tenors and music hall acts that at the time put traditional music in the background.

Maurice's notion of 'playing to the gallery' echoed the opinions of other respondents who felt that concert performances of Irish ballads were tourist-oriented. Inasmuch as 'playing to the gallery' implies entertainment, it could be deemed as inauthentic in the first person sense. The emphasis with which Maurice stated 'too much too late' suggested a strong belief in the anachronism of the genre. This was something taken up by Jimmy, albeit in a more political sense. For Jimmy, part of the concert ballad's in-authenticity arose from what he perceived as its negative relationship with 'organic' forms of Irish music. Jimmy's statement also suggested a type of socio-musical distinction, one which another interviewee, Fionnuala, put in more explicit terms when describing her response to the concert ballad genre: 'It talks

---

[4]   A comic derivative of the word 'Irish' that is often applied in a pejorative sense.

[5]   Comic term for a repertory of Irish traditional ballads that typically begin with the words 'Come all ye ...'.

to me maybe about a class situation in Ireland ... I didn't grow up in a family like that'.

Vallely (1997) distinguishes between two 'centres' of traditional music that are projected by and promoted through state-controlled media and other national institutions. First, there is the historical 'bourgeois centre' of national culture that Vallely associates with inauthentic genres ('proper' and heavily arranged versions of traditional music and song). Second, we have the emergence of a regional-based 'style centre', promulgated through specialist media channels and cultural agencies. These, he suggests, 'present and hone the "fashionable" or consensus view of what is "good" in traditional music' (Vallely, 1997: 109). Whereas most of the participants in this study deemed the concert ballad to be in-authentically Irish, a number of those who attended classical events did consider this music as Irish-sounding. This sub-group had something in common with Irish classical musicologists insofar as Irishness could be perceived in terms of repertoire and inherent elements. For other groups, authentic style was deemed to be a more important signifier of Irishness than musical substance. The apparent dominance of this latter view might be interpreted in the light of a newly constituted 'bourgeois centre' that increasingly validates 'regional' articulations of national culture (Vallely, 1997: 111).

Eoin and Mick, the youngest people that I interviewed, expressed no overt negative positions towards any of the Irish musicians that I mentioned, and in this they were quite unique. However, they thought it quite funny when I asked if groups such as The Irish Tenors had an Irish sound:

> *Eoin and Mick* ('Best of Irish')
> J: What do you think about groups like The Irish Tenors, The Celtic Tenors when they sing Irish ballads? Do they sound Irish?
> [Pause. Both laugh.]
> Mick: They sound like, eh ... did you ever see *Darby O'Gill and The Little People?*[6]

Rejections of what people believe to be inauthentic or kitsch representations of Irishness are similar to some of the 'deconstructive' principles applied in post-colonial critique. The kind of 'national baggage' that this implies is by no means unique to Ireland (for a discussion on 'tartanry' in Scottish music identity, see Symon, 1997: 204–5). However, as much as twee Irishness appears to come under attack in scholarly and commonsense views, stereotypical forms of representation can also accommodate new types of identity and meaning in a 'post-modern' Irish society. Such a pattern of identification comes through in various conceptions of nostalgia, as we shall see below. Additionally, it could be said that 'Irishry' has

---

[6] This was a Disney-produced movie of 1959 that presented stereotypical images of Irish culture and mythology. The 'little people' in question were leprechauns.

been re-packaged and re-presented in an era of cultural-economic entrepreneurship (see p. 43).

Authenticities of place and the construction of an Irish 'Other'

Nostalgia and 'The West'

A particular kind of place has consistently been invoked in constructions and imaginings of Irish national identity:

> ... the hegemonic image of the West of Ireland as the cultural heartland of the country was an essential component of the late nineteenth-century construction of an Irish nationalism which, in its dependence on a Gaelic iconography, was to prove exclusive rather than inclusive, particularly when its representations became fused with Catholicism. Strongly reinforced by the intellectual elite of early twentieth-century Ireland, the 'West' became an idealized landscape, populated by an idealized people who invoked the representative, exclusive essence of the nation through their Otherness from Britain. (Graham, 1997: 7)

Successive periods of economic growth and socio-political change have done much to question such an essentialist and exclusivist conception of Irish identity. However, it can be argued that mythical constructions of Irishness have more recently come to be appropriated by the interests of tourism and other industries (Duffy, 1997: 81; Gibbons, 1996: 88). More generally, mythologies of place have come to assume a new type of significance in many modern societies, and are often linked with ideas of nostalgia. Gibbons (1996: 85) comments on the emergence of such a phenomenon in late twentieth-century Ireland:

> The hankering for a return to nature and the simple life ... is a form of nostalgia for a world which was lost, and is simply an attempt to restore to the countryside an ideology which was taken from it in the first place. This view of rural nostalgia accords with Raymond Williams' definition of 'residual ideology', that is a value system which outlives its own era and survives in a new social order.

In previous chapters I have discussed how essentialist ideas of Irishness and music have increasingly come to be reworked in the creation of cultural products designed for both domestic and export markets. Arguably, this involves the cynical exploitation of collective imaginings of place and time on the part of cultural-economic entrepreneurs. However, cultural consumers may also be involved in the affirmation, negation or appropriation of such images and sounds. Identities of time and place are also grounded in real experience. Thus, while many of the interviewees in this study expressed idealized and nostalgic links between identity and Irish music, there were individuals among this group whose life histories and social experience seemed to 'fit' with the type of identifications in question. But there were also people whose histories and lifestyle patterns (including their musical tastes) contrasted sharply with such idealizations of Irishness and music. It could be argued then that the particular construction of, and nostalgia for a rural Irish cultural idyll involve processes of identification and authentication that are conceived in both first and second person senses. The following quotations show some different feelings and opinions of nostalgia:

> *Claire* (Dara gig)
> J: In terms of Irish sounding, how would you rate The Irish Tenors?
> Claire: It appeals to me for its nostalgia.
> J: Nostalgia? In what sense?
> Claire: Probably my country background.
> *Carmel* ('Best of Irish')
> J: What things do you think sound Irish about the music we heard tonight?
> Carmel: The airiness and the loneliness of things past is what I feel … and it captures a time and place.
> *Máire* (Hughes's pub)
> Máire: … it's sort of memories of the fact that it is more … something you identify with … . You see, my mam's family are originally from the West of Ireland.
> *Sophie* (Gerald Barry concert)
> J: Okay, the various types of albums based on The Irish Tenors, The Celtic Tenors … . In relation to their music, Irish-sounding or not?
> Sophie: Well, I was home the other night watching [the Irish tenors on] TV with my friend and her boyfriend and I was sitting there thinking, 'God, we have to turn it over, it's so ghastly'. And suddenly, as we were watching it, it went into the whole, kind of theatrical element of the *Gone with the Wind* Irishness and the sort of … you get swept away … . And I think it's absolutely awful and I'd never buy it, you know … but at the same time, I can see why … it's just kind of escapism, it's giving people what they want, something Irish that you can really switch on very quickly. It's sort of patriotic really.

Time and place feature in the responses of Carmel and Máire, and in both cases the context is the reception of live traditional music. The classical ballad genre is the subject of Claire and Sophie's responses and, although very different forms of identification are reported, the idea of nostalgia comes through in both cases. Sophie's response suggests an awareness of her split subjectivity as a listener in that she simultaneously de-authenticates and identifies (albeit in a removed fashion) with the same cultural product.

It is interesting to note how Claire and Máire, two Dublin-based interviewees, ascribe value to the rural origins of some Irish music. Overall, a dichotomy along the lines of Dublin/Rest of Ireland emerged with some consistency in the interviews. A tendency towards the same overarching division in the culture at large has been interpreted by Duffy (1997: 77), and in some ways relates to the 'bourgeois'/ 'regional' distinctions of Irish music observed by Vallely (1997). Among some of the Dubliners that I interviewed, it could be said that the mythological West represented a (desirable) cultural other, around which their identifications of musical Irishness were based. For example:

Jimmy (Noone's pub)
J: Can you tell me things about the music right now that you like?
Jimmy: The sound. The fact that, the music heard tonight, you could go back to hundreds of years ago. Maybe, as Maurice said, a shebeen[7] down in Connemara. You'd still hear the same music like nothing has changed. Like the music you hear tonight without the amplifiers and the modernization and that. It's still pre-*Riverdance.*

The Connemara region in West Galway has perhaps come to be one of the most symbolic of Irish places, not least because it holds a substantial Irish-speaking population, is an area of outstanding natural beauty and has provided a focus for much literary and artistic work from the late nineteenth century onwards. However, the assumption of an 'unchanged' musical tradition (and for that matter, the image of musicians performing in rundown, unlicensed drinking establishments) in Connemara and similar 'peripheral' regions is questionable, and has recently been challenged by scholarship in the field (for example, Uí Ógáin, 1999).[8]

In the previous chapter, I reported on how some people differentiated between the singers Dolores Keane and Mary Black not only on the basis of a perceived sound, but also in regard to their respective places of origin, Galway and Dublin. Even those people who regarded Mary Black as Irish-sounding, implied somehow that Dolores Keane was *really* Irish-sounding, as the following example shows:

Eoin
Well, it depends how you define Irishness. I mean, if you were in Australia, Mary Black is one hundred per cent Irish. There's no doubt about it. Whereas, Dolores Keane, you know, is different. She comes from a different Irish world than Mary Black's from ... and they're completely poles apart. But they're both distinctly Irish, do you know what I mean?

In this comparison, Irishness is discussed exclusively in terms of place, and the two singers are considered to be poles apart. Yet, unlike several other interviewees, Eoin does not deny the Irishness of Black's voice on the basis of her Dublin background, even though we can sense his identification with Keane's Irishness

---

[7] Shebeen (from the Irish *síbín*) is a bar premises in which alcohol is sold without licence.
[8] In many respects, present-day Connemara could be described as a rural-cosmopolitan region.

is more comfortable and immediate. However, when the comparative idea of place moves from an insider construct (Dublin/The West) to an outsider construct (Ireland/Rest of the World), then Eoin has no difficulty in affirming the Irishness of Mary Black. As it happens, the singer herself expresses a strong identity with the place of Ireland:

> When I asked Mary [Black] to describe any non-musical influences that might have influenced her music, she described Ireland. 'I do feel that a lot of music that I sing, it's like the landscape of Ireland. I know that might sound a little bit odd, but I really do feel that the music reflects a lot of what is really Irish, you know? Its landscape and the spirit of the people and, well, I hope that that is what it reflects'. (Digman, 2003: 17)

The material evidence would suggest that, along with other forms of Irish-produced music, traditional music is widely practised in Dublin. At a historical level also, it could be pointed out that the national organization CCÉ originated in Dublin, and that many of traditional music's greatest exponents – Séamus Ennis and Tommy Potts to mention but two – came from Dublin. It is possible that the tendency to perceive Dublin as less Irish arises from its former status as the centre of colonial administration and concomitant perceptions of 'residual Britishness'. (The potential power that a Dublin/ Ireland dichotomy might hold in the imagination of Irish people was brought home to me a number of years ago when a Dublin-based traditional music acquaintance told me that she believed her playing always improved whenever she 'got out of Dublin'.)

Links between Irishness, music and place may be constructed in relation to other styles of Irish-produced music. Musicologist Harry White (2003: 16, 2005: 34–5) suggests such an idea in his appraisal of contemporary Irish composers who from time to time engage with what might be described as 'non-sonic' markers of Irishness, notably, from literature, mythology and the idea of Ireland as a place. White distinguishes this general sense of cultural Irishness from contemporary composers whose work is largely based on 'the ethnic repertory', by which he means traditional music sources and/or references. Somewhere in between these two 'types' was composer E.J. Moeran who, as noted earlier, is regarded as Irish in some commentary by virtue of his father's nationality and through his eventual domicile in the south-west of Ireland. Not only was he an avid collector of folk music in both Ireland and England (Self, 1986: 47); it would also appear that Moeran identified strongly with the particular landscapes in which he composed:

> Nature was the eternal solace. He took a proprietary interest in favourite places ... . So crucial was setting for his music that he could not work or even complete a piece if the surroundings were wrong. Thus we can readily identify Norfolk music, or Kerry music, or that of Hereford. The early 1930s were, of course, a back-to-nature time ... . (Self, 1986: 247)

Illustration 8.1   Cover artwork for the compilation album *The Rough Guide to Irish Music* © World Music Network

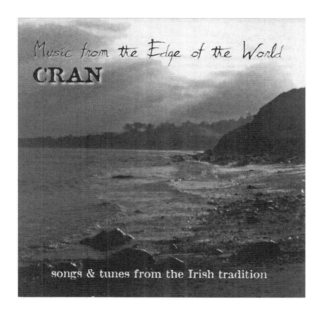

Illustration 8.2   Cover artwork for traditional group Cran's *Music from the Edge of the World* © Claddagh Records

The use of place names and/or the general idea of place continue to provide inspiration for many contemporary pieces of Irish-composed music. For example, the concert that I attended at UCH, Limerick included the piece 'Inishlacken' (a small island off the west coast of Ireland) by Bill Whelan, and an encore piece, 'Oileán' ['Island']⁹ by Mícheál Ó Súilleabháin. Whelan's piece in fact constitutes part of a trilogy entitled *Postcards from Connemara*, an area, which already noted, has come to connote a sense of mythological Irishness. One the pieces performed at the Gerald Barry retrospective concert was *The Road,* the title of which was inspired by the composer's memory of a quiet country road during his childhood in Co. Clare. Sophie and Fiona who attended this concert, had read the composer's notes in the programme that evening:

> *Fiona and Sophie* (Gerald Barry concert)
> Fiona: ... he, like, mentioned the visual imagery. I, like, was imagining this dirt road in the West of Ireland ... and I was imagining this kind of light. Then suddenly, the whole piece came to me visually.
> Sophie: I related it to a movie that I saw recently, *American Beauty*, and it was the whole feel of the plastic bag dancing in the street. And I was thinking, this is the whole plastic bag scene, you know. And, it's the West of Ireland as well.
> Fiona: I just had all these picture in my head like ... desolate landscapes and beautiful sunsets.

The idea of the visual image comes through quite forcefully here, and this is perhaps not surprising given the piece's title and accompanying programme notes.¹⁰ The juxtaposition of the images of dirt road, contemporary American film and West of Ireland landscapes perhaps illustrates just how many potential sounds and images can be in the head of a listening subject at any one time. Both Sophie and Fiona expressed awareness that the concert programme may have influenced how they imagined and heard the music that night. At most, we might say that the apprehension of Irishness in Barry's work on this occasion was associative. However, it is arguable that these associations are somewhat significant in the light of the composer's 'avant-garde' and highly individualistic style, and the fact that neither interviewee had heard his music before. In some respects, Fiona and Sophie's reception of *The Road* could be compared to 'post-modern' readings of

---

⁹ See White (2003: 26) for a comparison of this piece by Ó Súilleabháin with another composition bearing the same title by John Buckley.

¹⁰ My own perception of Barry's piece that night can be characterized in terms of a general 'shimmering' quality, which to my mind arose from the dense clusters of orchestral timbres and pitches, and from the pulsating though directionless drive of its temporal space. While not claiming to have reached the condition of synaesthesia, this sound-experience was closely linked with visual images arising from the title and programme notes.

the visual work *Irelantis*,[11] a series of surreal landscape collages by artist Seán Hillen, insofar as *Irelantis* can be interpreted as a superimposition of modernist and global imagery on conventional imaginings of Ireland as place (see Connolly, 2003: 4–6; Graham, 2001: 23–7).

Identity and difference

Very much linked to the imagery and idealization of The West is a tendency towards exoticism in conceptions of Irishness and music. While the idea of otherness in Irish music may go back centuries, it could be said that this view has steadily grown in currency since Seán Ó Riada (1982: 21) made the assertion that Irish music was 'not European'. Indeed, the aurally perceived alterity of Irish music has been linked to musical cultures as far afield as India and North Africa. This kind of theory was famously advanced by Quinn (1986: 19–21),[12] and has continued to feature in the discourse of many musicians, journalists and other commentators (for example, Ardagh, 1995; Ladd, 2002; Waters, 1994). Some of the perceived musical elements that may give rise to this thesis are the vocal timbres, microtonal intervals and florid ornamentations that feature in *sean nós* style, but there is no material evidence to date that can substantiate these views. 'Exotic' theories of Irish music have been critiqued by a number of traditional music scholars on the grounds that: (a) less attention is paid to English-language songs; (b) there is a tendency towards the 'fetishization of ornamentation'[13] and other 'exotic elements'; (c) regional and individual differences and/or contemporary influences are obscured (Coleman, 1997).

Whatever perceptions of mythical Irishness in music may or may not obtain, these are dialectically linked to people's mythological beliefs (or the absence of them) about Irishness in general. In many cultural commentaries, the musical genre of *sean nós* is regarded as inherently Irish, as the following statement from the 1999 edition of *World Music: The Rough Guide* illustrates:

> Songs in the Irish language are at the heart of the Irish tradition, freighted with significance as one of the few fragile links to the culture of Gaelic Ireland. The most important of them belong to a repertoire known as sean nós ... (O'Connor, 1999: 177)

As reported in Chapter 7, quite a number of interviewees identified a particular vocal timbre or 'nyaa' as the musical feature that most clearly defined the Irish

---

[11] As Hillen's title suggests, this is a conception that fantastically associates the entity of Ireland with the mythological city of Atlantis. The collages can be viewed on the website www.irelantis.com.

[12] Bob Quinn's *Atlantean* (1984) was originally broadcast as a three-part TV documentary (see O'Brien, 2004: 194–203).

[13] A term that Coleman (1997) attributes to *sean nós* singer and scholar Lillis Ó Laoire.

sound of singers like Dolores Keane, and the term *sean nós* was linked to this vocal quality on several occasions. There is no question that the 'nyaa' or individual timbre of singers can be regarded as unique. The critical issue here is how such subtle musical differences come to articulate and authenticate an apprehension of Irishness in some sounds and not in others. If anything, these examples have illustrated how what we believe affects what we hear and conversely, how what we hear reinforces our beliefs. It is not just a question of *what* musical elements people may or may not consider to be Irish-sounding but also *why* these are selected over others. The following statement by Seán Corcoran could well describe many of patterns observed in this book:

> Our perception of regionalism in Irish music depends greatly on the filters of mediation which stand between us and the reality of the social processes of popular music-making. Some of these are conscious cultural factors (Irish language song collectors ignoring the English language repertoire of their singers; collectors regarding melodies in a minor tonality as being more ancient and therefore more important; seeing certain regions as being more "Irish" than others …) and some are historical accident. (Corcoran, 1997: 28)

Common sense tells us that the general category of Irish music is more familiar to Irish people than it is to any other people. For this group and probably for others too, the musical style in which Irishness is generally believed to inhere is traditional music. While only a minority can be considered as insiders to its stylistic codes and conventions, most Irish people are familiar with traditional music as a 'generic sound'. For this majority group, the symbolic Irishness of traditional music does not necessarily correlate with their celebrations of music in general; it is, however, involved in particular processes of authentication and identification at the level of culture and nation.

General identifications of Irishness in music appear to involve both second and third person authenticities. The greater the remove there is between the listening subject and the imagined place and time of the music, the more that conceptions of 'us' and 'others' become blurred. Put another way, when the perception of inherent Irishness arises from idealizations of Irish musical culture along with the filtering out of unique and/or exotic musical elements, this suggests a dual process of authentication in which alterity and identity are simultaneously conceived. More specific identifications of Irishness in music may also relate to second and third person authenticities, but the hegemonic underpinning behind such conceptions are sometimes interrupted by the more immediate sense of first person authenticity where the musician 'speaks' directly to listener. For this reason, non-traditional performers with 'soul' and personality can also come to be regarded as essentially Irish (as apparently happens in the case of Sinéad O'Connor).

Just as authenticity does not reside in music, we can say that Irishness is not an essential quality of Irish-produced music. Yet, as with notions of musical authenticity, associations between Irishness and music may have real consequences insofar as they influence people's concepts, beliefs and behaviours in regard to that music. Perceptions of Irishness in music come to be mediated through style in a number of ways. First, the general style category of Irish traditional music is imbricated in most Irish people's conceptions of Irish music, though what is understood by 'traditional' and 'Irish' can vary considerably between and among different groups and individuals, depending on a range of social contexts and values (this is particularly the case with traditional-derived hybrids). Second, style, as it becomes linked to beliefs about musical authenticity, operates as a central articulatory principle when specific musical acts and/or musicians are appraised in terms of their potential Irishness *and* their musicality. This second sense of style may interrupt the assumed traditional-Irish apposition because, in some cases, Irishness may also be heard and felt in 'non-traditional' popular genres (but never, it would appear, in respect of Irish classical genres). Conversely, traditional-sounding music that is deemed to be stylistically inauthentic is not celebrated as Irish, though it may be acknowledged to be so.

Conclusion
Irishness and music 'inside out'

Aesthetic political representations of the Irish spirit currently fluctuate between discourses of communitarian essentialism and the transcendental homelessness of a race of angels. … Irish desire is torn between the object domains of Zooropa[1] and the rusty bicycle leaning against the wall of the pub in County Galway. Fearing that in Zooropa 'too much is not enough', Irish desire, Janus-like, also faces toward home in search of the holy grail of the authentic, but fears finding it also to be too much, too much that we may choke on it. (Keohane, 1997: 302)

As the above quotation from Kieran Keohane suggests, dominant representations of 'authentic' Irish culture attempt to reinstate aspects of essential Irishness – whether real, imaginary or a combination of both – into more recently formulated projections of a cosmopolitan and progressive Ireland. In this book I have set out to illustrate how such processes are to some extent mirrored in cultural commentary and in everyday views about Irish music, albeit with a degree of reflexivity that suggests a more fragmented sense of cultural belonging than heretofore. This arguably goes beyond a contestation of civic and ethnic conceptions of the national-musical field, since Irishness has also increasingly come to be exploited and, as a consequence, more widely considered in economic terms. Speaking about the current status enjoyed by Irish traditional music and its derivatives, Richard Middleton makes the following assessment:[2]

At first positioned as subaltern – as the music of a self-consciously postcolonial state – this has moved to a hegemonic position within the symbolic economy of musical nationalism, functioning as the dominant fraction of the 'Celtic connection' and as a widely admired model for 'post-traditional' musical politics. This move clearly maps the shift of the Irish state itself from 'developing' status into a 'Celtic Tiger' incorporated within the core of the transnational economy … . But at a deeper level what has happened here, surely, is that the music found that its previous Other had vanished, or at least had been transmuted into the shapeless flows of imperial capital; it was thus forced to fold back on itself ... assuming a position strangely *outside itself.* (Middleton, 2007: 198)

---

[1]   A reference to the *Zooropa* album released by U2 in 1993 (see also p. 106).

[2]   These observations by Middleton follow an essay I wrote in the same volume and in which I explored re-articulations of musical identity and authenticity in contemporary contexts of globality (O'Flynn, 2007).

There is an inherent irony here wherein Irish traditional and/or traditional-derived music is increasingly, though not exclusively, appraised in 'post-traditional' terms. The international visibility of these genres heightens the sense in which the same music can come to be perceived and, in some cases, celebrated by Irish people as 'ours'. At the same time, and as intimated by a number of interviewees in the previous chapter, this international success coupled with an ever-growing engagement with 'external' sounds and images might cause some people to experience a sense of loss and nostalgia for what is imagined to have been 'exclusively ours' in the past. In this respect, it would seem that idealized conceptions of Irishness and music exhibit a desire to engage with an 'other within'.[3] This 'other within' not only replaces what is imagined in an Irish cultural past, but may also symbolically act to supplant those less palatable aspects of international success which, as Middleton proposes, has to some extent placed the music 'outside itself'.

Indeed, not only does the general category of Irish music enjoy a high level of exposure in international markets; related to this trend and of equal significance is the impact that broader notions of Irishness can have in transnational contexts. It could be said then that the potential global significance of 'Irish music' arises no less from its ideological packaging than it does from the actual music that is consumed – and to a lesser extent, produced – by non-Irish populations around the globe. For example, Williams (2006) describes the involvement of many Japanese people in Irish traditional music scenes, and further comments on the sense of nostalgia with which the same music is generally associated in Japan. Negra (2004: 54) meanwhile explores changes in American identities following the bombing attacks of September 11, 2001, and highlights 'the politicised nature of the fantasies of nostalgia and innocence in which Irishness is so often embedded in the US'.[4] Undoubtedly, this was a period that saw a revival of interest among US audiences in artists such as U2 and Enya and, more generally, a rise in the international popularity of ostensibly Celtic artists. It seems reasonable to surmise that these political and cultural developments in the US and elsewhere have come to influence the production and marketing strategies of a number of Irish music acts. This is not to evaluate the artistic intent of those involved but rather to underline the sense in which much domestic production has become inextricably linked with international reception. Méav Ní Mhaolcatha, onetime member of the Celtic Woman ensemble alludes to this phenomenon when she states:

> I suspect that people leading an increasingly urban life want to go back to a
> simpler style of music. In the States, the romantic idea of Ireland is certainly
> part of the appeal … . Even though the place that they're thinking of may be

---

[3]   Bohlman (2000: 187–212) develops this term to describe a dialectic of identity/ difference regarding the historical reception of Jewish musical genres in Europe. I adapt this here to describe a process whereby recent articulations of an outward looking Ireland nonetheless retain a sentimental 'gaze' on an idyllic, rural and traditional past.

[4]   See also Negra (2006).

fast disappearing in modern Ireland, it's still part of our folk memory. (Ní Mhaolcatha, n. d.)

Once again, we can see the operation of an insider/outsider dialectic in this articulation of Irishness and music since, as Ní Mhaolcatha suggests, the same music can simultaneously be read as 'other' by contemporary Irish and international audiences. That said, I would propose that for Irish consumers, articulations of the 'other within' are read in more complex and problematic ways.

The previous chapter demonstrated the residual influence of colonial and nationalist ideas in individual and collective perceptions of Irish cultural otherness. This discourse continues to invoke the imagery of a peripheral place (the Atlantic 'fringe') and of exotic and liminal constructions of ethnicity (Gaelic-speaking and/or nomadic people). In a way, this adherence to a sense of periphery can be interpreted as a strategic denial of Ireland's contemporary position in the 'core' of political, cultural and economic alignments and flows. However, we have seen how, for some interviewees, the appropriation of traditional imagery was qualified by the juxtaposition of romantic and 'post-modern' markers of identification, reflecting perhaps a self-awareness of the contradictions lying between real and imagined aspects of Irish social experience. Other respondents displayed a distinct sense of unease with the blatant projection of Irishness or worse, Irishry, in aspects of domestic production and mediation. While not exactly stating that Irish music was in danger of 'eating itself', a number of people indirectly expressed a fear of 'choking' on a force-fed diet of reworked and repackaged 'Irish' musical products. As put by one interviewee, 'it's too much, too late'.

A sense of reflexivity notwithstanding, the Irishness of Irish music is predominantly constructed with reference to sonic features and cultural phenomena that are considered unique, filtered out as it were from the totality of music identifications experienced across a range of social groups. And yet, the material evidence presented in this book documents a field of music production and consumption that is engaged with a broad range of domestic and international genres. That said, Irish musical life does include a distinct and vibrant network of traditional music scenes, and it could be assumed that for the social actors in these milieux, identifications of Irishness in music are more closely integrated with general music preferences and behaviours. But, as is the case with all identifications in music, these are in turn subject to particular sets of contexts and values, thus leading to a wide range of interpretations and positions along the national-cultural spectrum.

What I wish to emphasize in this conclusion is the two-sided face of identity, and the variety of ways that this dialectic operates in positive and negative articulations of Irishness and music. The opening chapters of the book revealed an overarching hegemonic view of Irish musical life in which traditional music and classical music interest groups contest the national-cultural field in respect of emblematic status, institutional/educational support and other material resources. Representing, respectively, 'heritage/tradition' and 'high art' perspectives, these national elite groups effectively coalesce to exclude popular music from any consideration of Irishness or Irish culture. Related to this we can see how, depending on one's socio-cultural perspective and depending on the particular sound groups to which individuals may or may not belong and/or be associated, identity with a particular music style is to a large extent premised on what that music is not. Thus, in spite of increased patterns in hybridization and 'crossover' modes of presentation, it would appear that ideological delineations of the major style categorizations remain embedded in the culture at large.

Although a number of 'commonsense' theories concerning the Irishness of Irish music have been confirmed in this book, we have also seen the agency of listening subjects in negotiating the terms of their own discourse around such phenomena. Many were self-aware of the circular nature and apparent contradictions of their own definitions and perceptions. Others again illustrated how particular associations do not necessarily translate into essentialist views about either Irishness or music. While the opinions of some interviewees adumbrated a number of themes that were also advanced in journalistic and scholarly literature, it could not be said that any of these theoretical and/or ideological positions vis-à-vis Irish music were uncritically received.

Contradictory, 'globalized' trends in the domestic field of production and consumption bear further consideration. On the one hand, a narrow selection of Irish-produced music enjoys a disproportionately high share of international music sales; on the other hand, the totality of Irish-produced music represents a disproportionately low share of domestic markets. Paradoxically, these patterns can serve both to affirm and to negate assumptions about the inherent musicality of Irish people. However, in respect of the latter imbalance, it is perhaps worth reiterating that patterns of consumption across the entire national-cultural field are not defined by purchasing behaviour alone. In general, Ireland could be said to be awash with popular music, not only in regard to the widespread consumption of recorded and broadcast products, but also in respect of the extensive level of production activities (that include original music making), and the numerous live music and clubbing scenes throughout the country. This largely 'unsung' flowering of domestic popular music over the past four decades does not appear to have displaced the more established canons and practices of traditional music and classical music; indeed, all three style categories of Irish music can be said to have enjoyed sustained growth over the same period, albeit if each of these may have done so at different paces and with particular sets of conditions. As Smyth (2004a: 3, 2005: 1), has remarked on more than one occasion, 'the isle is full of noises'.

As much as this book has questioned homogenizing celebrations of Irishness and Irish music, it has also critiqued normative positions regarding Irish music and culture. Part of that analysis involved a materialist dimension, when I evaluated processes of mediation as they may bear on domestic production and consumption. To varying degrees the Irish state can be described as 'promotional' in respect of traditional music and classical music (although, for many observers including myself, this falls short of what might be expected from a comparatively wealthy country), and at best 'benign' in its neo-liberal position regarding domestic popular music (Cloonan, 1999, 2007: 141–4). As many sound groups and scenes – whether as part of participatory music or performance music or both – are excluded from dominant representations of Irish music, they come to occupy a newly aligned 'hidden Ireland' (Corkery, 1925). Arguably, it behoves those with an interest in Irish culture and society to worry less about the international image of Irish music or what Irish music *should* be, and to find out more about the musical practices of these and other 'hidden musicians' (Finnegan, 1989) and their audiences.

Notwithstanding its constant flux of negotiations, contestations and articulations, the hegemony of Irishness, both in a general sense and in specific relation to music, appears to be holding fast, especially when compared to comparative phenomena in other national entities.[5] This relative stasis in identity maintenance contrasts starkly with evidence of a diverse and often dynamic national-musical field, and is sustained by outsider perspectives that are refracted onto, and in turn utilized by, internal, post-traditional strategies of national representation. However, we have also seen how dominant representations of Irishness and music do not necessarily 'obliterate difference' (Hall, 1996: 3), and in an era marked by dramatic cultural, economic and demographic change, it seems likely that alternative voices from within Irish society will increasingly come to challenge homogenizing discourses of musical-national identity. In his critique of navel-gazing approaches to Irish cultural studies, writer Hugh Leonard (1989: 28) asks for 'a moratorium, not on Irishness but its celebration'. For future studies of Irish music, I would argue that, while we may still need to retain ideological factors within our gaze, the focus should now shift towards materialist inquiries about musical experience in contemporary Irish society.

---

[5] Zuberi (2001: 2), for example, regards the hegemony of Englishness to be in a state of crisis.

Bibliography

Acton, Charles (1978), *Irish Music and Musicians*, Dublin: Eason.

Adorno, Theodor (1976), *Introduction to the Sociology of Music*, trans. E.B. Ashton, New York: Continuum.

Allen, John (1996), CD programme notes for National Symphony Orchestra of Ireland, *Maritana*.

Anderson, Benedict (1991 [1983]), *Imagined Communities: Reflections on the Origin and Spread of Nationalism*, London and New York: Verso, revised and extended edition.

—— (2002), *National Identity, Popular Culture and Everyday Life*, Oxford: Berg.

Ardagh, John (1995), *Ireland and the Irish: Portrait of a Changing Society*, London: Penguin.

A.T. Kearney/Foreign Policy Magazine (2006), *Globalization Index*, Washington, DC: Foreign Policy.

Baily, John (1994), 'The Role of Music in the Creation of an Afghan National Identity, 1923–73', in Stokes, Martin (ed.), *Ethnicity, Identity and Music: The Musical Construction of Place*, Oxford and New York: Berg, pp. 45–60.

Barthes, Roland (1977), *Image–Music–Text*, trans. Stephen Heath, London: Fontana.

Barton, Ruth (2000), 'The Ballykissangelization of Ireland', *Historical Journal of Film, Radio and Television*, 20 (3), 413–26.

—— (2004), *Irish National Cinema*, London and New York: Routledge.

Becker, Howard (1963), *Outsiders: Studies in the Sociology of Deviance*, New York: The Free Press.

—— (1982), *Art Worlds*, Berkeley, CA: University of California Press.

Bennett, Andy (1997), 'Going down the pub!': The pub rock scene as a resource for the consumption of popular music', *Popular Music*, 16, (1), 97–108.

—— (2000), *Popular Music and Youth Culture: Music, Identity and Place*, Basingstoke, Hampshire: Macmillan.

—— (2004), 'Introduction Part 1: Music, Space and Place', in Whitely, Sheila, Bennett, Andy and Hawkins, Stan (eds), *Music, Space and Place: Popular Music and Cultural Identity*, Aldershot, England and Burlington, VT: Ashgate, pp. 2–8.

Bennett, H. Stith (1980), *On Becoming a Rock Musician*, Amherst: University of Massachusetts Press.

Bernstein, Basil (1997), 'Class and Pedagogies: Visible and Invisible', in Halsey, A.H., Lauder, Hugh, Brown, Philip and Stuart Wells, Amy (eds), *Education: Culture, Economy, and Society*, Oxford and New York: Oxford University Press, pp. 59–79.

Biddle, Ian and Knights, Vannessa (2007), 'Introduction', in Biddle, Ian and Knights, Vanessa (eds), *Music, National Identity and the Politics of Location*, Aldershot, England and Burlington, VT: Ashgate, pp. 1–15.

Bindl, Daniela (2008), Personal correspondence, 28 January.

Björnberg, Alf (2007), 'Return to Ethnicity: The Cultural Significance of Musical Change in the Eurovision Song Contest', in Raykoff, Ivan and Tobin, Robert D. (eds), *A Song for Europe: Popular Music and Politics in the Eurovision Song Contest*, Aldershot, England and Burlington, VT: Ashgate, pp. 13–24.

Björnberg, Alf and Stockfelt, Ola (1996), 'Kristen Klatvask fra Vejle: Danish pub music, mythscapes and "local camp"', *Popular Music*, 15 (2), 131–47.

Blacking, John (1995), 'Music, culture and experience', in Byron, Reginald (ed.), *Selected Papers of John Blacking*, Chicago and London: University of Chicago Press, pp. 223–42.

Blaukopf, Kurt (1992), *Musical Life in a Changing Society: Aspects of Music Sociology*, trans. David Marinelli, Portland, OR: Amadeus Press.

Bohlman, Philip V. (1988), *The Study of Folk Music in the Modern World*, Bloomington: University of Indiana Press.

—— (2000), 'Composing the Cantorate: Westernizing Europe's Other Within', in Born, Georgina and Hesmondhalgh, David (eds), *Western Music and Its Others: Difference, Differentiation and Appropriation in Music*, Berkeley: University of California, pp. 187–212.

—— (2004), *The Music of European Nationalism: Cultural Identity and Modern History*, Santa Barbara, CA: ABC-Clio.

Borthwick, Stuart and Moy, Ron (eds) (2004), *Popular Music Genres: An Introduction*, Edinburgh: Edinburgh University Press.

Bourdieu, Pierre (1984), *Distinction: A Social Critique of Taste*, Cambridge, MA: Harvard University Press.

—— (1993), *The Field of Cultural Production*, Cambridge: Polity Press.

Boydell, Barra (1996), 'The Iconography of the Irish Harp as a National Symbol', in Devine, Patrick and White, Harry (eds), *Irish Musical Studies 5: The Maynooth International Musicological Conference 1995 Selected Proceedings: Part Two*, Dublin: Four Courts Press, pp. 131–45.

—— (2007), 'Constructs of nationality: The literary and visual politics of Irish music in the nineteenth century', in Murphy, Michael and Smaczny, Jan (eds), *Irish Musical Studies 9*, Dublin: Four Courts Press, pp. 52–73.

Boyes, Georgina (1993), *The Imagined Village: Culture, Ideology and the English Folk Song Revival*, Manchester: Manchester University Press.

Bracefield, Hilary (1996), 'The Northern Composer: Irish or European?', in Devine, Patrick and White, Harry (eds), *Irish Musical Studies 4: The Maynooth International Musicological Conference 1995 Selected Proceedings: Part One*, Dublin: Four Courts Press, pp. 255–62.

Bradby, Barbara (1994), '"Imagining Ireland" Conference, Dublin, October 30th-31st 1993', *Popular Music*, 13 (1), 107–9.

Bradby, Barbara and Torode, Brian (1984), 'To Whom Do U2 Appeal?', *The Crane Bag*, 8 (2), 73–8.

Bradshaw, Brendan, Hadfield, Andrew and Maley, Willy (eds) (1993), *Representing Ireland: Literature and the Origins of Conflict, 1534–1660*, Cambridge/New York: Cambridge University Press.

Breathnach, Breandán (1977), *Folk Music and Dances of Ireland*, Dublin: Mercier.

Brewer, John D. (2000), *Ethnography*, Milton Keynes, England and Philadelphia, PA: Open University Press.

British Phonographic Industry (2001), *Statistical Handbook 2000*, London: British Phonographic Industry.

Broadcasting Commission of Ireland (2007), 'Press Release: JNLR figures for October 2006–September 2007', 15 November.

Brocken, Michael (1997), 'The British Folk Revival: An analysis of folk/popular dichotomies from a popular music studies perspective', unpublished Ph.D. thesis, Institute of Popular Music, University of Liverpool.

—— (2003), *The British Folk Revival 1944–2002*, Aldershot, England and Burlington, VT: Ashgate.

Buckley, Ann (1990), 'Musical Instruments in Ireland from the Ninth to the Fourteenth Centuries', in Gillen, Gerard and White, Harry (eds), *Irish Musical Studies 1: Musicology in Ireland*, Dublin: Irish Academic Press, pp. 13–57.

Burke, Andrew (1995), 'Employment Prospects in the Irish Popular Music Industry', *Journal of the Statistical and Social Inquiry Society of Ireland*, 27 (2), 93–120.

Cairns, David (1988), *Writing Ireland: Colonialism, nationalism and culture*, Manchester: Manchester University Press.

Campbell, Seán and Smyth, Gerry (2005), *Beautiful Day: Forty Years of Irish Rock*, Cork: Atrium.

Carroll, Jim (2000), 'Work Ethic Pop: Westlife rocks around the clock to keep themselves on top of the pops', *The Irish Times*, Saturday supplement, 18 November, 4.

Carson, Ciaran (1996), *Last Night's Fun*, London: Pimlico.

Central Statistics Office (2007a), *Census 2006: Preliminary Report*, Dublin: The Stationery Office.

—— (2007b), *Census 2006: Volume 5 – Ethnic or Cultural Background*, Dublin: The Stationery Office.

Chambers, Iain (1985), *Urban Rhythms: Pop Music and Popular Culture*, London: Macmillan.

Chapman, Malcolm (1994), 'Thoughts on Celtic Music', in Stokes, Martin (ed.), *Ethnicity, Identity and Music: The Musical Construction of Place*, Oxford and New York: Berg pp. 29–44.

Clampin, Fiona (1995), '"Those Blue Remembered Hills …": National Identity in English Music (1900–1930)', in Cameron, Keith (ed.), *National Identity*, Exeter: Intellect, pp. 64–79.

Clancy, Paula, Drury Martin, Kelly, Anne, Brannick, Teresa and Pratschke, Sheila (1994), *The Public and the Arts: A Survey of Behaviour and Attitudes in Ireland*, Dublin: The Arts Council.

Clancy, Paula and Twomey, Mary (1997), *The Irish Popular Music Industry: An Application of Porter's Cluster Analysis*, Dublin: National Economic and Social Council.

Clayton-Lea, Tony (1999), 'Welcome to Irish pop's sellout of the century', *The Irish Times*, 13 January, 16.

Clayton-Lea, Tony and Taylor, Richie (1992), *Irish Rock: Where it's coming from, where it's going*, Dublin: Gill and Macmillan.

Cloonan, Martin (1997), 'State of the Nation: "Englishness", Pop and Politics in the Mid 1990s', *Popular Music and Society*, 21 (2), 47–70.

—— (1999), 'Popular Music and the Nation-State: Towards a theorisation', *Popular Music*, 18 (2), 193–207.

—— (2007), *Popular Music and the State in the UK: Culture, Trade or Industry?*, Aldershot, England and Burlington, VT: Ashgate.

Cogan, Višnja (2006), *U2 An Irish Phenomenon*, Cork: The Collins Press.

Coleman, Steve (1997), 'Joe Heaney and Style in Sean Nós Singing', in Smith, Therese and Ó Súilleabháin, Mícheál (eds), *Selected Proceedings from BLAS: The Local Accent Conference*, Dublin and Limerick: The Folk Music Society of Ireland/Irish World Music Centre, University of Limerick, pp. 31–52.

Comhaltas Ceoltóirí Éireann (2002), 'New Arts Bill Welcomed', *Treoir*, 34 (2), 2.

—— (2003), 'Fleadh Cheoil', http://www.comhaltas.com/fleadh/index.html (accessed 23 January 2003).

Connell, John and Gibson, Chris (2003), *Sound Tracks: Popular Music, Identity and Place*, London and New York: Routledge.

Connolly, Claire (2003), 'Introduction: Ireland in Theory', in Connolly, Claire (ed.), *Theorizing Ireland*, Basingstoke, England and New York: Palgrave Macmillan, pp. 1–13.

Connor, Walker (1994), 'A Nation is Nation, is a State, is an Ethnic Group, is a ...', in Hutchinson, John and Smith, Anthony (eds), *Nationalism*, Oxford: Oxford University Press, pp. 36–46.

Contemporary Music Centre (1991–2004), *New Music News*.

—— (1998), 'News', *New Music News*, 8 (9), 3–6.

Corcoran, Frank (1982), '"I'm a composer" – "You're a what?"', *The Crane Bag*, 6 (2), 52–4.

Corcoran, Seán (1997), 'Conceptions of Regionalism in Irish Traditional Music', in Smith, Therese and Ó Súilleabháin, Mícheál (eds) (1997), *Selected Proceedings from BLAS: The Local Accent Conference*, Dublin and Limerick: The Folk Music Society of Ireland/Irish World Music Centre, University of Limerick, pp. 25–30.

Corkery, Daniel (1925), *The Hidden Ireland: A Study of Gaelic Munster in the Eighteenth Century*, Dublin: Gill.

Coulter, Colin (2003), 'The end of Irish history? An introduction to the book', in Coulter, Colin and Coleman, Steve (eds), *The End of Irish History? Critical Reflections on the Celtic Tiger*, Manchester and New York: Manchester University Press, pp. 1–33.

Courtney, Kevin (1999), 'Once Irish rock was down – then came the booze', *The Irish Times*, 'Business this Week' supplement (part two), 23 April, 1.

Cowan, Brian (2006), 'The Soul of Ireland is in Good Shape', in Mulholland, Joe (ed.), *The Soul of Ireland: Issues of Society, Culture and Identity*, Dublin: The Liffey Press, pp. 1–9.

Cox, Gareth (1998), 'The music of Gerald Barry as an introduction to contemporary Irish art-music: Twentieth-century music in the new Leaving Certificate syllabus (1999–2001)', in Irwin, Liam (ed.), *Explorations: Centenary Essays*, Limerick: Mary Immaculate College, University of Limerick, pp. 61–72.

Cox, Gareth and Klein, Axel (eds) (2003), *Irish Musical Studies 7: Irish Music in the Twentieth Century*, Dublin: Four Courts.

Cronin, Michael (1996), *Translating Ireland: Translation, Languages, Culture*, Cork: Cork University Press.

Culture Ireland (n.d.), 'Culture Ireland', http://www.cultureireland.gov.ie/.html (accessed 22 January 2007).

Curran, Catherine (1999), 'Changing audiences for traditional Irish music', in Vallely, Fintan, Hamilton, Hammy, Vallely, Eithne and Doherty, Liz (eds), *Crosbhealach an Cheoil – The Crossroads Conference 1996: Tradition and Change in Irish Traditional Music*, Dublin: Whinstone Music, pp. 56–63.

Dasilva, Fabio, Blasi, Anthony and Dees, David (eds) (1984), *The Sociology of Music*, Notre Dame, IN: University of Notre Dame Press.

Davis, Leith (2005), *Music, Postcolonialism and Gender: The Construction of Irish National Identity 1724–1874*, Chicago: University of Notre Dame Press.

Deane, Raymond (1995), 'The Honour of Non-Existence: Classical Composers in Irish Society', in Gillen, Gerard and White, Harry (eds), *Irish Musical Studies 3: Music and Irish Cultural History*, Dublin: Irish Academic Press, pp. 199–211.

—— (1997), 'In Praise of Begrudgery', in Doyle, Niall (ed.), *The Boydell Papers*, Dublin: Music Network, pp. 26–32.

—— (2002), '"It's Just Town!" Review of "Horizons" broadcast on Lyric FM, 11 March 2002', *The Journal of Music in Ireland*, 2 (3), 12–13.

Deane, Seamus (2003), 'Heroic Styles: The Tradition of an Idea', in Connolly, Claire (ed.), *Theorizing Ireland*, Basingstoke, England and New York: Palgrave Macmillan, pp. 14–26.

Denselow, Robin (1989), *When the Music's Over: The Story of Political Pop*, London: Faber & Faber.

Department of Arts, Sport and Tourism (2003), 'Press Release: End of year statement by John O'Donoghue, T.D., Minister for Arts, Sport and Tourism', http://www.arts-sport-tourism.gov.ie/publications/release.asp?ID=429/html (accessed 6 February 2005).

—— (2006), 'Press Release: O' Donoghue announces additional €2.5m to the Arts Council', http://www.arts-sport-tourism.gov.ie/publications/release. asp?ID=1764/html (accessed 29 February 2007).

—— (n.d.), 'Business Expansion Scheme for Music', http://www.arts-sport-tourism. gov.ie/arts/music/business_expansion_scheme.html (accessed 2 March 2008).

Department of Education (1996), *The Leaving Certificate: Music Syllabus*, Dublin: Department of Education.

Diamond, Beverley (ed.) (1994), *Canadian Music: Issues of Hegemony and Identity*, Toronto: Canadian Scholars' Press.

Digman, Steven (2003), 'Looking Back: Steven Digman has a retrospective ramble with Mary Black', *Irish Music*, 9 (1), 16–17.

Dillane, Aileen (2005), 'What's in an "S"?', *The Journal of Music in Ireland*, 5 (4), 25–6.

Doyle, Niall (ed.) (1997), *The Boydell Papers – Essays on Music and Music Policy in Ireland*, Dublin: Music Network.

Doyle, Roddy (1989), *The Commitments*, London: Vintage.

Doyle, Roger (2002), 'Funding for Opera and the Arts Plan', *The Journal of Music in Ireland*, 2 (6), 24–5.

Duffett, Mark (2000), 'Going down like a song: National identity, global commerce and the Great Canadian Party', *Popular Music*, 19 (1), 1–11.

Duffy, Alan (2006), 'Irish bands aim for the big break', http://www.mazers.ie.html (accessed 18 November 2007).

Duffy, Patrick J. (1997), 'Writing Ireland: Literature and Art in the Representation of Irish Place', in Graham, Brian (ed.), *In Search of Ireland: A Cultural Geography*, London and New York: Routledge, pp. 64–83.

Dungan, Michael (1999), 'Money for Music', *New Music News*, 9 (2), 9–12.

—— (2001), 'Interview with Ronan Guilfoyle', *New Music News*, 11 (9), 9–11.

Eagleton, Terry (2000), *The Idea of Culture*, Oxford: Blackwell.

—— (2001), *The Truth about the Irish*, New York: St Martin's Press.

Fagan, G. Honor (2003), 'Globalised Ireland, or, contemporary transformations of national identity', in Coulter, Colin and Coleman, Steve (eds), *The End of Irish History? Critical Reflections on the Celtic Tiger*, Manchester and New York: Manchester University Press, pp. 110–21.

Featherstone, Mike and Lash, Scott (1995), 'Globalization, Modernity and the Spatialization of Social Theory: An Introduction', in Featherstone, Mike, Lash, Scott and Robertson, Roland (eds), *Global Modernities*, London: Sage, pp. 1–24.

Feld, Stephen (1994), 'Communication, Music, and Speech about Music', in Keil, Charles and Feld, Stephen, *Music Grooves*, Chicago and London: University of Chicago Press, pp. 77–95.

Finnegan, Ruth (1989), *The Hidden Musicians: Music-Making in an English Town*, Cambridge: Cambridge University Press.

Flynn, Paul (2008), Personal correspondence, 6 February.

Folkestad, Göran (2002), 'National Identity and Music', in MacDonald, Raymond, Hargreaves, David and Miell, Dorothy (eds), *Musical Identities*, Oxford: Oxford University Press, pp. 151–62.

Forgacs, David (ed.) (1988), *A Gramsci Reader*, London: Lawrence and Wishart.

Foy, Barry (1999), *Field Guide to the Irish Traditional Session: A Guide to Enjoying Irish Traditional Music in its Natural Habitat*, Niwot, CO: Roberts Rinehart Publishers.

Francmanis, John (2003), 'National music to national redeemer: The consolidation of a "folk-song" construct in Edwardian England', *Popular Music*, 21 (1), 1–25.

Frith, Simon (1991), 'Anglo-America and its Discontents', *Cultural Studies*, 5 (3), 263–9.

—— (1996a), 'Music and Identity', in Hall, Stuart and Du Gay, Paul (eds), *Questions of Cultural Identity*, London: Sage, pp. 108–27.

—— (1996b), 'Popular Music Policy and the Articulation of Regional Identities: The Case of Scotland and Ireland', in Rutten, Paul (ed.), *Music in Europe, Part II: Music, Culture and Society in Europe*, Brussels: European Music Office, pp. 98–103.

——(2000), 'The Discourse of World Music', in Born, Georgina and Hesmondhalgh, David (eds), *Western Music and Its Others: Difference, Differentiation and Appropriation in Music*, Berkeley: University of California, pp. 305–22.

Gellner, Ernest (1983), *Nations and Nationalism*, Oxford: Blackwell Publishing.

Gibbons, Luke (1996), *Transformations in Irish Culture*, Cork: Field Day/ Cork University Press.

Gilmore, Bob (2005), 'Donncha Dennehy: Composition as Vandalism', *The Journal of Music in Ireland*, 5 (6), 29–33.

Gilroy, Paul (1993), *The Black Atlantic: Modernity and Double Consciousness*, London and New York: Verso.

Goodbody Economic Consultants (2003), *Report on the Economic Significance of the Irish Popular Music Industry*, Dublin: Music Board of Ireland.

Graham, Brian (ed.) (1997), *In Search of Ireland: A Cultural Geography*, London: Routledge.

Graham, Colin (1999), '"… maybe that's just Blarney": Irish Culture and the Persistence of Authenticity', in Graham, Colin and Kirkland, Richard (eds), *Ireland and Cultural Theory: The Mechanics of Authenticity*, Basingstoke and London: Macmillan, pp. 7–28.

—— (2001), *Deconstructing Ireland*, Edinburgh: Edinburgh University Press.

Graydon, Philip (2003), 'Modernism in Ireland and its cultural context in the music of Frederick May, Brian Boydell and Aloys Fleischmann', in Cox, Gareth and Klein, Axel (eds), *Irish Musical Studies 7: Irish Music in the Twentieth Century Ireland*, Dublin: Four Courts, pp. 56–79.

Green, Lucy (1988), *Music on Deaf Ears: Musical meaning, ideology and education*, Manchester: Manchester University Press.

—— (1997), *Music, Gender, Education*, Cambridge: Cambridge University Press.

—— (1999), 'Ideology', in Horner, Bruce and Swiss, Thomas (eds), *Key Terms in Popular Music and Culture*, Malden, Massachusetts/ Oxford: Blackwell, pp. 5–17.

—— (2001), *How Popular Musicians Learn: A Way Ahead for Music Education*, Aldershot, England and Burlington, VT: Ashgate.

—— (2002), 'From the Western classics to the world: Secondary teachers' changing perceptions of musical styles, 1982 and 1998', *British Journal of Music Education*, 19 (1), 5–30.

Guilbault, Jocelyne (1993), *Zouk: World Music in the West Indies*, Chicago: University of Chicago Press.

Hall, Stuart (1996), 'Introduction: "Who needs identity?"', in Hall, Stuart and Du Gay, Paul (eds), *Questions of Cultural Identity*, London: Sage, pp. 1–17.

Hamilton, Hammy (1999a), 'Session', in Vallely, Fintan (ed.), *The Companion to Irish Traditional Music*, Cork: Cork University Press, pp. 345–6.

—— (1999b), 'Innovation, Conservatism, and the Aesthetics of IrishTraditional Music', in Vallely, Fintan, Hamilton, Hammy, Vallely, Eithne and Doherty, Liz (eds), *Crosbhealach an Cheoil – The Crossroads Conference 1996: Tradition and Change in Irish Traditional Music*, Dublin: Whinstone Music, pp. 82–7.

—— (2001), 'Tradmyth: The Myth of Traditional Music's Popularity', *The Journal of Music in Ireland*, 1 (4), 18–22.

Harker, Dave (1985), *Fakesong: The manufacture of British 'folksong': 1700 to the present day*, Milton Keynes: Oxford University Press.

Harper, Colin and Hodgett, Trevor (2004), *Irish Folk, Trad and Blues: A Secret History*, Cork: The Collins Press.

Hegarty, Neil (2004), *Waking Up in Dublin: A Musical Tour of the Celtic Capital*, London: Sanctuary.

Heneghan, Frank (1995), 'Music in Irish Education', in Gillen, Gerard and White, Harry (eds), *Irish Musical Studies 3: Music and Irish Cultural History*, Dublin: Irish Academic Press, pp. 153–98.

—— (2001), 'The Music Education National Debate', unpublished report, Dublin: Dublin Institute of Technology.

—— (2002), 'The MEND Report: What Next for Irish Music Education?', *The Journal of Music in Ireland*, 2 (6), 19–23.

Henigan, Julie (1999), 'Sean nós technique', in Vallely, Fintan (ed.), *The Companion to Irish Traditional Music*, Cork: Cork University Press, pp. 338–9.

Hesmondhalgh, David (2002), 'Popular Music Audiences and Everyday Life', in Hesmondhalgh, David and Negus, Keith (eds), *Popular Music Studies*, London: Arnold, pp. 117–30.

Hibernian Consulting, Insight Statistical Consulting and Drury, Martin (2006), *The Public and the Arts 2006*, Dublin: The Arts Council.

Hill, Sarah (2007), *'Blerwytirhwng?': The Place of Welsh Pop Music*, Aldershot, England and Burlington, VT: Ashgate.

Hoctor, Michelle (ed.) (1998), *Directory of Musicians in Ireland*, Dublin: Music Network.

Hogan, Eileen (2007), 'Enigmatic Territories: Geographies of Popular Music', Critical Public Geographies Working Paper, University College Cork.

Hot Press (1998), *The Hot Press Yearbook 1998*, Dublin: Hot Press.

—— (2007), *The Hot Press Yearbook 2007*, Dublin: Hot Press.

Hot Press Newsdesk (2002), 'Press Release: Separate but equal?', 4 December.

Hudson, Robert (2007), 'Popular Music, Tradition and Serbian Nationalism', in Biddle, Ian and Knights, Vanessa (eds), *Music, National Identity and the Politics of Location*, Aldershot, England and Burlington, VT: Ashgate, pp. 161–78.

Hunt, Una (2006), 'George Alexander Osborne, a Nineteenth-Century Irish Pianist Composer', unpublished PhD thesis, National University of Ireland Maynooth.

Huss, Fabian (2007), 'Inspiration, influence and stylistic development in the symphonies and concertos of E.J. Moeran', unpublished MA thesis, Mary Immaculate College, University of Limerick.

Hyder, Rehan (2004), *Brimful of Asia: Negotiating Ethnicity on the UK Music Scene*, Aldershot, England and Burlington, VT: Ashgate.

IBEC Music Industry Group (1998), *Raising the Volume: Policies to Expand the Irish Music Industry*, Dublin: Irish Business and Employers Confederation.

—— (n.d.), 'Education and State Support', http://www.mig.ie/business.html (accessed 7 February 2003).

International Federation of the Phonographic Industry (1998), *The Recording Industry in Numbers 1997*, London: IFPI.

—— (1999), *The Recording Industry in Numbers 1998*, London: IFPI.

—— (2000), *The Recording Industry in Numbers 1999*, London: IFPI.

—— (2001), *The Recording Industry in Numbers 2000*, London: IFPI.

—— (2002), *The Recording Industry in Numbers 2001*, London: IFPI.

—— (2003), *The Recording Industry in Numbers 2002*, London: IFPI.

—— (2004), *The Recording Industry in Numbers 2003*, London: IFPI.

—— (2005), *The Recording Industry in Numbers 2004*, London: IFPI.

—— (2006), *The Recording Industry in Numbers 2005*, London: IFPI.

—— (2007a), *The Recording Industry in Numbers 2006*, London: IFPI.

—— (2007b), 'Press Release: IFPI publishes Digital Music Report 2007', IFPI, 17 January.

—— (n.d.), '2006 CD Sales Per Capita – Top Markets', http://www.ifpi.org/content/section_statistics/index.html (accessed 27 January 2008).

Irish Recorded Music Association (2006–08), 'The Irish charts – all there is to know', http://www.irishcharts.ie.html (accessed 15 October 2007).

Irish Traditional Music Archive (n.d.), 'Irish Traditional Music Archive: Databases and catalogues', http://www.itma.ie/English/DatabasesCatalogues.html (accessed 27 September, 2005).

Jameson, Kate (2008), Personal correspondence, 11 February.

Johnson, Sherry (2000), 'Authenticity: Who needs it?', *British Journal of Music Education*, 17 (3), 277–86.

Kearney, Richard (1989), 'The Transitional Crisis of Modern Irish Culture', in The Princess Grace Irish Library (eds), *Irishness in a Changing Society*, Totowa, NJ: Barnes and Noble Books, pp. 78–94.

Keegan, Niall (1996), 'Literacy as a Transmission Tool in Irish Traditional Music', in Devine, Patrick and White, Harry (eds), *Irish Musical Studies 4: The Maynooth International Musicological Conference 1995 Selected Proceedings: Part One*, Dublin: Four Courts Press, pp. 335–42.

—— (1997), 'The Verbal Context of Style in Traditional Irish Music', in Smith, Therese and Ó Súilleabháin, Mícheál (eds), *Selected Proceedings from BLAS: The Local Accent Conference*, Dublin and Limerick: The Folk Music Society of Ireland/Irish World Music Centre, University of Limerick, pp. 116–22.

Kelly, Mary and O'Connor, Barbara (eds) (1997), 'Introduction', in *Media Audiences in Ireland: Power and Cultural Identity*, Dublin: University College Dublin Press, pp. 1–16.

Kelly, Olivia (2002), 'Minister agrees to change section of bill affecting traditional arts', *The Irish Times*, 18 December, 7.

Keogan, Gillian (ed.) (2000), *Irish Music Handbook (2nd edition)*, Dublin: Music Network.

Keohane, Kieran (1997), 'Traditionalism and Homelessness in Contemporary Irish Music', in Mac Laughlin, Jim (ed.), *Location and Dislocation in Contemporary Irish Society: Emigration and Irish Identities*, Cork: Cork University Press, pp. 274–303.

Kiberd, Declan (1996), *Inventing Ireland: The Literature of the Modern Nation*, London: Vintage.

Kirby, Peadar, Gibbons, Luke and Cronin, Michael (eds) (2002), *Reinventing Ireland: Culture, Society and the Global Economy*, London: Pluto Press.

Kirschner, Tony (1998), 'Studying Rock: Towards a Materialist Ethnography', in Swiss, Thomas, Sloop, John M. and Herman, Andrew (eds), *Mapping the Beat: Popular Music and Contemporary Theory*, Malden, MA/Oxford, England: Blackwell, pp. 247–68.

Klamer, Arjo, Petrova, Lyudmilla and Mignosa, Anna (2006), *Financing the Arts and Culture in the European Union*, Brussels: European Parliament.

Klein, Axel (1996), 'Irish Composers and Foreign Education: A Study of Influences', in Devine, Patrick and White, Harry (eds), *Irish Musical Studies 4: The Maynooth International Musicological Conference 1995 Selected Proceedings: Part One*, Dublin: Four Courts Press, pp. 271–84.

—— (1997), '"An old eminence among musical nations"': Nationalism and the Case for a Musical History in Ireland', in Mäkelä, Tomi (ed.), *Music and Nationalism in 20th-century Great Britain and Finland*, Hamburg: Von Bockel Verlag, pp. 233–43.

—— (2001), *Irish Classical Recordings: A Discography of Irish Art Music*, Westport: CT: Greenwood Press.

—— (2003), 'Roots and directions in twentieth-century Irish art music', in Cox, Gareth and Klein, Axel (eds), *Irish Musical Studies 7: Irish Music in the Twentieth Century*, Dublin: Four Courts, pp. 168–82.

Kneafsey, Moya (2003), '"If it wasn't for the tourists we wouldn't have an audience": The case of tourism and traditional music in North Mayo', in Cronin, Michael and O'Connor, Barbara (eds), *Irish Tourism: Image, Culture and Identity*, Clevedon, England and Buffalo, NY: Channel View Publications, pp. 21–41.

KPMG Stokes Kennedy Crowley (1994), *A Report on the Irish Popular Music Industry*, Dublin: Temple Bar Properties.

Kruse, Holly (1998), 'Fields of Practice: Musical Production, Public Policy, and the Market', in Swiss, Thomas, Sloop, John M. and Herman, Andrew (eds), *Mapping the Beat: Popular Music and Contemporary Theory*, Malden, MA/ Oxford, England: Blackwell, pp. 187–201.

Kuhling, Carmen and Keohane, Kieran (2002), 'Celebrity. Case studies in the localisation of the global', in Corcoran, Mary and Peillon, Michael (eds), *Ireland Unbound: A Turn of the Century Chronicle*, Dublin: Institute of Public Administration, pp. 103–18.

Kuhling, Carmen, Donncha, Kavanagh and Keohane, Kieran (2006), 'The Creative Scene of Riverdance: Artrepreneurship and the Celtic Tiger', *Taighde: The Research Journal of the Faculty of Commerce*, 1 (2), University College Cork, 56–76.

Ladd, Michael (2002), 'The Arab Influence on Irish Traditional Music', *The Journal of Music in Ireland*, 2 (6), 16–18.

Laffey, Seán (2001), 'Interview with Dervish', *Irish Music*, 7 (3), 14–15.

Laing, Dave (1992), 'Sadeness, scorpions and single markets: National and transnational trends in European popular music', *Popular Music*, 11 (2), 127–41.

—— (1996), 'The Economic Importance of Music in the European Union', in *Music in Europe*, Brussels: European Music Office, pp. 4–60.

Lanier, S.C. (1999), '"It is new-strung and shan't be heard": Nationalism and memory in the Irish harp tradition', *British Journal of Ethnomusicology*, 8, 1–26.

Leonard, Hugh (1989), 'The Unimportance of Being Irish', in The Princess Grace Irish Library (eds), *Irishness in a Changing Society*, Totowa, NJ: Barnes and Noble Books, pp. 18–29.

Long, Siobhán (2001), 'Reeling in Rio', *Hot Press*, 25 (2), 58–61.

Loyal, Steve (2003), 'Welcome to the Celtic Tiger: Racism, immigration and the state', in Coulter, Colin and Coleman, Steve (eds), *The End of Irish history? Critical Reflections on the Celtic Tiger*, Manchester and New York: Manchester University Press, pp. 74–94.

Mac Aoidh, Caoimhín (1999), 'The Critical Role of Education in the Development of Traditional Music in the Republic of Ireland', in Vallely, Fintan, Hamilton, Hammy, Vallely, Eithne and Doherty, Liz (eds), *Crosbhealach an Cheoil –*

The Crossroads Conference 1996: Tradition and Change in Irish Traditional Music, Dublin: Whinstone Music, pp. 107–11.

—— (2006), 'Traditional Music – A Reflection of Who We Are', in Mulholland, Joe (ed.), *The Soul of Ireland: Issues of Society, Culture and Identity*, Dublin: The Liffey Press, pp. 134–40.

McCann, Anthony (2001), 'All That is Not Given is Lost: Irish Traditional Music, Copyright and Common Property, *Ethnomusicology*, 45 (1), 89–106.

McCann, May (1995), 'Music and Politics in Ireland: The Specificity of the Folk Revival in Belfast', *British Journal of Ethnomusicology*, 4 (special issue), 51–75.

MacCarthy, Jimmy (2001), *No Frontiers: The Jimmy MacCarthy Songbook*, Dublin: Waltons.

McCarthy, Marie (1995), 'The Transmission of Music in the Formation of National Identity in Early Twentieth-Century Ireland', in Devine, Patrick and White, Harry (eds), *Irish Musical Studies 5: The Maynooth International Musicological Conference 1995 Selected Proceedings: Part Two*, Dublin: Four Courts Press, pp. 146–59.

—— (1997), 'Irish Music Education and Irish Identity: A concept revisited', *Oideas*, 45, 5–22.

—— (1998), 'Music Education in the Emergent Nation State', in Pine, Richard (ed.), *Music in Ireland 1848–1998*, Cork: Mercier, pp. 65–75.

—— (1999), *Passing It On: The Transmission of Music in Irish Culture*, Cork: Cork University Press.

—— (2004), 'Changing Cultural Landscapes: The Co-existence of Musical Genres in Irish Culture and Education', *Irish Studies Review*, 12 (1), 51–62.

McConnell, Daniel (2006), 'U2 move their rock empire out of Ireland', *The Irish Independent*, 6 August, 1–2.

McCrone, David (1998), *The Sociology of Nationalism*, London and New York: Routledge.

McGlynn, Mary (2006), 'Garth Brooks in Ireland, or, Play that Country Music, Whiteboys', in Negra, Diane (ed.), *The Irishness in Us: Irishness, Performativity and Popular Culture*, Durham, NC and London: Duke University Press, pp. 196–219.

McGrail, Steve (2002), '"It's getting bland, and Ireland was never bland": An Interview with Singer/Songwriter Jimmy Crowley', *The Journal of Music in Ireland*, 2 (1), 26–7.

McGurk, Tom (1995), 'Celebrating Irish Music or the Onset of Traditional "Musac"', *Treoir*, 27 (2), 25–6.

Mac Laughlin, Jim (1997a), 'The Music of Daniel O'Donnell – An Oasis of Innocence in a Cruel and Wicked World', in Crowley, Ethel and Mac Laughlin, Jim (eds), *Under the belly of the tiger: Class, race, identity and culture in the global Ireland*, Dublin: Irish Reporter Publications, pp. 139–48.

—— (1997b), 'Ireland in the Global Economy: An End to a Distinct Nation?', in Crowley, Ethel and Mac Laughlin, Jim (eds), *Under the belly of the tiger:*

Class, race, identity and culture in the global Ireland, Dublin: Irish Reporter Publications, pp. 1–20.

McLaughlin, Noel (1999), 'Pop and Periphery: Nationality, Culture and Irish Popular Music', unpublished DPhil thesis, University of Ulster.

—— (2004), 'Bodies swayed to music: Dance culture in Ireland', *Irish Studies Review*, 12 (1), 77–85.

McLaughlin, Noel and McLoone, Martin (2000), 'Hybridity and national musics: The case of Irish rock music', *Popular Music*, 19 (2), 181–99.

McLoone, Martin (ed.) (1991), *Culture, Identity and Broadcasting in Ireland: Local Issues, Global Perspectives*, Belfast: Institute of Irish Studies, Queen's University.

—— (2004), 'Punk music in Northern Ireland: The political power of "what might have been"', *Irish Studies Review*, 12 (1), 29–38.

McLoughlin, Dermot (2003), Personal correspondence, 10 March.

Magaldi, Cristina (1999), 'Adopting imports: New images and alliances in Brazilian popular music of the 1990s', *Popular Music*, 18 (3), 309–29.

Magowan, Fiona (2005), 'Drums of Suffering in Belfast's European Capital of Culture Bid: John Blacking on Music, Conflict and Healing', in Rogers, Victoria and Symons, David (eds), *The Legacy of John Blacking: Essays on Music, Culture and Society*, Crawley, WA: University of Western Australia Press, pp. 56–78.

Maley, Willy (1999), 'Nationalism and revisionism: Ambiviolences and dissensus', in Brewster, Scott, Grossman, Virginia, Becket, Fiona and Alderson, David (eds), *Ireland in Proximity: History, Gender, Space*, London and New York: Routledge, pp.12–27.

Malm, Krister and Wallis, Roger (1992), *Media Policy and Music Activity*, London and New York: Routledge.

Manuel, Peter (1988), *Popular Musics of the Non-Western World*, Oxford and New York: Oxford University Press.

—— (1998), 'Chutney and Indo-Trinidadian cultural identity', *Popular Music*, 17 (1), 21–43.

Martin, Peter (1995), *Sounds and Society: Themes in the Sociology of Music*, Manchester: Manchester University Press.

Mathieson, Kenny (2001), 'Introduction', in Mathieson, Kenny (ed.), *Celtic Music*, London: Outline Press, pp. 4–9.

Meek, Bill (1987), *Paddy Moloney and the Chieftains*, Dublin: Gill and Macmillan.

Middleton, Richard (1990), *Studying Popular Music*, Milton Keynes: Open University Press.

—— (ed.) (2000), *Reading Pop: Approaches to Textual Analysis in Popular Music*, Oxford: Oxford University Press.

—— (2007), 'Afterword', in Biddle, Ian and Knights, Vanessa (eds), *Music, National Identity and the Politics of Location*, Aldershot, England and Burlington, VT: Ashgate, pp. 191–203.

Miller, David (1995), *On Nationality*, Oxford: Clarendon Press.

Moore, Allan (2002), 'Authenticity as authentication', *Popular Music*, 21 (2), 209–33.

Moylan, Terry (2001), 'Humpty Dumpty and Acoustic Bicycles', *The Journal of Music in Ireland*, 1 (4), 8–13.

Mulholland, Joe (ed.) (2006), *The Soul of Ireland: Issues of Society, Culture and Identity*, Dublin: The Liffey Press.

Murphy, Peter (1998), 'King of the Independents', *Hot Press*, 22 (15), 32–3.

Music Board of Ireland (2003), *A Strategic Plan for the Development of the Music Industry in Ireland*, Dublin: Music Board of Ireland.

Music Industry Group (1995), *Striking the Right Note*, Dublin: Irish Business and Employers Confederation.

Music Network (2003), *A National System of Local Music Education Services: A Report of a Feasibility Study*, Dublin: Music Network.

Nederveen Pieterse, Jan (1995), 'Globalization as Hybridization', in Featherstone, Mike, Lash, Scott and Robertson, Roland (eds), *Global Modernities*, London: Sage, pp. 45–68.

Negra, Diane (2004), 'Irishness, Innocence and American Identity: Politics Before and After 11 September', in Barton, Ruth and O'Brien, Harvey (eds), *Keeping it Real: Irish Film and Television*, London: Wallflower Press, pp. 54–68.

—— (ed.) (2006), *The Irishness in Us: Irishness, Performativity and Popular Culture*, Durham, NC and London: Duke University Press.

Negus, Keith (1996), *Popular Music in Theory: An Introduction*, Cambridge/ Oxford: Polity Press/Blackwell.

—— (1999), *Music Genres and Corporate Cultures*, London and New York: Routledge.

Ní Chathasaigh, Máire (1999), 'Modes', in Vallely, Fintan (ed.), *The Companion to Irish Traditional Music*, Cork: Cork University Press, pp. 243–4.

Ní Mhaolcatha, Méav (n.d.), 'Interview with Méav', www.celticwoman.com/index.asp.html (accessed 14 August 2006).

O'Brien, Harvey Thomas (2004), *The Real Ireland: The Evolution of Ireland in Documentary Film*, Manchester: Manchester University Press.

O'Brien Moran, Jimmy (2007), 'Irish folk music collectors of the early nineteenth century: Pioneer musicologists', in Murphy, Michael and Smaczny, Jan (eds), *Irish Musical Studies 9*, Dublin: Four Courts Press, pp. 94–113.

Ó Canainn, Tomás (1978), *Traditional Music in Ireland*, London: Routledge and Kegan Paul.

—— (2006), 'The Magic of Traditional Music', in Mulholland, Joe (ed.), *The Soul of Ireland: Issues of Society, Culture and Identity*, Dublin: The Liffey Press, pp. 141–7.

Ó Cinnéide, Barra (1999), 'The *Riverdance* Phenomenon: Crosbhealach an Damhsa', in Vallely, Fintan, Hamilton, Hammy, Vallely, Eithne and Doherty, Liz (eds), *Crosbhealach an Cheoil – The Crossroads Conference 1996: Tradition and Change in Irish Traditional Music*, Dublin: Whinstone Music, pp. 148–55.

—— (2002), *Riverdance: The Phenomenon*, Dublin: Blackhall Publishing.

O'Connell, Anne (2001), 'Press Release: Public Call for Submissions to the Music Board of Ireland', Dublin: Music Board of Ireland.

O'Connor, Barbara (1998), 'Riverdance', in Peillon, Michael and Slater, Eamonn (eds), *Encounters with Modern Ireland: A Sociological Chronicle, 1995–1996*, Dublin: Institute of Public Administration, pp. 51–60.

—— (2003), '"Come and daunce with me in Irlande": Dance and Globalisation', in Cronin, Michael and O'Connor, Barbara (eds), *Irish Tourism: Image, Culture and Identity*, Clevedon, England and Buffalo, NY: Channel View Publications, pp. 122–38.

O'Connor, Nuala (1991), *Bringing it all Back Home: The Influence of Irish Music*, London: BBC Books.

—— (1994), 'Irish Soul', in Broughton, Simon (ed.), *World Music: The Rough Guide*, London: Rough Guides Ltd., pp. 5–15.

—— (1999), 'Ireland: Dancing at the virtual crossroads', in Broughton, Simon and Ellingham, Mark (eds), *World Music: The Rough Guide, Volume 1*, London: Rough Guides Ltd., pp. 170–88.

Office of the Attorney General (1969), 'Exemption of certain earnings of writers, composers and artists', *Irish Statute Book, Finance Act 1*, No. 21 (2).

—— (1998), *Irish Statute Book, Education Act 1998*, No. 51.

—— (2003), *Irish Statute Book, Arts Act 2003*, No. 24.

—— (2006), *Irish Statute Book, Finance Act 2006*, No. 6.

O'Flynn, John (2005a), 'Irish Diaspora', in Shepherd, John, Horne, David and Laing, Dave (eds), *Continuum Encyclopedia of Popular Music of the World, Volume Seven: Locations*, New York and London: Continuum, pp. 218–20.

—— (2005b), 'Ireland', in Shepherd, John, Horne, David and Laing, Dave (eds), *Continuum Encyclopedia of Popular Music of the World, Volume Seven: Locations*, New York and London: Continuum, pp. 205–13.

—— (2006a), 'Vernacular music-making and education', *International Journal of Music Education*, 24 (2), 140–47.

—— (2006b), 'Interpreting Celtic Music'. Paper read at IASPM UK and Ireland Biennial Conference, University of Birmingham, 2 September.

—— (2007), 'National Identity and Music in Transition: Issues of Authenticity in a Global Setting', in Biddle, Ian and Knights, Vanessa (eds), *Music, National Identity and the Politics of Location*, Aldershot, England and Burlington, VT: Ashgate, pp. 19–38.

Ó Giolláin, Diarmuid, (1997), 'The Stagnant Pool and the Stream: New and Old Symbols of Irish Identity', in Crowley, Ethel and Mac Laughlin, Jim (eds), *Under the belly of the tiger: Class, race, identity and culture in the global Ireland*, Dublin: Irish Reporter Publications, pp. 35–42.

Ó hAllmhuráin, Gearóid (1998), *A Pocket History of Irish Traditional Music*, Dublin: The O'Brien Press.

O'Kelly, Eve (1995), 'Finding Our Voice: Music in Ireland Today', *Brio*, 32 (2), 94–102.

Ó Laoire, Lillis (2005), 'Music', in Cleary, Joe and Connolly, Claire (eds), *The Cambridge Companion to Modern Irish Culture*, Cambridge: Cambridge University Press, pp. 267–84.

O'Leary, Jane (1996), 'Contemporary Music in Ireland: Developments in the Past Twenty Years', in Devine, Patrick and White, Harry (eds), *Irish Musical Studies 4: The Maynooth International Musicological Conference 1995 Selected Proceedings: Part One*, Dublin: Four Courts Press, pp. 285–95.

Ó Murchú, Labhrás (1987), *An Ród Seo Romhainn – A Future for Irish Traditional Music*, Cork: The Irish Traditional Music Society/University College Cork.

Onkey, Lauren (2006), 'Ray Charles on Hyndford Street: Van Morrison's Caledonian Soul', in Negra, Diane (ed.), *The Irishness in Us: Irishness, Performativity and Popular Culture*, Durham, NC and London: Duke University Press, pp. 161–95.

Ó Riada, Seán (1982), *Our Musical Heritage*, Dublin: The Dolmen Press.

Ó Seaghda, Barra (1999), 'Crash Course', *Graph: Irish Cultural Review*, 3 (3), 29–32.

O'Shea, Helen (2006–07), 'Getting to the Heart of the Music: Idealizing Music Community and Irish Traditional Music Sessions', *Journal of the Society for Musicology in Ireland*, 2, 1–18, http://www.music.ucc.ie/jsmi/index.php/jsmi/issue/view/4.html (accessed 11 November 2007).

Ó Snodaigh (2001), 'Nua traditional/Ceol Nua Dúchasach, *The Journal of Music in Ireland*, 1 (3), 10–12.

Ó Súilleabháin, Mícheál (1982a), 'Irish Music Defined', in *The Crane Bag Book of Irish Studies*, Dublin: The Blackwater Press, pp. 915–9.

—— (1982b), 'The Art of Listening', *The Crane Bag*, 6 (2), 59–61.

—— (1985), 'Out of Tune with Reality: Music and the School in Ireland', *Irish Educational Studies*, 5 (1), 44–57.

—— (1994), '"All our central fire": Music, mediation and the Irish psyche', *Irish Journal of Psychology*, 15, (2/3), 331–53.

—— (1998), '"Around the House and Mind the Cosmos": Music, Dance and Identity in Contemporary Ireland', in Pine, Richard (ed.), *Music in Ireland 1848–1998*, Cork: Mercier, pp. 76–86.

—— (1999), 'Crossroads or twin track? Innovation and change in Irish traditional music', in Vallely, Fintan, Hamilton, Hammy, Vallely, Eithne and Doherty, Liz (eds), *Crosbhealach an Cheoil – The Crossroads Conference 1996: Tradition and Change in Irish Traditional Music*, Dublin: Whinstone Music, pp. 175–99.

Pickering, Michael and Green, Tony (eds) (1987), *Everyday Culture: Popular Song and the Vernacular Milieu*, Milton Keynes: Open University Press.

Pine, Richard (ed.) (1998), *Music in Ireland 1848–1998*, Cork: Mercier.

—— (2002), 'In Dreams Begin Responsibility', *The Journal of Music in Ireland*, 2 (2), 5–9.

—— (2005), *Music and Broadcasting in Ireland since 1926*, Dublin: Four Courts Press.

Potter, John (1998), *Vocal Authority: Singing Style and Ideology*, Cambridge: Cambridge University Press.

Power, Vincent (2000 [1990]), *Send 'Em Home Sweatin': The Showband Story*, Cork: Mercier Press, revised edition.

Prendergast, Mark (1987), *Irish Rock: Roots, Personalities, Directions*, Dublin: The O'Brien Press.

Quinn, Bernadette (1996), 'The sounds of tourism: Exploring music as a tourist resource with particular reference to music festivals', in Robinson, Mike, Evans, Nigel and Callaghan, Paul (eds), *Tourism and Culture, Towards the 21st Century*, Sunderland: Centre for Travel and Tourism and Business Education Publishers, pp. 383–96.

—— (2003), 'Shaping tourism places: Agency and interconnection in festival settings', in Cronin, Michael and O'Connor, Barbara (eds), *Irish Tourism: Image, Culture and Identity*, Clevedon, England and Buffalo, NY: Channel View Publications, pp. 61–80.

Quinn, Bob (1986), *Atlantean: Ireland's North African and Maritime Heritage*, London: Quartet Books.

Quinn, Toner (2008), 'Martin Hayes and the Tradition', *The Journal of Music in Ireland*, 8 (2), 20–24.

Raykoff, Ivan and Tobin, Robert Deam (eds) (2007), *A Song for Europe: Popular Music and Politics in the Eurovision Song Contest*, Aldershot, England and Burlington, VT: Ashgate.

Regev, Motti (1992), 'Israeli rock, or a study in the politics of "local authenticity"', *Popular Music*, 11 (1), 1–13.

—— (1996), 'Musica mizrakhit, Israeli rock and national culture in Israel', *Popular Music*, 15 (3), 275–84.

Reiss, Scott (2003), 'Tradition and Imaginary', in Stokes, Martin and Bohlman, Philip V. (eds), *Celtic Modern: Music at the Global Fringe*, Lanham, MD and Oxford, England: The Scarecrow Press, pp. 145–70.

Richards, Shaun (1999), 'Foreword', in Brewster, Scott, Grossman, Virginia, Becket, Fiona and Alderson, David (eds), *Ireland in Proximity: History, Gender, Space*, London and New York: Routledge, xi–xvi.

Rolston, Bill (1999), 'Music and Politics in Ireland: The Case of Loyalism', in J. Harrington and E. Mitchell (eds), *Politics and Performance in Northern Ireland*, American Conference for Irish Studies/University of Massachusetts Press, pp. 29–56.

—— (2001), '"This is not a Rebel Song": The Irish Conflict and Popular Music', *Race and Class*, 42 (3), 49–67.

Román-Velázquez, Patria (1999), 'The embodiment of salsa: Musicians, instruments and the performance of a Latin style and identity', *Popular Music*, 18 (1), 115–31.

Ryan, Joseph (1995), 'Nationalism and Irish Music', in Gillen, Gerard and White, Harry (eds), *Irish Musical Studies 3: Music and Irish Cultural History*, Dublin: Irish Academic Press, pp. 101–15.

—— (2001), 'The Tone of Defiance', in White, Harry and Murphy, Michael (eds), *Musical Constructions of Nationalism: Essays on the History and Ideology of European Musical Culture 1800–1945*, Cork University Press, pp. 197–211.

Sanjek, David (1999), 'Institutions', in Horner, Bruce and Swiss, Thomas (eds), *Key Terms in Popular Music and Culture*, Malden, MA/Oxford: Blackwell, pp. 46–56.

Schiller, Rina (1999), 'Gender and traditional Irish music', in Vallely, Fintan, Hamilton, Hammy, Vallely, Eithne and Doherty, Liz (eds), *Crosbhealach an Cheoil – The Crossroads Conference 1996: Tradition and Change in Irish Traditional Music*, Dublin: Whinstone Music, pp. 200–05.

Self, Geoffrey (1986), *The Music of E.J. Moeran*, London: Toccata.

Shepherd, John and Giles-Davis, Jennifer (2000), 'On the Negotiation of Meaning', in Scott, Derek (ed.), *Music, Culture and Society: A Reader*, Oxford: Oxford University Press, pp. 218–20.

Shields, Hugh and Gershen, Paulette (2000), 'Ireland', in Rice, Timothy, Porter, James and Goertzen, Chris (eds), *The Garland Encyclopedia of World Music, Volume 8: Europe*, New York and London: Garland Publishing, Inc., pp. 378–97.

Shuker, Roy and Pickering, Michael (1994), 'Kiwi rock: Popular music and cultural identity in New Zealand', *Popular Music*, 13 (3), 261–78.

Simpson Xavier Horwath Consulting (1994), *A Strategic Vision for the Irish Music Industry*, Dublin: Simpson Xavier Horwath Consulting.

Skinner Sawyers, June (2000), *The Complete Guide to Celtic Music*, London: Aurum Press.

Slater, Eamonn (1998), 'Becoming an Irish *flâneur*', in Peillon, Michael and Slater, Eamonn (eds), *Encounters with Modern Ireland: A Sociological Chronicle, 1995–1996*, Dublin: Institute of Public Administration, pp. 1–6.

Slobin, Mark (1993), *Subcultural Sounds: Micromusics of the West*, Hanover, NH: University Press of New England for Wesleyan University Press.

—— (ed.) (1996), *Returning Culture: Musical Changes in Central and Eastern Europe*, Durham, NC: Duke University Press.

Smaczny, Jan (2007), 'Musical national traditions in Ireland and the Czech lands in the nineteenth century', in Murphy, Michael and Smaczny, Jan (eds), *Irish Musical Studies 9*, Dublin: Four Courts Press, pp. 278–92.

Small, Christopher (1987), *Music of the Common Tongue*, London: John Calder.

Smith, Anthony D. (1991), *National Identity*, Harmondsworth: Penguin.

Smith, Christopher J. (2003), 'The Celtic Guitar: Crossing Cultural Boundaries in the Twentieth Century', in Coelho, Victor (ed.), *The Cambridge Companion to the Guitar*, Cambridge, England: Cambridge University Press, pp. 33–43.

Smith, Therese (2001), 'The Study of Oral Traditions in Music', *Irish Folk Music Studies/Éigse Cheol Tíre*, 5 & 6, 17–28.

Smyth, Gerry (1992), 'Who's the greenest of them all? Irishness and popular music', *Irish Studies Review*, 2 (3), 3–5.

—— (2002), '"The Same Sound but with a Different Meaning": Music, Repetition, and Identity in Bernard Mac Laverty's "Grace Notes"', *Éire – Ireland: Journal of Irish Studies*, 37 (3/4), 5–24.

—— (2004a), 'Introduction: The Isle is full of noises: Music in contemporary Ireland', *Irish Studies Review*, 12 (1), 3–10.

—— (2004b), 'Ireland unplugged: The roots of Irish folk/trad. Con (Fusion)', *Irish Studies Review*, 12 (1), 87–97.

—— (2005), *Noisy Island: A Short History of Irish Popular Music*, Cork: Cork University Press.

—— (2007), 'Listening to the Future: Music and Irish Studies', in Harte, Liam and Whelan, Yvonne (eds), *Ireland Beyond Boundaries: Mapping Irish Studies in the Twenty-first Century*, London: Pluto Press, pp. 198–214.

State Examinations Commission (2003), *Leaving Certificate Examination 2003, Music: Chief Examiners' Reports*, Athlone, Ireland: State Examinations Commission.

Stefani, Gino (1987), 'A theory of musical competence', *Semiotica*, 66 (1–3), 7–22.

Stokes, Martin (1994), 'Introduction: Ethnicity, Identity and Music', in Stokes, Martin (ed.), *Ethnicity, Identity and Music: The Musical Construction of Place*, Oxford and New York: Berg, pp. 1–28.

Stokes, Martin and Bohlman, Philip V. (2003), 'Introduction', in Stokes, Martin and Bohlman, Philip V., *Celtic Modern: Music at the Global Fringe*, Lanham, MD and Oxford, England: The Scarecrow Press, pp. 1–26.

Stokes, Niall (2000), 'Introduction', in *The Hot Press Yearbook 2000*, Dublin: Hot Press, p. 5.

—— (2001), 'One nation under a groove', *Hot Press*, 25 (23), 47.

—— (2003), 'Introduction', in *The Hot Press Yearbook 2003*, Dublin: Hot Press, p. v.

Strachan, Rob and Leonard, Marion (2004), 'A Musical Nation: Protection, Investment and Branding in the Irish Music Industry', *Irish Studies Review*, 12 (1), 39–49.

Sullivan, Caroline (2001), 'Established stars are making too much damn money', *Guardian Unlimited*, http://www.guardian.co.uk/Archive Article/0,4273, 4127337,00.html (accessed 23 January 2002).

Swan, Alan (2003), *From the Cradle to the Stage: Irish Music Greats, A Chronicle of their Early Years*, Dublin: Poolbeg Press.

Swanwick, Keith (1999), *Teaching Music Musically*, London: Routledge.

Symon, Peter (1997), 'Music and national identity in Scotland: A study of Jock Tamson's Bairns', *Popular Music*, 16 (2), 203–16.

Tansey, Séamus (1999), 'Irish Traditional Music – the melody of Ireland's soul; its evolution from the environment, land and people', in Vallely, Fintan, Hamilton, Hammy, Vallely, Eithne and Doherty, Liz (eds), *Crosbhealach an Cheoil – The Crossroads Conference 1996: Tradition and Change in Irish Traditional Music*, Dublin: Whinstone Music, pp. 211–13.

Taylor, Cliff (2003), 'Ireland ranked as the most globalised of 62 states due to exports', *The Irish Times*, 8 January, 8.

Taylor, Timothy (1997), *Global Pop: World music, World markets*, London and New York: Routledge.

The International Arts Bureau (2000), *A Comparative Study of Levels of Arts Expenditure in Selected Countries and Regions*, Dublin: The Arts Council.

The Journal of Music in Ireland (n.d.), 'The Journal of Music in Ireland, Ireland's bi-monthly music magazine', http://www.thejmi.com/html (accessed 10 November 2007).

The Northern Ireland Music Industry Commission (n.d.), 'Welcome to NI music', http://www.nimusic.com/html (accessed 4 December 2007).

Tovey, Hilary and Share, Perry (2000), *A Sociology of Ireland*, Dublin: Gill and Macmillan.

Townshend, Charles (1999), *Ireland: The 20th Century*, London: Arnold.

Uí Ógáin, Ríonach (1999), '"Camden Town go Ros a Mhíl" – Athrú ar ghnéithe de thraidisiún amhránaíochta Chonamara' ['"Camden Town to Ros a Mhíl" – changes in the Conamara singing tradition'], in Vallely, Fintan, Hamilton, Hammy, Vallely, Eithne and Doherty, Liz (eds), *Crosbhealach an Cheoil – The Crossroads Conference 1996: Tradition and Change in Irish Traditional Music*, Dublin: Whinstone Music, pp. 226–33.

Vallely, Fintan (1997), 'The migrant, the tourist, the voyeur, the leprechaun …', in Smith, Therese and Ó Súilleabháin, Mícheál (eds), *Selected Proceedings from BLAS: The Local Accent Conference*, Dublin and Limerick: The Folk Music Society of Ireland/Irish World Music Centre, University of Limerick, pp. 107–15.

—— (1999a), 'Céilí bands', in Vallely, Fintan (ed.), *The Companion to Irish Traditional Music*, Cork: Cork University Press, pp. 60–61.

—— (1999b), 'Comhaltas Ceoltóirí Éireann (CCÉ)', in Vallely, Fintan (ed.), *The Companion to Irish Traditional Music*, Cork: Cork University Press, pp. 77–81.

—— (2002), 'Knocking on the castle door – a place for traditional music in third level education?', *The Journal of Music in Ireland*, 2 (5), 12–15.

—— (2003), 'The Apollos of Shamrockery: Traditional Musics in the Modern Age', in Stokes, Martin and Bohlman, Philip V. (eds), *Celtic Modern: Music at the Global Fringe*, Lanham, MD and Oxford, England: The Scarecrow Press, pp. 201–8.

—— (2004a), 'Singing the Boundaries: Music and Identity Politics in Northern Ireland', in Kockel, Ullrich and Nic Craith, Máiréad (eds), *Communicating Cultures*, Münster: Lit Verlag, pp. 129–48.

—— (2004b), *From fifth column to pillar of society: Observations on the political implications of popular revival and education in Irish traditional music in modern Ireland*, Cork: The Traditional Music Archive/ University College Cork.

—— (2006), *Protestant Rejection of Traditional Music in Northern Ireland: Jigging at the Crossroads*, Dublin: Irish Academic Press.

Van De Port, Mattijs (1999), 'The articulation of soul: Gypsy musicians and the Serbian Other', *Popular Music*, 18 (3), 291–308.

Veblen, Kari (1994), 'The Teacher's Role in Transmission of Irish Traditional Music', *International Journal of Music Education*, 24 (1), 21–30.

Vignoles, Julian (1984), 'What is Irish Popular Music?', *The Crane Bag*, 8 (2), 70–72.

Wade, Peter (1998), 'Music, blackness and national identity: Three moments in Colombian history', *Popular Music*, 17, (1), 1–19.

Waldron, Janice (2006), 'Learning, Teaching and Transmission in the Lives of Two Irish Musicians: An Ethnographic Case Study', *International Journal of Community Music*, 4, http://www.intljcm.com/articles/Volume%204/ Waldron%20Files/Waldron.pdf.html (accessed 2 January 2007).

Wallace, Arminta (2002), 'Considering the art of the matter', *The Irish Times*, 29 October, 12.

Walser, Robert (1993), *Running with the Devil: Power, Gender and Madness in Heavy Metal Music*, Hanover, New England: Wesleyan University Press.

Walsh, Michael (1996), 'Emerald Magic', *Time*, 147 (11), 78–80.

Waters, John (1994), *Race of Angels: The Genesis of U2*, London: Fourth Estate Limited.

White, Harry (1995), 'Music and the Irish Literary Imagination', in Gillen, Gerard and White, Harry (eds), *Irish Musical Studies 3: Music and Irish Cultural History*, Dublin: Irish Academic Press, pp. 212–27.

—— (1998a), The Keeper's Recital: Music and Cultural History in Ireland, 1770–1970, Cork: Field Day/Cork University Press.

—— (1998b), 'Music, Politics and the Irish Imagination', in Pine, Richard (ed.), *Music in Ireland 1848–1998*, Cork: Mercier, pp. 27–36.

—— (1998c), '"A book of manners in the wilderness"': The Model of University Music Education and its Relevance as Enabler in General Music Education in Ireland', *College Music Symposium*, 38, 47–63.

—— (2001), 'Nationalism, Colonialism and the Cultural Stasis of Music in Ireland', in White, Harry and Murphy, Michael (eds), *Musical Constructions of Nationalism: Essays on the History and Ideology of European Musical Culture 1800–1945*, Cork: Cork University Press, pp. 257–71.

—— (2003), 'The Divided Imagination: Music in Ireland after Ó Riada', in Cox, Gareth and Klein, Axel (eds), *Irish Musical Studies 7: Irish Music in the Twentieth Century*, Dublin: Four Courts, pp.11–28.

—— (2005), *The Progress of Music in Ireland*, Dublin: Four Courts Press.

—— (2007), 'Cultural theory, nostalgia and the historical record: Opera in Ireland and the Irishness of opera during the nineteenth century', in Murphy, Michael and Smaczny, Jan (eds), *Irish Musical Studies 9*, Dublin: Four Courts Press, pp. 15–35.

Wilgus, Donald K. (1965), 'Review of "British Tradition"', *The Journal of American Folklore*, 78 (307), 88–91.

Williams, Seán (2006), 'Irish Music and the Experience of Nostalgia in Japan', *Asian Music*, 37 (1), 101–19.

Williamson, John and Cloonan, Martin (2007), 'Rethinking the Music Industry', *Popular Music*, 26 (2), 305–22.

Zaplana, Esther and Biddle, Ian (2000), 'Flamenco and the politics of voice: Vocalities/ identities/ regionalities'. Paper read at Popular Music and National Identities Conference, University of Newcastle, 12 September.

Žižek, Slavoj (1993), *Tarrying with the Negative: Kant, Hegel, and the Critique of Ideology*, Durham, NC: Duke University Press.

Zuberi, Nabeel (2001), *Sounds English: Transnational Popular Music*, Urbana and Chicago: University of Illinois Press.

Zuk, Patrick (2004), 'Words for Music Perhaps? Irishness, Criticism and the Art Tradition', *Irish Studies Review*, 12 (1), 11–27.

Select discography

Artist/composer

Afro-Celt Sound System, *Afro-Celt Sound System Volume 2: Release* (Realworld, CDRW76, 1999).

Altan, *Altan Collection* (Eureka, EURCD701, 1998).

Barry, Gerald, *Orchestral Works* (Marco Polo, 8.225006, 1998).

Black, Mary, *Mary Black – Collected* (Dara Records, CD046, 1992).

Bothy Band, The, *Old hag you have killed me* (Mulligan, B000024WYS, 1976).

B*witched, *B*witched* (Epic, 4917042, 1998).

Celtic Tenors, The, *The Celtic Tenors* (EMI Classics, CDC 5570482, 2001).

Celtic Tenors, The, *We are not islands* (Dara TORTVCD 1166, 2005).

Chieftains, The, *The Very Best of the Claddagh Years* (Claddagh Records, CC66CD, 1999).

Clannad, *Clannad, The Ultimate Collection* (RCA, 74321 48674-2, 1997).

Corrs, The, *Forgiven Not Forgotten* (Atlantic/East West, 7567926122, 1996).

Cran, *Music from the edge of the world, songs and tunes from the Irish tradition* (Claddagh, 004, 2002).

Cranberries, The, *Everybody else is doing it, why can't we?* (Island, 0630892, 1993).

Dara, *The Eye of the Clock* (Sony, 498328.2, 2000).

Dempsey, Damien, *Seize the Day* (Attack, 86010, 2003).

Dennehy, Donncha, *Elastic Harmonic* (NMC Recordings, NMCD133, 2007).

Dervish, *Spirit* (Whirling Discs, WHRL007, 2003).

Enya, *Watermark* (WEA/Warner, 2292438752, 1988).

Enya, *A Day without Rain* (WEA International, 85986, 2001).

Frames, The, *For The Birds* (Plateau, 1, 2001).

Gallagher, Rory, *Live in Europe* (Capo, CAPO103, 1999).

Hansard, Glen and Irglová, Markéta, *The Swell Season* (Overcoat Recordings, 25, 2006).

Hayes, Martin, *Under the Moon* (Green Linnet, GLCD115501, 1995).

Hayes, Martin and Cahill, Denis, *Live in Seattle* (Green Linnet, GLCD1195, 1999).

Horslips, *Dancehall Sweethearts* (Edsel, 0000663EDS, 2000).

Irish Chamber Orchestra, *Silver Apples of the Moon* (Black Box, BBM1003A, 1997).

Keane, Dolores, *Solid Ground* (Dara Records, CD065, 1994).

Kíla, *Tóg é go bog é* (Kíla Records, KRCD005, 1999).

Lunny, Donal, *Coolfin* (Hummingbird Records, CDHBRTE221, 1999).

MacCarthy, Jimmy, *The Song of the Singing Horseman* (Mulligan Records, LUNCD053, 1991).

Moeran, Ernest J., *The Complete Solo Piano Music* (ASV, CDDCA1138, 2003).

Moeran, Ernest, J., *Symphony in G minor / Sinfonietta* (Naxos, 8.555837, 2002).
Moore, Christy, *Ride On* (WEA, 40407, 2007).
Moving Hearts, *The Storm* (Tara, 3014, 1985).
O'Connor, Sinéad, *So Far ... The Best of Sinéad O'Connor* (Chrysalis, 21581, 1997).
O'Donnell, Daniel, *The Daniel O'Donnell Irish Collection* (Rosette, ROSCD2025, 2002).
Ó Riada, Seán, *Mise Éire* (Gael-Linn: CEFCD080, 1979).
Ó Súilleabháin, Mícheál, *Becoming* (Virgin, CDVE937, 1998).
Ó Súilleabháin, Mícheál, *Templum* (Virgin, CDVE955, 2001).
Picturehouse, *Picturehouse Live: Bring the House Down* (Arc, CD001, 2001).
Planxty, *Cold Blow and the Rainy Night* (Shanachie, SHANCD9011, 1994).
Rice, Damien, *O* (Vector Recordings, 48507, 2003).
Saw Doctors, The, *If this is rock and roll I want my old job back* (Shamtown, SAWDOC001CD, 1991).
Sweeney's Men, *Sweeney's Men* (Transatlantic, 2000, 1969).
Thin Lizzy, *Live and Dangerous* (Mercury, 5322972, 1996).
Turner, Pierce, *Pierce Turner* (Beggar's Banquet, BEGL2010CD, 1998).
U2, *The Joshua Tree* (Island, 422-842298-2, 1987).
U2, *War* (Island, 811148, 1990).
U2, *Zooropa* (Island, 314-518047-2, 1993).
Wallace, William, *Maritana* (Marco Polo, 8.223406-07, 1996).
Walls, The, *Hi-Lo* (Dirtbird Records, 2000).
Westlife, *Westlife* (RCA, 74321728512, 1999).
Whelan, Bill, *Riverdance: Music from the Show* (Celtic Heartbeat, KCD38002, 1995).

Compilation albums and soundtracks

A Woman's Heart Volume 1 (Dara, DART3158, 1993).
A Woman's Heart Volume II (Blix Street, 10014, 1995).
Classical Ireland (Cosmic Sounds, COSCD100, 2003).
Contemporary Music Centre, *Contemporary Music from Ireland, Volume Six* (Contemporary Music Centre, CMC CD06, 2006).
Go Move Shift (Know Racism/*Hot Press*, CDMPOIRL/1, 2002).
In the Name of the Father Soundtrack (Island, 518841, 1994).
Irish Dance Athems Volume 1 (Emerald, CD9000, 2003).
Late Night Radio (EMI, CDNIGHT1016, 2002).
Louis Walsh's History of Irish Pop (Solid Records, ROCD26, 2003).
The Commitments Soundtrack (MCA: MCAD10286, 1991).
The Rough Guide to Irish Music (World Music Network, 1006, 1996).
Tom Dunne's 30 Best Irish Hits Volume 1 (Solid Records, ROCD25, 2001).
Tom Dunne's 30 Best Irish Hits Volume 2 (Solid Records, ROCD28, 2002).
Warmer for the Spark – The Songs of Jimmy MacCarthy (Dara, TORTVO94CD, 2002).

Filmography

Byrne, Gay (1993), *The Late Late Irish Music Special.*
Cameron, James (1997), *Titanic.*
Carney, John (2007), *Once.*
Dewhurst, George (1926), *Irish Destiny.*
Donaghy, David (2006), *Celebrity Jigs and Reels.*
Duane, Paul (1996), *Ballykissangel.*
Heffernan, David (2000), *Out of Ireland: From a Whisper to a Scream.*
Howard, Ron (1992), *Far and Away.*
Jackson, Peter (2001), *The Lord of the Rings: The Fellowship of the Ring.*
Keady, Billy (2002), *Ceol Tíre.*
Keating, Bill (1968), *Like Now.*
King, Philip (1991), *Bringing it all Back Home.*
King, Philip (1994), *Christy.*
King, Philip (1995), *A River of Sound.*
MacQuaid, Lynda (2002), *Popstars.*
MacQuaid, Lynda (2002), *You're a Star.*
Mendes, Sam (1999), *American Beauty.*
Morrison, George (1959), *Mise Éire.*
Ní Chinnéide, Dairena (1998), *Treo?*
Nichols, Mike (2004), *Closer.*
O'Brien, Sinéad (1999), *Luke.*
Parker, Alan (1991), *The Commitments.*
Quinn, Bob (1984), *Atlantean.*
Sheridan, Jim (1993), *In the Name of the Father.*
Stevenson, Robert (1959), *Darby O'Gill and the Little People.*

Index

References to illustrations are in **bold**.

accent, and Irishness 155–6
Adorno, Theodor 7
    social theory of music 134
Afro-American 22, 29 fn11, 107
Afro-Celt Sound System 35, 42, 61, 93
    Irishness 136–7
Agnew, Elaine 71, 84
    Wait and See 74
aisling 42
Altan 2, 35, **36**, 37, 61, 92, 93, 180
    authenticity 176
    Irishness 162
America
    Irish Diaspora 26, 101
    Irishness 198
American Beauty film 192
Anglo-American rock 30, 31, 108
Anúna choral group 97 fn1
Ardagh, John
    Ireland and the Irish 106
    on Irishness and music 106–7
'art world' concept (Becker) 183
Arts Act (2003) 46–7
arts funding 47
Arts, Sport and Tourism, Department,
        budget 45
Aslan 32
Association of Irish Musical Societies 49, 84
audiences, classical music 75–6
authenticity 176
    Altan 176
    classical music 173
    commercialism, incompatibility 177–80
    definition 174–5
    Dervish 176
    and ethnicity 173
    interviewees' views 174
    Keane 176
    Moore on 174, 175

in music 175
    performance modes 175
    pluralities, varying articulations of 174
    Stokes (Martin) on 174
    theories 173–5
    see also inauthenticity

B*witched 31, 34, 94, 115, 140, 179
    perceived inauthenticity 178
Balfe, Michael 41
    'I dreamt that I dwelt in marble halls'
        97, 140
    The Bohemian Girl 74, 97
ballad
    concert, inauthenticity 185–6
    folk/traditional 26, 33, 72, 73, 99, 150,
        168
    groups 36, 37
    opera 71, 74, 84, 97, 99, 116
    political 36
    rock 99
'ballad boom', 1960s 26, 27, 67
Ballykissangel TV series, music 150
Bang on a Can All-Stars 41
Barry, Gerald 42, 71, 84, **97**, 114
    Lyric FM festival 86
    music, perceived (non-) Irishness 96,
        164
    Piano Quartet No. 1 96
    The Conquest of Ireland 73–4
    The Road 73
        repetition in 164
        West of Ireland landscapes 192
Baudelaire, Charles, *flâneur* concept 122
beat groups 29
Becker, Howard, 'art world' concept 183
BellX1 32
Benedict, Julius, *The Lily of Killarney* 74
Bennett, H.S. 7
Black Box label 62
Black, Mary 33, 69, 189
    Irishness 189, 190

singing style 154, 155, 156
Blackness, Irishness, association 107
blues-rock 29
bodhrán 28 fn9, 72, 74, 95, 104
    Irishness 159, 160
Bono, on Irish music 105
The Boomtown Rats 30
The Bothy Band 35, 37
Bourdieu, Pierre 18, 88
bouzouki 35, 68, 72, 166
Boydell, Brian 41, 151
Boyzone 31
Brady, Glen 32
Brady, Paul 5, 33, 35, 46, 81
bricolage 123, 130
Bringing it all Back Home
    book 101
    TV series 101, 127
Britain, Irish Diaspora 101
Britishness 4, 6, 178, 190
Britpop 31
broadcast music 62–4
    see also radio play
Broadcasting Commission of Ireland 62
broadcasting organizations 62
Buckley, John 42
Business Expansion Scheme for Music 48

Cahill, Denis 68, 72, 80, 81, 166
Casey, Paddy 33
Cassidy, Patrick 42
céilí bands 28, 166
Celebrity Jigs and Reels TV series 40
Celtic, Gaelic, distinction 182 fn3
Celtic genres, Irish music 44
    see also New Age/Celtic
The Celtic Tenors 43, 71, 75, **85**, 142
    crossover music 75, 85
    presentation mode 86
    recordings
        'Ireland's Call' 85
        'Spanish Lady' 86
        We are not islands, cover artwork **85**
'Celtic Tiger'
    economy 10, 45, 121, 197
        non-economic factors 132
    hagiographies 134
Celtic Tiger show 43

'Celtic twilight' 182
Celtic Woman ensemble 2, 44, 198
Ceol, traditional music museum 128
Ceoltóirí Chualann 28, 35
charts, international repertoire,
    domination 60
The Chieftains 2, 35, 127, 180
Civic/ethnic dichotomy 9–10, 55, 114–15,
    173
The Clancy Brothers 26
Clannad 35, 37, 44
classical music 3, 14, 40–43, 66
    Anglo-Irish associations 6, 41
    authenticity 173
    composers 42
    education 53
    festivals 51
    'Finding our Voice' exhibition 128
    Irish-composed 40, 41–2
    Irishness 113, 114
    live events 69–70, 73–5
        audiences 75–6
    national institutions 113
    non-Irishness 95, 99
    O'Kelly on 114
    performances, national anthem at 14, 84
    presentation mode 83–7
    record sales 57, 58
    recordings 61–2
    venues 70
Closer film 33
Cogan, Višnja 17
Comhaltas Ceoltóirí Éireann 26, 46, 49,
    53, 67, 118, 190
commercialism, authenticity,
    dichotomy 177–80
The Commitments film 107
*The Companion to Irish Traditional
    Music* 157
competitions 51
Concorde group 41
Connemara, symbolism 189
consumerism
    and *flâneur* concept 122
    and Irish identity 122–4
Contemporary Music Centre 49, 62, 114
    'Finding our Voice: Music in Ireland
        Today' 128

Conway, Zoë 75
Corcoran, Frank 113
Corcoran, Seán 194
Cork International Choral Festival 51
The Corrs
    book cover 1, 34, 93, 179
    Irishness 135, 140, 161–2
    perceived inauthenticity 178
Coughlan, Eoin 33
Coulter, Phil 5, 85
country and Irish music 32, 62, 142
Cowan, Brian, on Irish culture 126
Cox, Gareth 96
Cran, *Music from the Edge of the World*,
    cover artwork **191**
The Cranberries 2, 31, 103, 104
The Crash Ensemble 41, 42
Create 49
Crowley, Jimmy 179
'The Cruisheen Lawn', Irishness 97–8
Culture Ireland 48
    music programmes 128
Cumann Násiúnta na gCór 49

dance forms, traditional music, association
    148–9
dance scene 32
dance tunes, and Irishness 150
Dara 69, 72, 76, 82
    Irishness 98–9, 117
    see also O'Toole, Dara
Darby O'Gill and the Little People film 186
Davey, Shaun 42, 62
Dé Dannan 35
Deane, Raymond 42, 113, 152
Dempsey, Damien 37
Denmark, record sales, domestic vs
    international 58
Dennehy, Donncha
    Aisling Gheal 42
    on classical music 114
    Grá agus Bás 42
Dervish 35, 37, 61, 102, 103
    authenticity 176
discography 225–6
Doherty, Josie 72
Dolphin Records 59, 61
Doyle, Niall 130–31

Doyle, Roddy 116
Doyle, Roger 42
Dublin
    colonial associations 190
    events/venues 68, 69, 70, 71
    Ireland, dichotomy 190
Dublin County Choir 75
The Dubliners 26, 86, 127

Eagleton, Terry 21
Electric Picnic festival 50
emigration 121, 139
Englishness 31 fn16, 163, 178, 201 fn5
Ennis, Séamus 190
Enya 2, 35, 198
    Irishness 149–50
    recordings
        A Day without Rain 151
        The Lord of the Rings, music 151
ethnicity
    and authenticity 173–4
    and national identity 9
    see also Irish ethnicity
Eurovision Song Contest 9, 37
    Irish participation 29
    Irish success 29 fn10
events, and venues 67–71

Faith of Our Fathers 43
Far and Away film, music 150
Farrell, Eibhlís 42, 114
FÁS 55
Federation of Music Collectives 50
Feeney, Julie 33
Feis Ceoil 51
Festival of World Cultures 51
festivals
    classical music 51
    increase 60
    intercultural music 51
    jazz 51
    rock 50
    traditional music 50
fiddle playing, Irishness 153, 160
Field, John 41
filmography 227
flâneur concept, and consumerism 122
Flatley, Michael 43

Fleadh Cheoil 50, 51
fleadhanna ceoil 27
Fleischmann, Aloys 151
Folk Music Society of Ireland 49
folk musicians 26
folk/blues genre 33
folk/traditional, associations and
    distinctions 5 fn7, 26–7, 37
Forum for Music in Ireland 49
fragmentation, Irish identity 122, 124
The Frames 33, **34**, 164
France, record sales, domestic vs
    international 58
The Frank and Walters 32
Frankfurt Book Festival 127
Friday, Gavin 104 fn5, 179

Gael Linn 51, 61
Gaelic
    Celtic, distinction 182 fn3
    term 6 fn9
Gaelic Storm 150
Gaeltacht 143
Gallagher, Rory 29
Galway Arts Festival 129
gender issues, Irish music 152
Gerald of Wales 73
Germany, record sales, domestic vs
    international 58
Gilsenan, Matthew 75
Glass, Philip 82
globalization 122, 123
    and Irish culture 125
Go Move Shift CD 135–6, 137
Graham, Brian 8, 13
Graydon, Philip 151
Greece, record sales, domestic vs
    international 58
Gribbin, Deirdre 42
Guilfoyle, Ronan 54
guitar 160, 163, 166
    'Celtic' 44

Hansard, Glen 33
harp, and Irish nationhood 159
Hayes, Gemma 33
Hayes, Helen 68, 72
    singing style, Irishness 154

Hayes, Martin 68, 72, 78, 81, 82, 148, 166
    presentation mode 80–82
    on traditional music 102
hegemony concept, Irish music 12–13, 55,
    100
Heineken Green Energy Festival 50
Helix Centre, Dublin 70
heterophony 165, 166, 167
Hillen, Seán, *Irelantis* collages 193
hip-hop 7, 33, 34, 62, 67, 88, 89, 173, 179
Holmes, David 32
homology
    theories 10
    traditional music, Irishness 91–3, 100,
        103, 111
Horslips, 'Johnny's Wedding' 29
Hot Press 63
    Go Move Shift CD 135, 137
    popular music museum 128
The Hothouse Flowers 32, 164
HQ venue 69 fn5
Hunt, Fionnuala 75
Hunt, Una 74
    on Moeran 86–7
hybridity
    concept 17
    Ó Súilleabháin's *Hup!* 96
    and syncretism 17
Hyperborea 34

immigration 121
In the Name of the Father film 104
inauthenticity (perceived)
    B*witched 178
    concert ballad 185–6
    The Corrs 178
    see also authenticity
Independent Broadcasters in Ireland 62
independent labels 61
innovation
    tradition, dichotomy 47, 180–84
    traditional music 182
instrumental style
    Irishness 153
    regional differences 153–4
    see also fiddle playing
instruments *see* musical instruments

International Federation of the
    Phonographic Industry 56
interviewees
    authenticity, views on 174
    on Irish identity and music 108–13
    Irish music, responses to 136–43,
        147–50, 200
    musical analysis, reluctance 147
    musical interests 87–90
    nostalgia 140–41
        views on 188
    performance activity 89, 141
Ireland
    agrarianism 15
    annual festivals 50
    arts policy 45
    economic success 3
    identity *see* Irish identity
    independence 6
    'most globalized' country 59–60
    music *see* Irish music
    as social construction 13
    social stratification 6
Irglová, Markéta 33
Irish boy/girl bands 31
Irish Chamber Orchestra 74
Irish Council for Traditional Music 49
Irish culture
    branding 132
    Cowan on 126
    economic appropriation 131–3
    essentialism 118, 132, 182 fn3
    and globalization 125
    and Irish music 10, 200
Irish Destiny film 43
Irish Diaspora 4, 33
    Britain 101
    North America 26, 101
Irish ethnicity 4, 101, 132, 134, 159
Irish identity 10
    and consumerism 122–4
    essentialism 121, 187
    fluidity 129
    fragmentation 122, 124
    future directions 124–7
    and music 87
    Ó Cúiv on 124–5
    and the West of Ireland 187–90, 192–3

    writings on 13
    see also Irish musical identity
Irish language, and Irish music 37, 51,
    117–18
Irish music
    Adorno's social theory of music 134
    alterity 193
    Bono on 105
    Celtic genres 44
    commodity, vs non-commodity forms 66
    compilations 62
    definition 4–5
    discography 225–6
    domestic market 57
    economic perspective 130–31
    essentialism 8, 21, 127, 128, 130, 134,
        168
    exotic theories, critique of 193
    folk music as 21
    gender issues 152
    government funding 45
    haunting quality, attribution 149–50,
        151, 152
    hegemony concept 12–13, 55, 100
    international market 2, 56, 134,
        150–51, 200
    interviewees' responses 136–43,
        147–50, 200
    and Irish culture 10, 200
    and Irish identity 87, 108–13
    and Irish language 37, 51
    Irishness of 1, 18, 19, 21–3, 52, 56,
        91–119, 147–8, 199
        Ardagh on 106–7
        data 19–20
        interviews 19–20
        style-mediated 195
    live music 66
    lively quality, attribution 147–8, 152
    Ó Riada, on 27–8
    Paddy Mad/Paddy Sad persona 152
    and place 192
    presentation modes 78–87
    production modes **66**
    recent history of 25–44
    record sales 57, 58
    representations 127–9
    stereotypes 152

studies 14–17
style categories 5–8, **66**, 146
supporting organizations 49
traditional music as 21, 94, 99, 101,
    109, 113, 174
    see also classical music; popular
        music; traditional music
Irish Music magazine 39, 67
Irish Music Rights Organization 56
Irish musical identity 1, 17, 87, 108–13, 114
    and difference 193–5
    diversity 135–43
    narrow base 3
Irish Musical Studies 49 fn12, 113
Irish pop 31, 32, 131
    commercial success 179
    non-Irishness 178
Irish psyche 16-17, 22, 104
Irish Recorded Music Association 56
'Irish Ring' operas 71, 74, 75
    Joycean associations 116
    live commentary 84
    non-Irishness 97, 116
    nostalgia 140–41
Irish rock 2, 30, 131
    non-Irishness 99
Irish soul 22, 103, 104, 107–8, 158, 171, 177
    see also soul music, Irish
Irish sound 21, 91, 104, 108, 171
The Irish Tenors 43, 142
    perceived (non-) Irishness 98, 185
    nostalgia 188
Irish Traditional Music Archive 49, 61
Irish-language music 51
Irishness
    and accent 155–6
    Afro-Celt Sound System 136–7
    Altan 92, 162
    America 198
    Black 189, 190
    Blackness, association 107
    bodhrán 159, 160
    civic/ethnic dichotomy 114–15
    classical music 113, 114
    The Corrs 135, 140, 161–2
    'The Cruisheen Lawn' 97
    cultural 21–2, 113–19
    and dance tunes 150

Dara 98–9, 117
economic, and music 22–3, 129–35,
    197
Enya 149–50
essentialism 128, 187
ethnic/ ethnic specific 11, 95, 123, 130,
    173, 184
and feeling Irish 99–100
fiddle playing 153, 160
hegemony of 201
idea of 1, 96
idealized conceptions of 198
and inherent musicality 22, 52, 53, 56,
    73, 116, 195, 200
instrumental style 153
of Irish music 1, 18, 19, 21–3, 91–119,
    147–52, 199
Kila 137–8
The Lily of Killarney 98
MacCarthy 99, 139, 168, 170, 185
minor keys 166–7
Moeran 86–7, 117, 167, 190
musical instruments 159–64
musical structures 164–7
mythical, and music 23, 187
and place 189–93
reinventions 129
and repetition 164–5
and rhythm 165
Riverdance 38–9, 132, 135
singing style 154–9
song lyrics 167–8, 170
spiritual 101
traditional music, homology 91–3, 100,
    103, 111
Turner 99, 138–9, 179
twee 23, 185, 186
uileann pipes 159, 160, 161
    see also non-Irishness
Irishry 108, 133, 186–7, 199
Irvine, Andy 35, 69, 81, 82

Jack L 33
Japan, record sales, domestic vs
    international products 58
jazz festivals 51
JJ72 32
John Field Room, NCH 70–71, 74, 116

The Johnstons 26
The Journal of Music in Ireland 1, 128
Joyce, James 74, 116, 117

Kavanagh, Mark 32
Keane, Dolores 33, 92, 194
    accent 155
    authenticity 176
    singing style, Irishness 154, 155, 156,
        157, 159, 189
Keating, Ronan 31
Kelly, Thomas C. 41
Keohane, Kieran 106, 197
Kila 37, 61
    Irishness 137–8
King, Philip 104, 127
    on music as cultural resource 125–6
    on traditional music 101–2
Kitt, David 33
Klein, Axel 14

Laffey, Seán 176
Lambeg drum 104
The Late Late Irish Music Special 127
The Late Late Show 127
Leonard, Hugh 201
The Lily of Killarney, Irishness 98
L'Imaginaire Irlandais arts festival 127
live music 66–87
Lloyd Webber, Andrew 43
Lord of the Dance 43
The Lord of the Rings, Enya's music 151
Lunny, Dónal 35, 81, 180
    Coolfin 184
Lyric FM 40, 63, 76
    Barry festival 86

Mac Aoidh, Caoimhín, on traditional music
    102, 126
McCabe, Mark 32
MacCarthy (McCarthy), Jimmy 33, 69, 76,
    92, **169**
    Irishness 99, 139, 185
    presentation mode 83
    recordings
        'Mystic Lipstick' 170
        No Frontiers songbook, cover
            artwork **169**

songwriting, Irishness 167–8, 170
McCarthy, Marie 15, 17, 51
MacColl, Ewan, 'Go Move Shift' 135 fn7
McGill Summer School 126
McGlynn, Michael 42
McGowan, Shane 108
McGurk, Tom 181
Mac Laughlin, Jim 129, 131–2, 142
McLaughlin, Noel 15–16, 32, 105–6, 178
Mac Laverty, Bernard 116
MacNamara, Mary 68, 72, 80
The McPeake family 26
Maoin Cheoil an Chláir 53
Marco Polo label 62
Marsh, Patrick 68, 72
May, Frederick 41
    String Quartet in C Minor 151
Metisse 35
Middleton, Richard 146, 197
Millstreet Arena (Cork) 69
minor keys, Irishness 166–7
Mitchell, Shane, on traditional music 102–3
modernity, Irish 122
modes
    of audience interaction 33
    of cultural engagement 123
    of music production **66**, 180, 181
    of music transmission 15
    musical 166–7
    performance 175
    of presentation 11, 19, 26, 44, 65,
        78–87, 200
Moeran, E.J. 41, 71, 74, 76, 84
    Irishness 86–7, 117, 167, 190
    landscape, identification with 190
    Rhapsody No. 2: 165
    Symphony in G Minor 86
    'The Lake Island' 167
Molloy, Angela 84
Moloney, Paddy 46
Moore, Allan, on authenticity 174, 175
Moore, Christy 33, 35, 36, 46, 69, 81, 92
    accent 155
    'Go Move Shift' 135 fn7
    'moral entrepreneurs' 11
Morris, Niall 75, 86
Morrison, Van 107, 108
Mosaik 35

Moving Hearts 35, 37
Moy, Johnny 32
Moylan, Terry, on traditional music 100–101
Mumba, Samantha 31
Mundy (Edmund Enright) 33
music
    Adorno's social theory of 134
    anti-racism, Stokes on 135–6
    authenticity in 174–5
    commodification 122, 123
    as cultural resource, King on 125–6
    and Irish identity 87
    and national identity 8–13
    significations 146
    social mediation 11
    see also Irish music
Music Board of Ireland 48, 56, 130
music education 52–6
    classical 53
    degrees 54
    popular music 54–5
    traditional music 53–4
    see also music schools
Music Education National Debate 15, 49
Music Industry Group 56
Music Network 49, 81, 128
music schools 53
musical analysis
    interviewees' reluctance 147
    and meaning 145–7
musical instruments, Irishness 159–64
musical structures, Irishness 164–7
Musicians' Union of Ireland 50

national anthem, at classical music
        performances 14, 84
National Concert Hall, Dublin 70, 71
national identity
    characteristics 9
    and ethnicity 9
    ideal types 9–10
    and music 8–13
    see also Irish identity; Irish musical
        identity
National Symphony Orchestra 41, 61, 73
Naxos label 61
Nelson, James 75
New Age/Celtic genre 35, 44

New Music News 40
Ní Chathasaigh, Máire 151
Ní Dhomhnaill, Nuala 125
Ní Mhainnín, Roisín 74
Ní Mhaolcatha, Méav 198–9
non-Irishness (perceived)
    Barry's music 96, 164
    classical music 95, 99
    Irish pop 178
    '"Irish Ring" operas' 97, 116
    The Irish Tenors 98, 185
    Ó Súilleabháin's Hup! 95
    rock music 99
    The Three Irish Tenors 95
    traditional sounds 93–4
    U2's music 107
    see also Irishness
Northern Ireland 4, 36, 49
nostalgia
    interviewees' 140–41
        '"Irish Ring" operas' 140–41
        views on 188
    The Irish Tenors 188
    rural 187
    and West of Ireland 187
'nyaa' 154, 155, 157, 193–4,

O'Brien, Edel 74
Ó Canainn, Tomás, on traditional music 126
Ó Cinnéide, Barra 16, 132, 133
O'Connor, Nuala 104, 107, 108, 154, 157
    Bringing it all back Home 101
O'Connor, Sineád 2, 31, 37, 158
    singing style, Irishness 157–8
Ó Cúiv, Eamon, on Irish identity 124–5
O'Donnell, Daniel 32–3, 142
O'Donoghue, John 46–7
Ó Giolláin, Diarmuid 129
O'Kelly, Eve, on classical music 114
O'Leary, Jane 42
Ó Lionaird, Iarla 42
Ó Murchú, Labhrás, on traditional music 100
Ó Riada, Seán 11, 41, 42, 166, 193
    on Irish music 27–8
    Mise Éire 27, 37
    traditional music, influence on 28
O'Riordan, Dolores 31, 104
O'Rourke, Declan 33

Ó Seaghda, Barra 114
Ó Snodaigh, Rossa 137
Ó Súilleabháin, Mícheál 4, 16–17, 41, 42,
    43, 62, 71, 181–2
    Hup! 74, 84
        hybridity 96
        perceived (non-) Irishness 95
        music, perceived inauthenticity 184
        'Oileán' 192
O'Toole, Dara 72, 82
Oireachtas na Gaeilge 51
Once film 33
opera, official funding 47
Osborne, George Alexander 87
Out of Ireland: From a Whisper to a
    Scream TV series 105, 127, 128
Oxegen festival 50

Paddy Mad/Paddy Sad persona, Irish music
    152
Patrick Street 35
performance modes, authenticity 175
Phonographic Performance Ireland 56
Picture House 69, 82
Pine, Richard 14
place, and Irish music 192–3
Planxty 35, 37, 81, 166
Point Theatre (Dublin) 69
political ballad/song 36–7
pop *see* Irish pop
Popstars TV series 31
popular music 15, 16, 66
    education 54–5
    genres 32–5
    Hot Press museum 128
    live events 69
        audiences 76
    official policies 48
    performer/audience interaction 82–3
    radio play 62–3
    ubiquity of 200
    venues 69
population, non-Irish nationals 121
Potts, Tommy 190
pub sessions, traditional music 27, 67–8,
    71–2
    interviewees' views 76–8

Quinn, Bernadette 128–9

The Radiators from Space 30
radio listening 62
radio play
    live music 63–4
    popular music 62–3
rebel songs 36
record labels, independent 61
record sales
    classical music 57
    digital downloads 61
    Ireland-produced vs international
        products 57, 58, 59
    non-industry recorded 61
    per capita 59
Recorded Artists and Performers 50
recording activity 61–2
recording studios 60
Reel 34
reflexivity 122, 123, 197, 199
repetition, and Irishness 164–5
residual ideology concept 187
The Revs 32
rhythm, and Irishness 165
Rice, Damien, *O* 33
Richardson, Stephen 73
A River of Sound TV series 102, 127, 181–2
Riverdance 2, 16, 22, 27, 37–40, 130, 149,
    151, 181
    influence 43, 129
    international market 39, 124, 129, 132
    Irishness 39, 135
RnaG radio station 63, 64
The Rough Guide to Irish Music, cover
    artwork **191**
Royal Dublin Society 69
RTÉ 62
    Like Now TV series 29
RTÉ Concert Orchestra 61
RTÉ Music 61
Ruby Horse 32
Ryan, Joseph 14

The Saw Doctors 33, 152
Sawyers, Ruth Skinner, *The Complete*
    Guide to Celtic Music 107
Scottishness 163

sean nós 37, 42, 84, 95, 108, 118, 143, 155,
 157, 193–4
Self, Geoffrey 165
'selloutism' 133, 180
session/seisiún 67, 68, 71, 76–7, 81
set dancing 88 fn19, 89, 148
Shannon, Sharon 81, 127
showbands 28, 29, 173
signification 122, 123
 music 146
singer/songwriters 33
singing style, Irishness 154–9
Slater, Eamonn 122, 123
Slógadh 51
The Smiths 103, 104
Smyth, Gerry 16, 17, 35, 200
 on Irish music stereotypes 152
social groups, sound groups, distinction 27
social mediation, music 11, 12
Society for Musicology in Ireland (SMI) 49
song lyrics, Irishness 167–8, 170
songs, Irish-language 37, 193
soul music
 Afro-American 22, 107
 Irish 107, 108, 171
 see also Irish soul
sound groups 64, 81, 89, 101, 143, 146,
 181, 200, 201
 social groups, distinction 27
Stanford, Charles Villiers 41
Stokes, Martin, on authenticity 174
Stokes, Niall 131
 on anti-racism and music 135–6
supergroups, traditional music 35
Sweeney, Eric 42, 114
Sweeny's Men 29, 35
Switch 34

Tansey, Séamus 182
Tara label 61
Temple Bar Music Centre 69
Theatre Royal, Wexford 70
Thin Lizzy 29
The Three Irish Tenors 43
'three tenors' formula 43
The Thrills 32
tin whistle, Titanic film 129–30
Titanic film

 music 150
 tin whistle 129–30
tonality, traditional music 165–7
tradition, innovation, dichotomy 47, 180–84
traditional music 5–7, 66
 antiquarian collections 6
 Ceol museum 128
 commodification 181
 and continuity 110
 dance forms, association 148–9
 education 53–4
 essentialism 21, 100, 160, 182
 ethnicity of 13, 114
 festivals 27, 50
 formal settings 79–81
 Hayes on 102
 heterophony 165, 166
 innovation 182
 instrumental 26
 instruments 72, 159–61, 166
 as Irish music 21, 94, 99, 101, 109,
  113, 174
 Irish-sounding [more] 114, 115
 Irishness, homology 91–3, 100, 103, 111
 Japanese involvement 198
 King on 101–2
 Mac Aoidh on 102, 126
 Mitchell on 102–3
 Moylan on 100–101
 national/regional 186
 Ó Murchú on 100
 official patronage 46–7
 Ó Riada's influence 28
 performer/ audience interaction 79–82
 popularization 35–7
 privileging 26
 professionalization 180, 181
 pub sessions 27, 67–8, 71–2, 79
  audiences 76–7
 'renaissance' 26, 39
 sessions 67, 68, 71, 76–7, 81
 singing style 157
 status 197
 supergroups 35
 tonality 165–7
 TV documentaries 127
 venues 68
traditional sounds, non-Irishness 93–4

Treo? TV documentary 124, 125
Trimble, Joan 41, 87
Turner, Juliet 5, 33
Turner, Pierce 69, 72–3, 76, 179
    Irishness 99, 138–9
    lyrics 73
    music, eclecticism 73
    presentation mode 82–3

U2 2, 17, 30, 103, 106, 198
    move of business to Netherlands 48
    music, perceived (non-) Irishness of 107
    recordings
        Joshua Tree 107
        'Sunday, Bloody Sunday' 37
        War 37
        Zooropa 106 fn9, 197 fn1
uileann pipes 37, 72
    Irishness 159, 160, 161
UK, record sales, domestic vs international 58
University Concert Hall, Limerick 70, 71

Vallely, Fintan 182, 186, 189
Van De Port, Mattijs 159
venues 32, 43
    classical music 70
    and events 67–71
    improvements 60
    outdoor 50
    popular music 69
    traditional music 68
Vignoles, Julian 30

The Virgin Prunes 30
Volans, Kevin 42

Wallace, Arminta 46
Wallace, William Vincent 41
    Maritana 74, 97
    'Scenes that are brightest' 97
The Walls 32, 69, 82
Walsh, Louis 31
Waters, John, on Irishness in music 103–4
Welsh popular music 25, 37
West of Ireland
    as cultural other 189
    and Irish ethnicity 159
    and Irish identity 187–90, 192–3
    and nostalgia 187
Westlife 31
    Coast to Coast 179
Wexford Festival Opera 14, 51, 70, 129
Whelan, Bill 37, **38**, 42, 71, 181
    Inishlacken 74, 94, 149, 192
    Postcards from Connemara 192
    see also Riverdance
White, Harry 6, 14, 42, 95, 112, 114, 190
Williams, Raymond, residual ideology concept 187
The Wolfe Tones 36
Worby, Rachel 84
world music 2, 89, 129, 173
World Music: The Rough Guide 107, 154, 193

You're a Star TV series 31

DATE DUE	RETURNED
MAR 2 0 2013	MAR 1 4 2013